ALL DAY

A Year of Love and Survival Teaching
Incarcerated Kids at Rikers Island

LIZA JESSIE PETERSON

CENTER
STREET

New York   Nashville

Copyright © 2017 by Liza Jessie Peterson

Jacket design by Jody Waldrup
Jacket copyright © 2017 by Hachette Book Group, Inc.

Center Street
Hachette Book Group
1290 Avenue of the Americas, New York, NY 10104
centerstreet.com
twitter.com/centerstreet

First edition: April 2017

Center Street is a division of Hachette Book Group, Inc. The Center Street name and logo are trademarks of Hachette Book Group, Inc.

The publisher is not responsible for websites (or their content) that are not owned by the publisher.

Library of Congress Cataloging-in-Publication Data has been applied for.

ISBNs: 978-1-4555-7091-1 (hardcover), 978-1-4555-7090-4 (ebook)

Printed in the United States of America

LSC-C

10 9 8 7 6 5 4 3 2 1

For Leslie, my sister, my bookey, my heart.
Eternally

Contents

Foreword by Abiodun Oyewole   ix

Introduction   xi

1. Summer Substitute   1
2. Sizing Me Up   8
3. I Got This, *Not*   25
4. Danny Gunz   43
5. One, Two, *Poof*   62
6. Rug Rat Roll Call   83
7. Africa Prince tha Don   94
8. King Down   114
9. This Is Some Bullshit   143
10. Artist vs. Civilian   171
11. Paradigm Shift   188
12. The Hardest Part   193
13. MoMo and Friends   203

Afterword   231

Acknowledgments   237

Rikers Rug Rat Slang   239

Foreword

All Day is a tremendously powerful story of a warrior writer, Matrix Momma, beautifully bold and blessed sister who has an undying love for her people fueled by her passion to make a difference in the lives of Black youth in trouble. Liza Jessie Peterson has captured the essence, the humor, the intellect, and the psychology of the lives of young people (especially young Black men) trying to survive in the penal systems of America. Her narrative takes you to Rikers Island and into the classroom—into the minds and souls of some of our most precious treasures, the children. I was captivated by the characters. I could see them, smell their musk, feel their attitudes, and hear their voices to a point where I felt I knew them and would recognize any one of them if I bumped into them on the street.

Peterson's perspective and the insights and wisdoms she so powerfully shares will make any teacher a better teacher and any person a better person. It was a pleasure and very refreshing to know that there are real, live angels among us who are doing God's work, which is to bring out the God in each of us so in some way we can be a blessing to ourselves. Liza Jessie Peterson is a tall Amazon, caramel-brown, laser-eyed sister who also just happens to be very attractive. Her presence alone is positive and powerful. She presents herself in such a way that demands respect. Her words are sharp, witty, provocative, passionate, and Black. She is not afraid to show love in a way that is never misunderstood.

The stories, the characters, the talent, the conflicts, and the love are all there with a message: There must be a better way to raise our youth among us who have gone astray than to warehouse them in penal institutions throughout the land. The number of young Black men in jail is embarrassing. This country was built on the backs of many of these young people's ancestors. For them to be labeled as bad seeds or as incorrigibles destined to a life of crime speaks volumes about the shame and callousness America has shown its benefactors. *All Day* is a must-read for anyone who cares about children and believes in the possibilities that arise from affording them the opportunity to have the brightest of futures.

Abiodun Oyewole

Founding member of the Last Poets

Author of *Branches of the Tree of Life*

Introduction

Most New York City transplants come to the Big Apple with a dream of doing something extraordinary. I first came to New York by way of Philadelphia with a dream of becoming a supermodel. I did the Paris–New York–Milan couture romp for several years, not achieving supermodel status, but I managed to walk the runway for some of the fashion industry's best designers. The luster and glam quickly lost its shine, as I found it unfulfilling to be judged solely on my looks. I was searching for my identity, my voice, my calling. Walking away from modeling, I decided to take a theater class and immediately felt alive and a spark was lit. I experienced an unshakable desire to express myself; I had something to say and it was through character that I discovered a passion for acting and journaling, which would quickly unveil my dormant poet and playwright. Both the stage and the page became a refuge for my creative spirit. I studied classical theater at Stella Adler and the National Shakespeare Conservatory in New York and later with the legendary Susan Batson (acting coach for the stars). I took classes religiously, auditioned frequently, and landed several independent feature films. But it was at the renowned Nuyorican Poets Cafe in lower Manhattan that I would nurture my calling as a poet and playwright. I performed on HBO's *Def Poetry Jam*, on PBS's *Between the Lions*, and virtually all over New York wherever there was a mic reserved for poets.

The poems evolved into monologues, which evolved into plays, and when I looked up I had a one-woman show under my belt with a second one gestating. When my sophomore solo show, *The Peculiar Patriot,* was born I performed it in more than thirty-five adult prisons around the country. From model, poet, and playwright to teaching in prison, this book is a testimony about my experiences once I stumbled upon teaching incarcerated boys as a full-time GED teacher at Island Academy, the high school for inmates detained on Rikers Island. Initially starting out as a teaching artist conducting poetry and creative writing workshops, I was merely looking for a steady job that would pay more than the poetry gigs, enabling me to pay my rent and get on my feet financially. It was supposed to be temporary, but a funny thing happened when passion met purpose, and so it's been eighteen years and counting that I've been working in multiple capacities with incarcerated youth.

My hope is that this book will give you an insight into a draconian subworld where so many of our children languish and allow you to understand the plight of adolescent boys behind bars and feel, as I do, that they are worth our love and attention. *All Day* is a story of my journey finding love and purpose in an unexpected dark place.

CHAPTER ONE

Summer Substitute

2008

As I make my way down the dingy gray hallway of Rikers Island C-74 at 7:30 a.m., correctional officers (COs) are already stationed at their desks on the school floor while other staff are gathered in the poorly lit teachers' lounge, putting their lunch in the large refrigerator as the TV plays a random, early morning news show. I pop my green tea into the microwave so I can have something warm and comforting to hold on to in hopes of easing my anxiety. I notice most teachers are carrying large, hideous "Department of Corrections" see-through plastic tote bags, which I later find out are mandatory for security purposes—to make visible any contraband that might sneak in and inadvertently wreak havoc, like cell phones, matches, cigarettes, sharp objects, pocketknives, glass bottles, and aluminum cans.

The microwave beeps. I grab my tea and head to the main office, which is across the hall from the teachers' lounge, to clock in. I search for my name on the row of time cards hoisted on the wall. The teacher behind me introduces herself. "Good morning. I'm Ms. G." She is a tall, thin, sassy fashionista with perfectly manicured sandy-brown dreadlocks pulled up into a perfectly coiffed chignon.

She appears younger than she probably is and I wonder how she navigates the boys crushing on her.

"I'm Liza Peterson," I reply as I slide my time card into the clock, which punches 7:38 a.m. A lump forms in my stomach. Time cards. I am officially a time-card-punching worker bee, a common pedestrian. For any hardwired artist like myself, creativity and freedom is paramount. I have an aversion to time cards. I associate them with assembly line jobs, factory culture, and becoming so mechanical that creative expression is replaced with groupthink. The shit makes me anxious. I swear I can faintly hear the clink of a chain gang in my head. My breath gets shorter. This is going to be a major adjustment. I take a deep breath and tell myself, *This is a blessing, girl. You were broke and now you're able to pay your rent, and you're even eligible for benefits. This is a blessing.*

There are only two more weeks left in June before summer break starts for all New York City public schools, and Phil, the principal here at Island Academy, the high school located on Rikers Island, asked if I could substitute for a teacher who couldn't finish the semester due to a family emergency. The gig lands me back on my old stomping grounds. I first touched the Rock* back in 1998 when I taught poetry workshops over in the Six building (C-76), where most of the sentenced adolescent boys are housed and attend classes. What was supposed to be just a three-week teaching-artist gig turned into three years straight, and I became the unofficial poet in residence at Rikers. When I first started, I was a bright-eyed poet who had never been to prison for any reason, *ever*. Rikers Island became my introductory crash course about the prison industrial complex and, over a span of ten years, I evolved into a seasoned vet working with incarcerated teenagers. Barbed wire, correctional officers, and the sound of gates opening and slamming shut had become

---

***Rock:** a synonym for Rikers Island that was borrowed from the nickname used for Alcatraz, which had the appearance of being a giant "rock" on an island. Like Alcatraz, Rikers is on an island, located in New York's East River.

routine—familiar even. But the river of Black and Brown boys streaming up and down the hallways was unsettling and pricked at my spirit. With a daily inmate population of roughly 12,300 at any given time, approximately 800 of the prisoners at Rikers Island are sixteen- to eighteen-year-old kids; 746 boys and roughly 45 girls. The adolescents are housed separately from the adults until they turn nineteen, and even though they can't legally buy alcohol until the age of twenty-one, in jail they're considered old enough to be housed with the grown-ups. Rikers Island is its own altered reality, a sub-universe, an ugly island surrounded by dookey-brown stinky water. It's a mammoth jail, one of the largest in the country. It's where I planted seeds and grew roots. A lotus in the swamp.

I've always enjoyed being an artist who teaches poetry and theater. It's a really cool gig with flexible hours. I can prance from class to class and school to school and never feel stuck. I'm the rocking, cool poetry lady who comes into the class for one or two periods and wows the kids with my poetry mojo. I tap into their creative self-expression, inspire them to write, and get them hyped about poetry. My workshops are a break from their regular academic class schedule. I bring the magic and the fun. As a teaching artist, I'm in and I'm out, spending no more than an hour and a half, tops, sometimes just forty-five minutes, in each class. My poetry teaching artist swag is tight. I flow like honey and the kids gravitate to me like bees. I rock that shit.

But today, the next day, and the next three weeks will be *very* different. I will be teaching incarcerated boys a pre-GED curriculum all day. From 7:50 a.m. to 2:30 p.m. I'll be with the *same* group of boys in the *same* class teaching *all* subjects, all day. Jesus, take the wheel. Lord knows I don't want to do this. I'm an artist! I love the freedom of making my own schedule and not being confined to any one place for any extended length of time, like being in a classroom all day—or worse, sitting in an office cubicle, a graveyard for dreams. But dammit, I need the money, and my artist coins aren't consistent enough to support me on their own. I find myself frequently jumping from teaching-artist gig to teaching-artist gig like an urban frog on a concrete lily pad. And summers are always financially tight because there's no school. No school generally means no teaching gigs. Summer school teaching-artist programs are scarce, and I have only one lined up, with just a couple of paid poetry performances sprinkled throughout the summer to help me eke through till September. It's a constantly unpredictable hustle. Landing this temporary substitute teaching gig at Rikers was perfectly timed. The universe has thrown me a three-week money branch. I should count my blessings. *Punch the clock, heifer.*

I was drifting when Ms. G brought me back: "Whose class are you covering today?"

I'm not sure how she knows I'm a sub, probably because I'm a new face among the regulars who are greeting each other with familiarity. It takes me a second to remember. "Umm, I'm subbing for Ms. Morgan until the last day of classes."

Ms. G looks at me with pity. "Oh God, they put you with the goons. That's a tough class. Good luck, girl!" My deer-in-the-headlights expression beckons her to continue. "Put your foot down right away, and if you have any problems, don't hesitate to call a CO." She smiles and tries to reassure me. "You'll be fine, though." Ms. G is Brooklyn-fly, talking to me with Gucci sunglasses perched on her petite cinnamon face. And her shoe game is tight. I know we're going to be cool. Sometimes divas clash, sometimes they connect. We connect.

I stand there trying to convince myself she is right, that I *will be* all right. Hell, I've worked with these kids before; I've been teaching poetry workshops here at Rikers for ten years. I have nothing to be afraid of. Ms. Barron was never afraid. She was a teacher I worked with back in 2002 when I taught an eight-week poetry workshop with her class. I remember watching her on this very same school floor wield her iron fist in a velvet glove.

Ms. Barron had a way of nurturing the boys with tough love. She said things like, "I don't care if you try to intimidate me, but there are certain things I won't allow in my class! You might want to punch me in my face. I might want to choke your neck. But the bottom line is I care about you learning and getting an education. I want you to get to know who you are and learn to like yourself! I care enough to say no. It's much easier for me to sit back and let you do what you want. But that's not who I am. I'm consistent and persistent. And you will most certainly work hard and use your brain while you're in my class. Believe that. If you can't get with the BOE [Board of Education], then you'll have to deal with the DOC [Department of Corrections], and I'm team BOE."

Ms. Barron would frequently bring the boys breakfast bars because they often came to class hungry, complaining they hadn't eaten. Some mornings they'd have to wake up at four thirty for breakfast. Since most of them stayed in bed, the boys generally wound up missing morning chow. She knew it was impossible for them to focus and learn if their stomachs were growling and ribs were touching. "Make sure I get every wrapper back. If the officers find out I'm giving y'all snacks, I could get in trouble, and they'll dead the snacks," she'd say. They would gobble up the breakfast bars and diligently return the wrappers.

I'd met Ms. Barron through a mutual friend and, after talking with her at length, I couldn't wait to teach a series of poetry workshops with her class. She was the real deal. Her love for her students was palpable and, coupled with her passion and brutal honesty, it created a unique bond between her and her students. She constantly challenged them to think critically. She'd tongue-lash them when they were wrong and praise them when they were right. And, in a place where they were seen as criminals, dangerous minds, a booking case number, and a menace to society, she saw them as her sons.

Ms. Barron taught at Rikers for over fifteen years and felt God put her there for a reason. Her son is incarcerated, serving a twenty-five-year-to-life sentence in a maximum security adult penitentiary. He was convicted when he was sixteen, the same age as many of her students. When she shared that information with her class, it got so quiet you could have heard a mouse piss on cotton. Heads just nodded, followed by a couple of "wows." Losing her only son to prison when he was a teenager was the catalyst for her embarking upon a deeply personal journey to teach incarcerated adolescent boys, in an attempt to heal. It was a classic case of transference indeed, and yet every boy who came through Ms. Barron's class was better off because of it. She was a stand-in mother; she stood in the maternal gap when their own mothers could not.

Whenever some of her students would get on her bad side, their act was nothing short of self-sabotage, because they'd be denied the mother's love they all craved and needed. Even though many of Ms. Barron's students rebelled, they soon found themselves back at her door like hungry puppies, humble and apologetic, wanting her thug mama hug, which she always gave.

Ms. Barron was genuine and real and, in spite of her going ballistic on her students at times, they knew she cared. Urban kids recognize *real* and pick up on *phony* instantly. They are masters of quickly reading and sizing people up—a skill they need to have in order to survive the streets. Ms. Barron left an indelible imprint on my teaching style, and thinking of her gave me a boost of confidence. If she could run a classroom without being afraid, why couldn't I?

I was trying to convince myself but couldn't, because teaching in *this* capacity, as a full-time teacher, is still terrifying. It's a far cry from a poetry workshop; this is the Marine Corps for teachers. Plus, I was going to be a substitute teacher, aka a "sub," the lowest level on the teacher food chain. Even the kids know it. When I went to school the same was true…substitute teachers always got played and suckered, all day, every day.

"Girl, you'll be just fine," Ms. G said as I took a sip of tea. She sucked her teeth. "You ain't no punk. Where you from?"

"I'm originally from Philly, but now I live in Brooklyn."

"Awww yeah, Brooklyn in the house!" Ms. G made me laugh. "You got this, girl, but they're gonna test you, so remember it's better to start off hard at first and then soften up. Not the other way around. If they see you're soft, then it's game over and *they* run the class."

"Okay" is all I can manage to say. My head is still spinning from punching a time card in a time clock at seven-fucking-thirty in the morning.

"I'm two doors down from you," she continues. "I'll check in on you during my prep."

I'm glad I met someone who clearly knows the ropes and is friendly to me, willing to guide me through this morass of I-don't-know-what-the-fuck-I-have-gotten-myself-into.

"Oh, and one *very* important thing to remember...see that class list you're holding in your hand? Don't lose it. You'll need it to take attendance so you know *exactly* who's supposed to be in your class and who's not. They know you're new so they're gonna try to have all their little friends up in your class, and you'll have more drama and ruckus than you need. Take attendance *first thing* when they come in, and don't hesitate to send whoever is not on your list out of your class, immediately."

"Thanks for that, Ms. G, will do."

She proceeds with the warning: "You don't want to be caught with a student who's not supposed to be in your class, because if a fight breaks out and one of them is not on your student roster, *you're* gonna be the one asked why was so-and-so in your class in the first place. Get to know who's in your class ASAP."

"Thanks for the heads-up, Ms. G. I really appreciate it."

"No problem, Ms. Peterson. I got you, girl. I'll stop by your class later," she chirps in her friendly way as she struts out of the office.

I walk down the hot, musty hallway to my classroom thinking, *Oh great, I've got the thuggest of thugs in my class. Well, isn't this just dandy?* Thank God it's only for three weeks and, since it's the end of the school year, I'll just be babysitting until June 23 anyway. I can manage that, goons and all.

CHAPTER TWO

Sizing Me Up

By 7:50 a.m. the class begins to trickle in as the students are brought up from their respective housing areas to the school floor. They are much more quiet and orderly than I expected. But it's early, too early for me, and they seem to be feeling the same way. They shuffle along, escorted by correctional officers. Some enter my class and sit, while others linger in the doorway, talking to other students who pass by on their way down the hall. Most of the boys have on their street clothes because they have not yet been sentenced and are detainees, not city or state property. Their fate is still being gambled and negotiated in court. New York is one of two states in America that try sixteen- and seventeen-year-olds as adults, even for nonviolent crimes. Some kids have been sentenced to serve a City Year* at Rikers (which is eight months); some will be released on their next court date; some have been going back and forth to court for over a year; some are waiting to be sentenced. Very few are able to post bail, and most just sit in jail while their court dates get repeatedly

---

*City Year: the eight months an inmate serves under a twelve-month sentence. For every thirty days of an inmate's incarceration, ten days are reduced from their sentence. These ten days are considered "good days" or "good time." For example, an inmate sentenced to thirty days in jail will actually serve twenty days; an inmate sentenced to one year will serve eight months.

adjourned month after month after month. The majority of the kids have an overworked, underpaid, inattentive, court-appointed Legal Aid lawyer, which means they will likely wind up taking a plea deal* from the district attorney, who wants a conviction and usually gets it. Around 90 percent of all criminal defendants in the United States plead guilty without a trial because they can't afford a paid lawyer. The risk of taking it to trial to prove your innocence means the defendant will languish in jail, sometimes for years, awaiting trial and the DA will raise the stakes very high by offering a horrendous amount of time for the crime should the jury reach a guilty verdict. Blowing trial is way too risky so plea deals are the norm, especially for a kid who is scared and wants to go home, even if it means they'll have a felony on their record.

From misdemeanors to felonies, and from criminal mischief[†] to murder, all the guys on the school floor have one thing in common: They are embroiled in a justice system that criminalizes Black and Latino youth. As I look at the faces of these kids, still young enough to outgrow their shoes, I wonder what they did to land themselves in jail.

I am stunned to find out how normal adolescent rebellious behavior can land a Black boy in prison. A school fight can brand him a criminal with an assault charge, whereas white kids are often easily forgiven, getting nothing more than detention and a slap on the wrist. In predominately Black schools, discipline-related issues that a school dean or principal should normally handle are now handled by police officers and settled in a court of law.

Jerome, a tall, lanky skater boy, was charged with assault and petty larceny because he got into a fistfight at school and stole the other kid's phone...Bernard jumped the turnstile and had a warrant for missing a court date...Kevin sold drugs...Maurice got caught

---

*Plea deal: in criminal proceedings, where the district attorney will offer the defendant a lesser sentence if the defendant agrees to plead guilty to the charge and waives their right to a trial.

†Criminal mischief: committing acts of vandalism, graffiti, or destruction of property.

with a gun…Cedrick smart-mouthed a cop…Russell stole a car…
Victor set a trash can on fire…Sammy graffitied a wall…Johnathan
snatched a purse…Daniel robbed a bodega…Nasiem got caught
with illegal firecrackers…Jeremy violated probation…Wilson had
dirty urine…Shaleik hustled bootleg DVDs…Stephon got caught
with a gun…Craig tried to kill somebody…Shane *did* kill somebody…James refused to snitch…Michael didn't cooperate with the
cops…Devante took the fall for a gang member in order to protect
his family…Kevin had mistaken identity…Jalil was a booster*…
Tyshaun was a burglar…Kareem sold weed…

The list goes on and on, but one thing connects them all:
Whether innocent or guilty, charged with crimes that are violent or
petty, they are all in the same boat: teenagers at Rikers Island mandated to go to school—and to my class.

Several students are wearing state-issued, beige khaki pants with
matching khaki button-down shirts, which indicate they have been
sentenced and have a release date. The khaki kids are sprinkled in
with the vast majority of kids, who haven't been sentenced and are
wearing the clothes they were arrested in. Most have on jeans and
T-shirts. Despite the semi-freedom of the nonsentenced kids, who
are able to wear their street clothes, giving them some semblance of
individuality, there are still very strict Department of Corrections
regulations that prohibit certain colors (no red, no blue for obvious Blood/Crip gang-related reasons), and no brand-name labels (a
restriction that reportedly reduces violence).

For adolescents, not being able to wear designer labels is a painful sentence to no-frills purgatory, since they are all at that annoying
stage of *being* what they wear, equating designer tags with personal
value and self-worth. Sad but true. (I too succumbed to that teenage malaise and became a proud victim of materialism. I was a high
school Gucci girl, to be exact. Without my Gucci bag and gaudy

---

*Booster: a person who steals items and sells the goods on the black market.

labels, I felt incomplete, naked, *less than,* and corny. It was a phase.)
I can relate to their materialistic pain.

Almost all of the kids are wearing state-issued, bright neon
orange slip-on canvas sneakers, but a few of them are sporting
regulation black Reeboks or the old-school white-on-white Nike
Uptowns. The Reebok/Nike kids were either wearing them at the
time of arrest or a loved one had been kind enough to send them
a pair so they could avoid the mandatory super-ugly, nondescript
canvas slip-ons. Most of the fancy designer sneakers have removable innersoles where contraband and weapons can be hidden,
making them a security risk. But since the black Reeboks and Nike
Uptowns don't have removable insoles, and because of their generic
color (all black or white), they're allowed. Timberland boots are
banned because they have steel toes. When it comes to security, the
DOC leaves no stone unturned. The fancy, trendy, fresh, fly sneakers the boys might have been sporting out on the town and at the
time of arrest wind up being taken from them and placed in property, along with other items like their wallets, jewelry, and jackets
(including money). Sometimes items in property turn up "missing,"
and an inmate rarely has recourse. Almost all of the boys wind up
being issued the Patakis,* which the kids brilliantly nicknamed
pumpkin seeds† because of their neon orange color and shape. By
the end of my three weeks, I will have a complete jailhouse lexicon.
The poetry and figurative language that flows effortlessly from their
foul mouths amazes me.

The first student who makes his way into my class is Naquan,
wearing a brown extra-large sweatshirt and gray sweatpants too
tight for his big ass. He takes the seat closest to the door, stretching
his oversize body across the desk, peering out the door to see who's

---

*Patakis: official name and synonym for "pumpkin seeds," the bright neon orange,
state-issued canvas slip-on sneakers named after former governor George Pataki.
†Pumpkin seeds: state-issued kung fu–style slip-on canvas sneakers. They are bright
neon orange in color, like a pumpkin, and shaped like a seed; also called Patakis.

coming down the hall. He occasionally throws up gang signs to his comrades, who briefly enter my class to give him the ritualistic handshake that resembles a funky finger-puppet soul minuet.

"Nigga, that's why your breath smells like diaper shit!" yells a short skinny kid with his hair half-braided and half-afroed before flipping Naquan the middle finger. Naquan jumps up and runs to the doorway yelling, "Nigga, that's why I saw you in the town with a patent leather Wu-Tang jacket on, nigga!"

The entire hallway cracks up laughing.

Naquan is sizing me up now. More students come in. As I continue taking attendance, about eight guys are sitting in my class who aren't supposed to be. I shoo them out.

"But miss, this is my class, my name's just not on the list cuz I just got here..." One of the guys tries to swindle me.

"I was born at night, but not last night. You can't stay in my class. Go where you're supposed to be."

Surprisingly, he doesn't give me much of a fight as he swivels from out of the desk he tried to occupy. "Yo, son, she don't play, but she mad cute though, ya heard, miss?"

"Ummhmm, go where you're supposed to go," I say in a stern voice with an ice-grill face.

"Good morning." I make it a point to greet each young man who comes in the room. "Good morning," I repeat, sometimes with a soft smile. "Good morning," sometimes with a stoic face. This is a balancing act. Can't appear too nice, but can't be too mean at first. I have to be flexible, keep them on their toes so they can't peg me right away. Most don't respond to me, some grumble, and some return the greeting.

I put my name, Ms. Peterson, on the board, but immediately they begin to call me Ms. P, since they refuse to try to remember my name, and nicknames are standard hood ritual. *Ms. P.* I guess I'll have to be.

"Yo, Ms. P, where you from? Brooklyn I bet," asks one kid.

"Naw, nigga, she look like a Harlem chick!" another kid yells from the back of the class. He's brushing his hair, slouched down in his seat, looking at me from head to toe with a gaze too grown for his adolescent baby face. He thinks he's cool.

"Excuse me but I am not a chick. I'm a grown woman, and it doesn't matter where I'm from, because right now I'm at C-74, just like you." I have to put my grown-woman foot down and set a boundary for how I will and will not be addressed. They're feeling me out.

As I begin to write an assignment on the board a kid with pimples yells out, "I know you don't expect us to do work. You can't be serious. You going hard-body, miss, and it ain't that serious!"

Using my strongest theater voice to project loudly and sternly without yelling, I say, "I have high standards. And as long as I'm here, trust and believe, we will do work, brother."

"Miss, this jail! We criminals!" the pimply-face kid shoots back.

"Malcolm X said, 'To have once been a criminal is no disgrace. To remain a criminal is the disgrace.' Elevate your mind, Black man. And as long as I'm here teaching, that's what we're going to do...elevate."

"Tell it, sister girl!" yells Xavier, a tall, slim diesel kid with deep mahogany skin, chiseled features, and high cheekbones. His face is a gorgeous African mask. And he is clearly the drama king and alpha male in class. Many students defer to him, making it obvious that he has some level of rank in the housing area.* He seems to take a liking to me. This will be helpful.

I ask Xavier in a familiar 'round-the-way tone, "What you know about Malcolm X?"

"Come on now, how you gonna play me, miss? That's my son. Malcolm, yo, that was a strong Black man right there. That's why *I'm* X too." He slaps his chest with pride.

"Nigga, you X cause your name is Xavier," Naquan quips. "You

---

*House or housing area: synonym for crib; the area where inmates are housed and kept; the open dorm-style area; cells.

ain't no Muslim nigga. I saw you buying pork rinds in commissary,* nigga."

Xavier snaps back in a half-joking, half-serious growl, "Yo, watch your mouth, nigga. They don't sell no fucking pork rinds in commo,† you dumb-ass nigga with them high-water skintight sweatpants on looking like bitch-ass capris. Nigga, shut the fuck up!"

The class is in hysterics, having big fun snapping on each other and playing the dozens, but I have to nip it in the bud or else this could escalate into chaos.

"All right, all right, relax," I say, laughing. "Ain't no niggas in here, and please don't use that word, at least not in my class."

Maxwell, a handsome kid with brown satin nutmeg skin, sits slouched in the back row brushing his hair with slow meditation-like strokes. Hair brushing isn't just for grooming; it's soothing, like hugging yourself or sucking your thumb. It calms them down, this jailhouse Zen of hair brushing. Having a brush is also a luxury and status symbol; it means someone loves you enough to send it to you *and* you are respected enough that no one has taken it from you.

Maxwell's donning a fresh haircut with shiny, soft waves rippling across his head and sporting crisp white-on-white Nike Uptowns. His beauty has a commanding presence similar to that of Xavier, but unlike loud-mouth X, who holds court like a skilled street corner ghetto jester, Maxwell's energy is old-school, cat-daddy smooth and mysterious. The boy is fine.

"Miss, come on!" he says. "You sound like my grandmother or something. This ain't like back in the old-timey days. When *we* say it, we mean it differently. It ain't negative no more. Everybody say 'nigga' now. We can't stop saying that word, miss. That's unrealistic, 'cause niggas gonna stay calling niggas niggas." He's being a smart-ass and has garnered an amen corner.

---

*Commissary: the jailhouse general store where snacks, toiletries, and goods are purchased.
†Commo: short for commissary.

Naquan chimes in, "Word! I ain't gonna never stop using that word son, ya feel me, my nigga."

This is never an easy discussion. Most urban kids use the word *nigga* uncontrollably like a noun, a pronoun, an interjection, a curse, and a compliment. They aren't even aware how much they say it. They inherited the word from older generations who were stumbling through post-traumatic slave syndrome and still are today. The elders bequeathed this mangled, controversial, and highly charged word to us. Today it has become that much more haunting, as the children casually swing it loudly in public and in front of white people, hitting the elders in the head, making them cringe and silently cry. It's a word that hurts, and I don't like hearing the kids use it because they have no frame of reference to its painful history, and they're so reckless with their ignorance. It feels like a pinch when I hear them drench conversations with it. And yet when I am in the private company of close friends, sometimes it rolls off my tongue comfortably. My father and uncles were great men, and they all used the word when holding court, talking shit or fussing. It's a contradiction and internal conflict I haven't quite resolved.

The word is as complex as our history. It can be used as a term of endearment or as an insult, depending on the context and tone. My dad said African-Americans are superhumans, magical niggas of the world who survived the Middle Passage, European diseases, and slavery. And we performed alchemy when we snatched the poison from the python by taking back the power of that whipping-stick word white people used on us. He said Black folks take slop, stir it in a pot, season it, and make song around it, for survival. *Nigga*. It's a word that *we* can use but white people can't—and definitely shouldn't. There's a subtext of power wherein Black people have something that white people don't have free access to. It's a word white folks have to whisper and sneak to say lest they be seen as ugly racists—or worse, get their ass beat. Yes, it's a double standard. Black folks have normalized a multitude of double standards living in a white-dominated society rooted in a long history of white supremacy. We know the rules. A young white man running down the street is just running; maybe he's late for school. A young Black man running down the street is seen as suspicious; he must have committed some crime. Police will stop him, maybe even shoot him. A white youth in a hoodie is just wearing casual sports gear; maybe he's about to go jogging. A Black youth in a hoodie is a thug,; he is probably a criminal, might have a gun. Police will stop and frisk him. A white woman who talks back to a cop might get a ticket or a warning. When a Black woman talks back to a cop, she's dragged out of her car, tased, arrested, and might be killed. A Black person will be sentenced more harshly in a court of law for the exact same crime that's committed by a white person. White people taking food from a grocery store for survival during Hurricane Katrina were "finding food"; Black people taking food were "looters." The Second Amendment protects white citizens, affording them the right to bear arms and openly carry shotguns in a mall. The mere sight of a Black man with a gun, even with a permit in an open-carry state, could mean an immediate death sentence. Black children with toy guns were shot by police in Baltimore and Cleveland. The list goes on and on. Black folks are used to it. It's not fair. But that's the way it is, currently. So yes, using the word *nigga* is a double standard, maybe the only one Black people own. Nigga, twisted and layered. Like our history.

"Ms. P, it's not that deep, and we're not saying *nigger,* we saying 'nigga,'" says Alex, a pudgy Pillsbury Doughboy–looking Latino kid with fuzzy cornrows.

"It's the same word. It doesn't matter how it's spelled. Come on," I argue.

"Naw, the 'er' makes the difference, miss."

"Alex, please. Give me a break. Do you hear Mexicans calling themselves *wetbacks* or Puerto Ricans referring to themselves as *spicks* or Jews calling themselves *kikes*? We're the only people who refer to ourselves using a demeaning term."

They paused to ponder that idea, but only for a brief moment.

"Miss, we gave that word a different meaning, so like we took lemons and made lemonade."

Dammit, he's right. They are beginning to frustrate me. I remember how Ms. Barron used to go ape-shit on the kids who used that word and even had it on her list of violations of classroom rules. Offenses in her class were categorized as either misdemeanors or felonies, and using the word *nigger* in her class was considered a felony. She grew up in the segregated South, and her family was chased out of town by the Klan. That word was salt in a wound for her. Not so much for me, but I still don't want the kids to say it.

I attempt to give a brief history lesson about the word. "That word has a violent history, and—"

Maxwell cuts me off. "I know the history. It was used to violate us and be like a putdown, but we changed all that."

I have to figure out a stronger argument. I thought about what my good friend, mentor, and homie-for-life Abiodun Oyewole (aka Dune) said to me about the word *nigga*. A poet, philosopher, cultural icon, Harlem shaman, and founding member of the legendary Last Poets, Dune has always been a staple in my toolbox for teaching. His love, passion, and understanding of Black people is an ancient cosmic root that reaches beyond galaxies. His tongue is a sacred blade, and his words are medicine. His poems inspire and heal, and his stories are hilarious. His life is revolutionary. I'm always sitting by his knee, a young Jedi soaking in the bounty of wisdom from this uptown national gem. Yoda told me you can't get rid of the word *nigga* because there will always be niggas. Nigga is a character that exists in all Black people, and it has provided a shield against white supremacy. The nigga in us protects us and helps us back a motherfucker up off us; it's good for our break-glass-in-case-of-emergency moments. Dune also said that "instead of telling people to stop using that word, or having silly funerals for the word, be proactive. Start using the term *brother,* or create another word to use instead of *nigger,* because you can't take something away without replacing it with something else."

I try some of Dune's psychology on the boys.

"I'm not saying don't ever use that word. I'm not scared of that word, brotha. I'm just saying try to incorporate other words into your vocabulary to refer to each other so you don't sound ignorant all the time. Try using the term *brotha,* or 'my dude,' 'my man,' or 'my ninja.' Come on now—stretch your vocabulary, that's all I'm saying. Be aware of what's coming out of your mouth, because right now you're saying it without realizing you're even saying it and you never want to be in a position where you slip up and say it in the wrong environment and embarrass yourself by looking ignorant when you're not."

"I hear you, miss. Like if I'm at a job interview or something."

"Exactly! Or talking to an elder who would be offended."

Even though I cracked his argument, he tries desperately to cling to his position like a baby clutching an empty bottle. "But I can control it. I know when to say it and not to say it."

"No you don't. You're not conscious of what comes out your mouth, so I'mma be the reminder and help you be more conscious. I wouldn't be a righteous Black woman if I sat here and allowed you to talk reckless all day in front of me." I think I have momentarily stunned him with my passionate declaration, until the class clown trumps me.

"Power to the people, sister! Help these brothers not be ignorant niggas!" Xavier says, jumping out of his seat pumping his Black fist in the air for dramatic emphasis.

"All right, Xavier, take a seat please, thank you." I say "thank you" before he complies.

I think of how Abiodun would handle this situation. He told me once, "Baby, *nigga* is a Black family word. It's like pajamas; you wear your pajamas around people you're comfortable with. You don't wear your pajamas outside the comfort of your home. *Nigga* is like that. It has a time and a place." I carried Abiodun's philosophies and teaching with me like a talisman.

I sense this is going to be an ongoing debate. I'll need to create a thorough history lesson to tackle this subject. Nas's newly released album, aptly titled *Nigger*, immediately comes to mind. There are several songs that talk about the word *nigger*, with Abiodun appearing on two tracks. Plus, the album cover has a picture of Nas's scarred back, reminiscent of the iconic and historical photo of a slave's whipped and keloid back dated from the 1800s. Juxtaposing both images would be a great starting point, but I'll have to table this discussion for another day because right now, in this moment, I need to switch gears and come up with something for them to *do,* quickly.

The classroom is hotter than asphalt baking in the August sun or a crowded subway car with broken air-conditioning. Stifling and funky. And it's the last three weeks of school, so the kids think they don't have to do a lick of work. Even though I'm just a substitute covering the class, I can't have them talking and doing nothing all day. (I probably *could,* and I'm sure no one would judge me, but my personal code of ethics won't let me. I'm a teacher and that's what I came here to do, teach.) I need to figure out a way to keep them engaged and comply with actually doing some work. The chips are stacked against me, and the kids are getting antsy. I pull out my HBO *Def Poetry* performance card and hit them with a couple of my standard razzle-dazzle poems, which gets some applause, but more important, I have their attention and interest. It's a cheap trick, but it's working. Hey, I have to use what I have to get what I need: keeping them busy with a semblance of order.

"Miss, you was on TV?"

"You met Russell Simmons?"

"Did they pay you a lot?"

"So if you're famous, then why you here?"

"Yo, she was on TV, son. That's wavy."*

"I wanna hear another one of your poems."

"I don't write poetry but I can rhyme…"

Great. I have them engaged. This is the cool new teacher

---

*__Wavy:__ synonym for cool and hip.

honeymoon, but I have a feeling this won't sustain itself for three weeks, and the challenge is bound to come. It's the nature of children, particularly adolescents and especially the ones who have already bucked the law, challenging authority.

In order to get them to do some work and write, I am constantly making deals, like promising a movie for tomorrow if they do work today, or promising to play some music if they work while listening. I brought in Nas, Ghostface, Jay-Z, Mos Def, Dead Prez, and Tupac, but it's Lil Wayne who is the primo bargaining chip that can get them to do work, because they all fiend to listen to Weezy. The kids are actually writing, and I'm surprised how well they're complying with the assignment. Because I'm not their regular teacher and it's the last three weeks of school, I don't have the burden of having to teach the full pre-GED curriculum. I can freestyle what I want as long as they're engaged and learning. So, for the short time that I'm here, I'm leaning heavily on my strength—poetry and creative writing. Other teachers walking by are amazed to see the infamous class of goons behaving relatively orderly and writing.

I have the mojo. I can do this. I'm effective. I'm connecting. And, as long as I keep the classroom standard high and make unwavering demands of them, as long as I push them and encourage them, I'm seeing them rise. Even if just a little bit, they are actually rising.

Like a strategically planned prank laying in the cut for the right moment, the inevitable challenge I had anticipated, but forgot about, comes a few days before the last day of school. By now they are used to seeing me, and we have a good rapport. The day starts like all the others with my run-on mantra:

"Good morning…Good morning…Have a seat…Pull up your pants…Excuse me, I'm talking…Sit down, sir…Get your feet off the desk…Get out my chair, boy! Go sit down…Watch that word! No, he's not a nigger…Relax! Watch your mouth… Are you doing what I asked you to do? Put something on the paper, boy. What is wrong with you?…Pick up that piece of paper you just threw…Don't throw that pencil…Go get it…Thank you…Pull up your pants…Get your hands out of your pants…Don't spit in my class…Come get this tissue, please…Go to your class, sir. No, this is not your class…It's too much conversation…Fellas, this is not the barbershop…Watch your mouth…Don't be disrespectful…Don't make me have to make it hot* and call a CO…You're cruising for a bruising…Come here and let me see what you wrote…Very good. Now give me a couple more lines…See? I knew you could write. So stop fronting on me and do the work…You're doing great…Watch that word…Keep your voices down, fellas…" And on and on like that, all day, nonstop.

There are the consummate chatterboxes who sit in the back of class: Naquan, Maxwell, Blake, and Kev. I hear someone about to hog spit, and I immediately look up in the direction of the gross sound of mucus gathering in the throat. I see the culprit is Blake. He cuts his almond-shaped eyes at me, shooting me a quick glance before he continues talking to his friend. This is a dare. I wait a few seconds as I scroll down the class roster to remind myself of his name.

"Mr. Blake, can you come here for a minute?" I ask in a calm, nonconfrontational sweet tone laced with honey. When he reaches my desk, I hand him some tissue. "Would you please wipe up your spit, and next time would you be so kind as to get some tissue to spit in? I know it's jail, but let's keep our room sanitary." I call him by his last name to distinguish him from another student who has the same first name. It is the only way I can avoid confusion with the other Naquan, the class clown.

Blake's physical frame is sculpted for the gods. Standing at six feet one, all lean muscle mass, he could probably be an athlete if he didn't choose the streets. His cheekbones are so high his eyes practically sit on them. He stares at me momentarily before he says nothing. His wheels are turning, and he finally decides to just give me a chin-up,

---

*Making it hot: bringing unwanted attention to a situation from an authority, usually from a CO or teacher; creating a scene that could bring trouble; caliente.

I'm-so-cool nod of agreement. He wants to resist but for some reason chooses not to. Whew. Perhaps he appreciates that I didn't put him on blast in front of the class. I'm learning it's all in the approach, and it's a delicate split-second judgment call, situation by situation. This is a small victory, but Mr. Blake has more in store for me.

Later, Blake throws a balled-up piece of paper across the room at Reginald, a quiet kid with Magic Marker–looking tattoos on his neck and hand. (Why that boy did that to himself only God knows.) His skin is so dark that the tattoo is indistinguishable and looks smudged. Reginald ducks and laughs, then retaliates, hurling another balled-up piece of paper. I have to nip this paper-ball fight in the bud before it escalates into a full throttle free-for-all and something less "fun" gets thrown.

"Y'all cut that out right now and come get the piece of paper, Blake. You too, Reginald. Pick up that paper, please."

Blake ignores me and resumes talking to his buddies, the fly boys in the back row, while Reginald picks up the piece of paper that he threw. "Thank you, Reggie. I appreciate that. Mr. Blake, will you please pick up that piece of paper you just threw and throw it in the trash?"

Blake continues to ignore me. Thug mama is stirring in me; she is being summoned but not yet released from the lamp. My tone gets strong and confrontational. It's hot and my tolerance for foolish defiance is short today.

"Mr. Blake, I am talking to *you*. Pick up the piece of paper you just threw!"

"I ain't throw *that* paper! That's not my paper, miss!"

And, here we go . . . the power struggle.

"You know, that's something an immature boy would say." My octave is commanding the attention of the entire class now. The show has begun, and all eyes are on Mr. Blake and Ms. P. Whether consciously or not, he successfully pushed my buttons. And, like a genie in the lamp, he conjured my inner thug mama to whirl out as I belt, "A man acknowledges his mistakes. A man acknowledges when he's wrong. And when a woman politely asks a man to *please* pick up a piece of paper, a *man picks it up*! But a *boy* whines 'it's not my paper,' 'I didn't put it there.' A boy will find every excuse *not* to do something and blames everybody else for his wrongdoing, *But a man takes responsibility for his actions!*"

Blake is now standing up out of his seat and yells while beating his chest with one fist like King Kong, "I'm a man! I did a man's crime!"

"You did a man's crime with a child's mind!" I shoot back.

He looks shocked. Bull's-eye! I stung him. He doesn't have a comeback. There is a brief pause, and I seize it before he does. Thug mama puts on her velvet glove to deliver the rest of the bitter medicine a little more gently.

I soften my tone just a bit. "Learning how to become a man is not easy, and while you are not a full man, you are on your way to becoming one, and it ain't an easy thing. It can be very frustrating when you're trying to figure it out on your own. And I know this is an uncomfortable moment right now, but it's all for the good if you learn and grow from it. 'Cause that's what it's about. Learning from your mistakes and growing into a man. They call them growing pains for a reason. It's painful sometimes. It's embarrassing sometimes, like right in this moment. But it's *all* for your good. It's part of the process to your manhood, brotha."

Xavier is out of his seat, jerking his body in fake convulsions, pretending to catch the Holy Ghost as if he's in a Pentecostal church service. He starts running back and forth from one side of the room to the other, shouting with his hands in the air, "Ooooh, preach! Hallelujah, sista, praise the Lord! Ooooh, praise God! Can I get an amen, brothas?" The entire class, including me and Blake, start laughing hysterically. In a masterful instant, Xavier lightens the mood with brilliant comic relief. Genius timing. He is a true drama king who knows how to hold court, a true actor-comedian in need of a stage and audience.

"Boy, sit down with your crazy self," I say through my laughter.

And just like *that,* in a mystical snap, the mood shifts. Blake is chopping it up and laughing with his friends in the back row while listening to Xavier's church stories and urban lies. And my thug mama is back in the lamp.

It turns out to be a good day, and I feel like I earned a break. I damn sure need a rest after all of that, so I let them rock the radio and play board games for the last two periods. I'm exhausted. I don't want to battle them to get them to do more work. Shit, it's Friday, and school is finished next week. I made my point. I'm respected. I survived the goons. I'm feeling confident and proved to myself that I *can* do this. Word spread with staff and students that "Ms. P don't play. She handles her business and she'll turn it up."* In just three short weeks, I earned a reputation of respect.

As I make my way to the main office to clock out for the day, I run into Phil, the principal. Phil and I go way back to the days when he was the vice principal and I was teaching poetry workshops back in 1998 in the Six building (C-76). I like Phil. He's always been an advocate for arts and literacy, and he loves my poetry workshops; he even came out to see several of my poetry performances and my one-woman show in the city. His short, scruffy beard along with the tiny diamond-stud earring in his ear gives him a hint of a hippie past. Phil is a cool white dude.

"Liza! Well, you made it through. I knew you would. You always had a way with this population." He seems pleased. "There might be a teaching position we need covered for the new semester in September. Sort of like a permanent substitute where you'll have your own class. You're a good fit and would bring a lot to the guys. Will you be around? And would you be interested?"

"Of course, Phil, I'd love to."

I'm feeling confident and successful after surviving the three weeks thrown into the fire, and Phil's job offer validates my victory. I accept without hesitation. I damn sure need the steady reliable income. I can do this. And I'm learning how to flow, getting my full-time teacher's swag. It's on.

---

*Turn it up: to make it hot; to fight; to become hostile and belligerent.

CHAPTER THREE

I Got This, Not

Summer break is over. The elaborate, colorful, and very loud West Indian Day Parade on Labor Day in Brooklyn marks the end of my summer freedom. The boombastic calypso rhythms along with the massive steel pan bands collectively ring the "party over, y'all, back to work" alarm. No more spontaneous beach bumming on a weekday afternoon, writing till 3 a.m., or late-night saloon hangs at my favorite watering hole with my girls. It's officially time to set my alarm clock for 4:30 a.m. and go back to work at Rikers in the wee hours of the morning. The fun flew by in a flash. Dread is starting to creep up on me as the evening sun begins to set. Damn.

"No money, no man, I don't have *any* shows lined up for the fall, this rent is kicking my ass and I have to teach full-time at seven thirty a.m. every fucking day just to eke by and barely pay bills. What the hell is going on with my life? Something's gotta give, girl. I deserve a breakthrough, dammit. This country doesn't respect or support artists, only celebrities. And just because you're a celebrity doesn't mean you're an artist anyway. It's all bullshit."

My friend Sun quietly listens while we sit on my balcony as I ramble and rant about my life. She occasionally offers me a compassionate, "Mmhmm, I hear you, girl." She gets me. She's an artist, too—a singer and songwriter—who does freelance writing for online publications and copyediting. Her passion is music, but it doesn't pay the rent. She understands the hustle and grind of being an artist living in New York City, where juggling the passion of your art and paying bills usually means taking jobs that you don't really want to do.

All it takes is the right opportunity, the right person, to see or hear your work and for the right combination of events to happen, and the doors to the dream of *just being an artist* will swing open and, like magic, your art will pay the rent. All artists pray for that Lotto moment, but in the meantime, we bust our asses working various jobs, squeezing in time to create. Sometimes it feels like I'm chasing a unicorn. Yet the passion outweighs the frustration. I love acting, I love performing, and I *love* writing. My art keeps me breathing. I can't imagine living life without having the freedom to create and express myself artistically. It's the language I speak. It's how I make sense of the world. It's what I was put here to do. It's my first love.

"And it sure would be nice to come home to some loving arms, but *no,* what do I have? I have my cat meowing, begging me for food. Maybe I should get a sugar daddy?" I'm whining and getting on my own nerves. Sun is patient.

"Girl, if it was that easy, you would have already done it. Five minutes with one of those rich nig-nuts and you'd be cussing them out or yawning in their face. You can't fake it. *I know you.* Relax. Just breathe. You're on the right path. You're doing important work. Trust the Creator has your back."

Sun always has a way of unruffling my feathers. She's right. Compromising myself for money was never a consideration or option. I'm just working myself up into a tizzy talking crazy talk. Frustration and anger will do that. I'm angry that summer is over and I have to go back to grown-up world and work a full-time non-artist job. While I was initially grateful for the opportunity of steady, secure income, the rigid schedule I am now forced to face is making me a bit anxious and resentful. But as Sun rightfully reminded me, at least I am employed and rent will get paid. Sometimes I get so fixated on what I don't have and what I want that I miss the small blessings right in front of my face.

In order to get a good night's sleep, I calculate that I have to be in bed by at least 9:00 p.m., because I have to be dressed and out of the house by 5:30 a.m. to be at Rikers Island by 7:30, ready for class at 7:50. This is such an adjustment. What in cockamamie hell have I signed up for? I lie wide awake in bed at 9:15 p.m., not the least bit tired or ready for sleep. Thoughts about my being able to pay my rent and the solitude of living without a roommate help reinforce the idea of this being an *opportunity*. Perspective is everything. I try to play Jedi mind tricks with myself to quell the overwhelming resistance to this absurd schedule and to calm my artist's instinctual urge to act out, to run and not show up.

I wake up starting my morning off with a prayer that will become my daily mantra: *"Mother Father God, Infinite Great Spirit, NTR, show me what to teach, show me how to reach these children today, guide my words, use me as a tool to uplift and inspire. May your Light shine through me and as me."*

School buses are not even on the road by the time I leave the house, and it's still dark. The moon has slipped away, but night still hugs the sky. It's so early that even the sun hasn't begun to yawn and the birds aren't singing. And it's still too early to see kids trotting back to school with new book bags full of school supplies, donning new outfits and fresh hairdos. The kids I'm about to see are likely wearing the same underwear and clothes they were arrested in, wrinkled and musty.

Facing this god-awful early morning schedule feels like I'm diving underwater, submerged in a world so far removed from my art that it's beginning to threaten my self-esteem. *This isn't a three-week gig, sweetie. Naw, baby, you're in it for the long haul, the entire school year.* The three-week summer substitute stint was a measly warm-up, a light jog, in comparison to what I am about to face—a long-distance marathon. I was able to skate by and fluff with just my poetry and creative writing lessons over the summer,

but *now,* today, next week, next month and *all year,* it's the real deal, yo. I'll be expected to teach a full-fledged pre-GED curriculum in *all* subjects. I begin to feel small. I signed up to do something I'm not sure I can even do and truly don't want to do, but I've got crazy bills spilling out of my mailbox like an overstuffed mouth, with angry notices bulging, threatening to cut off this or that service. I don't even open it, but I slap the box each time I walk by, hoping the bills will get swallowed up. I can run but can't hide. My rent and past-due bills demand I be an adult and face the music: My art isn't making the cut financially. That is a hard pill to swallow. Becoming a schoolteacher, at this stage in the game, means I have failed as an artist. Despite my hard work and sacrifice, my dream has eluded me. The unicorn tricked me; the dream was just a mirage.

When Phil offered me the position I leaped because guaranteed income in a city where the rent is too damn high beats tenuous teaching-artist gigs that haven't even been secured yet; secure known money trumps dice-roll money. Dammit, I'm an artist. I don't want to teach full-time because it's a commitment I fear will significantly reduce (and maybe even annihilate) my creative energy. But I also don't want to fail the kids. I know that since I signed up for this I need to be the best teacher I can be and give the kids the best that I can offer. I take teaching our children seriously. Black and Latino kids need educators who care, particularly in a society where their lives are marginalized, criminalized, and rendered disposable. I feel a sense of obligation to show up in a way that will significantly empower them, even if my artist withers somewhat in the process. I suppose it's the activist in me.

Getting *to* the classroom is the challenge, but once I'm in, I commit. The kids keep me authentic; they bring out the nurturer in me. But what if I fall short and fail as a teacher, too? And what if the kids rebel, and what if I don't reach them or make an impact? Then that makes me a double failure. Teacher failure. Artist failure. The ANTs—automatic negative thoughts—are beginning to run amok. There's a lot of self-doubting chatter going on in this head of mine. I feel like curling up in my bed to cry and float in my river of self-pity, but I have to dash out of the house to be on time.

Crazy butterflies dance in my stomach as I ride the subway to Queens Plaza, where I catch the Q100 express bus to Rikers. I see Mr. Davis, a fellow teacher on the island, who takes a seat next to me on the bus, temporarily diverting my anxiety as he gives me a warm Black nationalist greeting.

"Hotep and good morning, my Black Nubian queen. Good to see you, sister!"

I'm relieved to see a familiar face. Mr. Davis's smile is warm and comforting. His caramel-colored face is heavily decorated with freckles and crowned by a short, sandy brown, almost red afro with a matching mustache. He's a tall, slender man in his fifties with a potbelly camouflaged by his green-and-gold embroidered African dashiki. The way he talks and carries himself reminds me of my father and uncles whom I grew up with who fought against white supremacy in the 1950s, '60s, and '70s. They were proud, strong men who experienced tsunamis of injustice, oppression, and racism and to this day refuse to be silent about it. Just like my father, Mr. Davis's rage is palpable and justified, earned from history. My dad was a decorated World War II veteran who risked his life to serve this country and "protect our freedoms" only to return home and be spit upon and denied those very same "freedoms."

When GIs returned to the States from fighting in the South Pacific, the Red Cross welcomed them with coffee and donuts. When my father reached for a cup of coffee and a donut, the white Red Cross nurse snatched her tray away and said the coffee and donuts were for the white GIs, not niggers. After that sledgehammer, upper-cut punch in the face, my dad vowed he would never give blood to the Red Cross, even if his own mother's life depended on it.

"How was your summer?" I ask Mr. Davis.

"My summer was too damn short! And I am certainly not enthused about waking up to come to this modern-day plantation where they have our brothers and sisters packed in here like slaves."

Mr. Davis keeps his fire stoked. "But while I *am* here, my Nubian sister, it is my duty and assignment to make sure I teach these young brothers in my class *everything* they need to know about who they *really* are. I teach them the true history of the Black man and not those European lies that have our people lost and downright ignorant."

"I know that's right," I reply.

It's too early for visiting hours, so the only people on this express bus to Rikers are other Board of Education and Department of Corrections employees. Mr. Davis takes pleasure in talking loud about Black history and the "miseducation of the Negro," while signifying 'bout whitey. It certainly doesn't take much to get Mr. Davis riled up, especially if he has an audience of white folks, the target of his ammunition.

As soon as he notices a white employee glance toward him and shift uncomfortably, he gets a little louder. "You see, my sister, I teach the brothers the truth about who they really are. You know how the kids say 'real recognize real'... Well, I keeps it real, sister. Can you imagine if I stood in class and taught our young brothers that Christopher Columbus discovered America? That's ancestral blasphemy! Some of these teachers can't teach because they were lied to their damn selves, so how can they teach *our* children when *they* don't even know the truth of our history? We are the only people who let the sons and daughters of our former slave masters teach our babies. Now that's something to think about."

The fire's ablaze and he's on a roll, despite it being 7:05 a.m. "Christopher Columbus was the original gangster. He was a true terrorist who killed thousands of Native Americans, brought over syphilis, and renamed the Caribbean Islands the West Indies because he thought he was in India! And these wicked people have a holiday for this stupid, diabolical man? Only thing good about Christopher Columbus is we get a day off the plantation for his ignorant ass. See, my sister, I teach our young brothers the truth, and they respect me for it."

I'm happy to bump into Mr. Davis on the bus before my first

day as a full-time schoolteacher. He gives me a lightning bolt energy charge, putting a battery in my back, reminding me why it's import- ant to impart untold history and unpopular truths to urban kids, because they don't know who they are. They lack knowledge of self, which is essential in shaping self-perception and behavior.

My parents instilled in me a strong sense of pride and frequently spoke about the genius and superhuman resilience of Black peo- ple. They made sure that I grew up with a positive self-image, not only of myself but also of my race. My older cousin ran with the Black Panthers, and our living room was powwow central. I heard a lot. Mr. Davis reminded me of my power-to-the-people cousins. I love talking with old heads well versed in Black history, because they keep Black scholarship alive. If our children knew how great a legacy they come from, maybe the generational tides of self-hatred could begin to turn with them. Mr. Davis was giving me a refresher course on what I needed to bring to my class besides the mechanics of English. I had to bring them history and self-pride.

Mr. Davis and I worked together, back in 2001, at Friends of Island Academy, a youth development reentry program for previ- ously incarcerated adolescents. He taught the GED classes, and I wore many hats working primarily with the young women. The kids called me Sista Liza, and I was known for holding mini-cyphers* about Black history as I sought to impart wisdom on the young, misdirected, wayward warriors. My desk was full of unconventional history books by Black scholars. I was determined to wake as many sleeping giants as possible.

Mr. Davis is exactly what I need this morning to temporarily quell my anxiety and reaffirm the warrior spirit in me, who, like him, is putting in work on the Underground Railroad with the youth.

Mr. Davis continues his rant: "Did you know, in 1921, we had our very own Black Wall Street in Tulsa, Oklahoma, and the white

---

*Cypher: a term used in hip hop to denote a circle of freestyle rap artists taking turns "spitting" or rhyming.

devils burned our entire community to the ground in three hours? Murdering thousands of Black men, women, and children? Three hundred businesses, homes, schools, banks, and hospitals burned to the ground by treacherous crackers? Talk about terrorism." He groans. "We know it quite well, my sister!"

As we cross the bridge over troubled water the stench from the garbage and methane gas seeps from the landfill that Rikers sits on, surrounded by the East River. Sometimes I forget and naively look around at the other passengers on the bus to see if I can detect who farted. It smells like rotten eggs. Awful. There's also a cluster of power plants to the left of the bridge, about a mile distance away from the island, that emit God only knows what kind of fumes and pollutants.

The bus pulls up to the Perry Building, where several seagulls sit on top of the dingy blue and dirty white one-story structure. Mr. Davis brushes the cascade of crumbs off his lap from the egg-and-cheese roll he chomped on. He throws me the Black power fist as he speedily strides off into the sea of employees entering through the first security check point and turnstile. I flash my Board of Education ID to the obese, porcelain-faced CO at the control turnstile, who surprisingly offers a morning smile. I remember him from the summer. He's usually stone-faced. I take the smiling CO's warm gesture as a sign from the universe: *It's going to be all right.*

Visitors, lawyers, and other volunteers have to wait in line to get a temporary DOC visitor's ID. They wait while the CO sitting behind the Plexiglas booth rummages through a jumbled folder stuffed with preapproved clearances that have been faxed over from headquarters. Sometimes people get turned away because someone somewhere in the rabbit hole of bureaucracy didn't submit the paperwork in time or it got lost or the officer simply overlooked it. I zip on by that hassle and extra lucky for me I don't have to take one of the old blue and orange rickety route buses that take employees to the various ten facilities across the 415-acre island. I can actually walk across the bus depot and parking lot that is conveniently directly across from my facility, RNDC (C-74). It's always super-windy because of the East River a rock-toss distance away, and the loud roaring engines from the steady stream of airplanes descending and ascending to and from LaGuardia Airport directly to the right of the island is initially jarring but soon becomes like white noise. The barbed wire is both shiny and rusted; the building is two stories, low, wide, and gray. The scent of fresh-cut grass momentarily overpowers the toxic stench as several adult male inmates in bright neon orange jumpsuits are mowing the small strips of lawn outside the facility.

Even though talking with Mr. Davis temporarily put me at ease and has me ready to charge into class with confidence, as soon as I enter the building, I feel a heavy lump in the pit of my stomach. Fear is dancing in my belly doing the cha-cha, shaking my colon and giving me gas. I look behind me; the coast is clear so I fart in the stairwell leading to the school floor.

When I reach the school floor, I am informed that there are no students today because it's classroom prep day. The day will be spent getting all of our class books in order and our classrooms set up. Nice! I let out an audible sigh of relief. I punch in and retrieve my class schedule from my mailbox. I read it and my stomach sinks again. I am expected to teach language arts, reading, writing, grammar, social studies, *and* science. I begin to have a mini panic attack, and the air around me suddenly gets thick. My heart feels abnormally heavy, and heat is coming over me. Sentence structure, grammar, social studies, and—oh God!—*science*. I feel inadequate and unprepared. I am terrified. How can I help these kids learn when I don't know a thing about science? And social studies? *Jesus.* I barely remember what I learned back in college. Even though I know how to speak the King's English and basic grammar rules, I'm not fit to teach the *mechanics* of it. I am totally out of my league. I am doomed. I haven't even started and I already suck. I'm gonna fail; I'll never make it past a week. The students need me in order to learn and advance in life, and I have *no* idea what the hell I'm doing! What I do know is that I'm drowning. Now I *really* feel like crying.

The other teachers are happily and effortlessly loading up their carts with books for their classroom library, moving through the halls with ease. They sit in the morning staff meeting looking uber-relaxed and some even seem a little annoyed because they are clearly *all* veterans who know the drill and are bored by the monotony of this routine, first-day-back-to-school meeting. But *not me*. I'm trying to keep my click-it-on-get-the-money poker face, while shitting bricks, in over my head. When the meeting is over, I walk up to Ms. G. I think I might be sweating.

"Hey, Ms. G," I pant.

"Hey, Ms. P!" she says all chippy.

I let out a deep sigh and shake my head. She notices the gravity in my voice and sees the terror in my eyes. "What's the matter, girl?"

"I don't even know where to begin. This is quite overwhelming. I don't even know what books to get for my library. And I don't know a lick about science."

I want to fall in her arms and sob, but I can't.

"Girl, go get a cart and meet me in the resource supply room. I'll show you what books I use. The first day is always daunting. It's normal. You'll be fine. Just breathe, girl. You did great over the summer. You *got* this."

I make an uncomfortable "yeah, right!" chuckle. I know she's trying to help me, but she doesn't know the degree of my fear.

As Ms. G. guides me through the rows of semi-organized shelves while pointing out which books are best to have for my class, my shoulders slowly slide back down. She piles reading books, pre-GED textbooks for each subject, pencils, erasers, paper, posters, and a spanking-new CD player onto my cart. As I look with awe at this shiny new boom box, an instrument that could really help soothe my nerves with music therapy, Ms. G says, "Girl, don't let them touch the radio, 'cause it will start arguments and wind up broke before you know it."

Ms. Harris, the gatekeeper of the teacher supply room, chimes in, loud and abrasive, "And you only get one for the year. If it breaks, that's it. No more. And you best ration out the erasers, because I don't have an unlimited supply, and since the rotten little criminals like to steal 'em and eat 'em like animals, I suggest you keep your erasers locked up." She seems mean and needs electrolysis. *Animals?* I don't like her for calling them that. She rubbed me the wrong way talking about the kids like they're garbage.

Ms. G adds her two cents regarding the classroom supplies, but she doesn't bark like the grumpy billy-goat troll. "Oh yeah, keep your pens locked up too, and if they ask you to borrow a pen, get their ID card. When they return the pen, they get their ID back. No exceptions. Pens are a valuable commodity around here because they'll sell 'em, and you only get a limited ration. Oh, and always, and I do mean *always,* keep your markers in sight. I keep mine in my ID pouch I wear around my neck. If one of those lil' suckers gets a hold of one and starts tagging up the walls, you could get in deep trouble for that."

My headache starts to get bigger. I think the drained look on my face must have prompted Ms. G to add some reassurance. "Girl, most of this shit is just common sense. You ain't from Kansas. Just be smart. You know they're slick, so establish boundaries and be firm. No one sits at your desk, and no one is allowed to walk behind your desk. Don't let up on that rule unless you want them rummaging through your drawers like some dingbat teachers, who I won't name."

"You mean some teachers actually let them go through their desk?" I gasp in shock.

Ms. G gives me the universal sista-gurl look with curled lips and tilted head. "Girl, *please.* Some teachers let the kids sit at their desk, have their feet up on the desk, and basically run the class. You'll see who's who. Just watch."

"Oh no, no, no," I respond self-righteously. "I might be new, but I don't play that, sitting at my desk . . . and feet up? Oh no, no." I start wagging my finger at this point.

"I know you don't play, girl. You held it down this summer, so you're gonna be fine. Set a standard of respect and they'll respond.

You're always gonna have one or two knuckleheads who will try you, so make an example of them and write them up ASAP. And trust me, they hate that, 'cause they lose privileges."

"Yeah, the orange slip is great leverage, huh?" It feels good to show Ms. G that I had learned a little bit of the classroom ropes from my summer run.

"Works like a charm in most cases," Ms. G says, "and when that don't work, call the CO. They'll pull them out of your class with the quickness. And as much as the boys grumble about being in school, they'd rather be in class than sitting in their cell all day."

"I'm glad I didn't have to do that," I say proudly.

"Oh, you will. I promise you, you will." She's shut down my little burst of three-week pride. What could I say? She's a vet.

Talking to Ms. G helps lift the boulder from my chest. I take a deep breath and inhale a little bit of my confidence. Slowly, I push my rickety cart piled high with books and supplies down the hall and around the corner to my newly assigned classroom.

It's so dusty, I sneeze. It looks horrendous, full of old paper and trash, a whirlwind of garbage everywhere. A damn junkyard. The teacher whose class this was may have been a formidable educator but they were also a disorganized hot-ass mess…a trifling slob. Just nasty. I can't work in these conditions, so I set out to make my classroom a clean sanctuary. Order will help me think clearly. I will definitely need some semblance of peace of mind in this place, so I'm going to create a feng shui vibe of virtue and order. The visual aesthetic and frequency in the class is important so I'm going to clean this shit up and elevate the energy. I roll up my sleeves and go in deep with rubber-glove action, scrubbing, bleaching, sweeping, and disinfecting the desks and shelves. The industrial-size garbage bag I'm using is full. I am not playing. I don't do *mess*. The energy is already changing.

Next, I put up brightly colored wall decorations and arrange the desks in straight, neat rows. I place cutout posters of all the planets in the solar system up high, close to the ceiling, all around the circumference of the room, giving it a cosmic vibe. I create a designated poetry wall, of course, but my personal favorites are the ancestor walls. There are several standard Board of Education Black history posters of inspirational figures that I put on display: Martin Luther King Jr., Rosa Parks, Malcolm X, Langston Hughes, Maya Angelou, and Jackie Robinson. But the most powerful and stunning images come from my personal collection that I copied and laminated from my library of classic coffee-table books. I have pictures of African kings and queens from the Old Kingdom, New Kingdom, and pre-dynastic eras in Egypt, the Great Temple of Ramses, the Great Pyramids, and beautiful, rare images from *One More River to Cross*. I also hang rare pictures—Marcus Garvey; a smiling Malcolm X; Martin Luther King Jr. (hugging Coretta); Malcolm and Martin shaking hands; Black men in uniform from the Civil War; Black men donning top hats and tuxedos, from Reconstruction; Frederick Douglass with a young protégé; Harriet Tubman; finely dressed Black women from the 1920s; wrinkled, stoic elders over one hundred years old; the Black Panthers; and Native American warrior chiefs. My ancestor wall *rocks*.

I prominently mount the images on both sides of the blackboard so that the boys will constantly be seeing their ancestors of antiquity and, hopefully, draw some inspiration from them through osmosis. The only thing missing is incense. I'm going in, tapping into my esoteric holistic healer. It soothes me.

Just at that moment, Mr. Young, the art teacher, who is pushing a squeaky cart full of art supplies piled in a colorful mound, pops his head into my room.

"Looking good, sis. Very artistic. Great composition."

"Thank you, Mr. Young. I appreciate that coming from you."

"Even if I didn't already know you were an artist, I would have guessed it just by the way you decorated your room. It feels good in here. Visually engaging; good vibes and very feng shui."

"That's exactly what I was trying to accomplish. You know about feng shui?" I ask excitedly.

"Oh yeah. Besides being a visual artist, I study martial arts. It's all connected. I'm into energy, the esoteric and the eclectic, and I could be wrong, but I get the sense that you are too."

My eyes light up. Another artist! "You know I am. Energy, the cosmos, the ancestors, all that's important for our youth...I love that you get it. And you can see I was up in here doing my feng shui like a motherfucker." We both laugh as I continue. "We in jail, so I gotta have my force field turned up high, you feel me? I want the energy in the room to make them feel good on a subconscious level. Only thing missing is my incense for the aromatherapy, which I know I can't burn in here."

"Sis, there's a simple solution for that. What I do is get essential oils like frankincense."

"I keeps me some frankincense in stock, always. I got some in my purse right now, son!"

Mr. Young laughs. "Cool. So what you do is take your oil and pour a little bit on a piece of tissue, and in the morning, before the guys get here, rub a little bit on each of the desks."

"Brilliant!"

"It's great, because you're spiritually anointing your room and each desk. And let's be real," Mr. Young adds, "the guys smell a little musty, so it keeps the room funk-free, and it really does chill them out. I notice a difference every time I do it."

We both laugh at the reality of how bad this place smells at times with rooms full of bad breath, farts, and guys who can't afford deodorant. "Mr. Young, you just made my day! Thank you for that!"

"Please, just call me Young. Mr.'s too formal. Or you can call me Killa. That's what the kids call me."

I laugh. "Killa? How'd you get a name like Killa? You don't look like no killer."

"The kids gave me that name when I first started working here around 1992, damn near twenty years ago, and sis, this place was *really* bad. There were stabbings and slashings on a regular, and stepping over pools of blood was the norm. It was crazy—"

"Damn. That's wild."

"You have no idea just how wild it really was. I was new to the joint and was trying to get used to this negative environment. I'm generally a happy person, sis, so coming in here was truly a spiritual battle. I was going through the fire."

I like how he put that. I immediately feel a kindred spirit in Mr. Young. Maybe I too am going through the fire, and this teaching assignment is a spiritual test. He tells me the story of gaining his jailhouse moniker.

"So, there was this guy named Spanky B...I'll never forget that guy's name. I knew he was an adult playing like he was an adolescent, because it was something about his energy and the way he carried himself. I could tell he was older and I think he knew that I knew. Sometimes when guys come in from bookings, they'll give a phony age and name. And back then, until their fingerprints came back from being run through the system, DOC had to put them with the adolescents—especially if they looked young, they could get away with it more easily.

"So Spanky B," he continued, "was extorting the kids. I didn't like the guy, and for some reason, he decided that he didn't like me. Our energies didn't mix, and we both knew it. One day we got into a minor verbal exchange, nothing serious, but a tit-for-tat kinda thing, and suddenly I became the butt of Spanky's jokes. The guys are laughing and getting him hyped, but what he didn't know was that I was a better comedian than he was. So I went in on him and started getting louder laughter from the class, which pissed Spanky B off.

"Well, he gets all embarrassed, and his only comeback was to try and intimidate me, so he says 'I should rob you' and proceeds to touch my pants pocket. I knew this was a challenge. So I told the dude, 'Don't touch my pockets,' and he ignored me. He put his hands in my pocket, and in a reflex reaction to block his hand I moved so quickly that I slapped him by mistake."

Killa stands to demonstrate what happened next. "There was like a three-second delay, because I was shocked. Spanky B was stunned and the class got silent. Then the entire class said 'ooooh,' and Spanky's nose flared like a bull and he charged at me. But I used his body weight against him and spun around like *this* and he hit the floor. I could hear the CO running to the class, and when he came in, he sees Spanky B lying on the floor and asked what happened. I said just as calmly, 'He fell.' The CO knew I was probably lying, but what could he say? He had to take my version of the story. So now at this point I've gained the respect of the class, because I didn't snitch. Spanky B got up and sat in the front row. I tried to continue with the lesson and turned my back to write on the board, but my hands and legs were shaking to the point where I couldn't even write. And I could hear Spanky fuming. He was breathing so heavy that I could hear his breath. Sis, I was scared. So I turned around and I said to him 'Look, I'm scared, and I don't like feeling like this, so if we gotta do this again, we might as well get it in right now…' And the class went dead silent."

"Oh my God, what the hell did Spanky B do?" I ask. My heart's racing as he tells the story. "Spanky B said 'Fuck this class!' and walked out, and the whole class went crazy saying stuff like 'Yo, this teacher is a Killa.' And from that point on the kids kept calling me that. The vice principal eventually asked me why the kids kept calling me Killa, and I told her it was an acronym for 'knowledge in living life adventurously.'"

I'm cracking up. Killa is a great storyteller. He's lanky, six foot four, with waist-length dreadlocks heavily streaked with silver strands of wisdom neatly pulled back in a rubber band. Mr. Young smiles a lot and has a youthful, bubbly demeanor. A jokester with a great sense of humor, Young's inner child is fully evident in his bouncy, childlike gait, walking on the balls of his feet.

"Well, sis, I'm not gonna talk your ear off, but I gotta share something with you before I get out of here."

"Killa, you're not talking my ear off at all. What you gotta tell me?"

"Well, it's kinda sad."

"Oh no, what happened?"

"Last night the police found a six-year-old boy wandering the streets and offered to take him home. The boy said, 'No, I don't want to go home, because my mom beats me.'"

I gasp and clutch my heart, bracing myself for the worst.

"The police asked, 'Well, what about your dad?' And the boy said, 'He beats me too.' So the police asked the boy, 'Where do you want to live?' and the boy replied, 'With the Dallas Cowboys. Because they never beat anybody.'"

Killa smirks. "I forgot to tell you I'm a comedian too."

"Ooh, I needed that laugh. I was feeling so overwhelmed, you have no idea how much I needed that."

"Sis, like I said earlier, working in this place really is a spiritual battle, and we artists have more difficulty adjusting to the energy here. But believe it or not, you're exactly what these guys need. No doubt about it. Just your strong presence alone is good for them. You're gonna be just fine. But remember, you're an artist. Don't let this place take that from you. Incorporate what *you* do best with the guys. Use your art. I remember you from when Ms. Barron brought you in to do your poetry workshop with the guys and then you came back another time to perform your one-woman show. That shit was dope. The guys were totally into it. You held their attention the entire time, and that ain't easy in an auditorium of a hundred and fifty adolescents, especially in this place. Your art is powerful, sis. And you got a big heart. That's who you are. Don't get trapped here."

Okay, now he is speaking to my soul. The tears are beginning to well up in my eyes, so I take a deep breath to avoid crying and opening the floodgates that his truth has tapped into. I am terrified that teaching in this full-time capacity could doom my dream of being an artist. Killa's simple warning—"don't get trapped"—reminds me to keep this teaching assignment in perspective, that it's just a temporary season in my life. This doesn't have to be the endgame because *I am an artist. Don't get trapped here.*

God, I needed that affirmation. I clasp my hands and bow. "Thank you, Killa."

"Anytime, sis. I'll be checking in on you. Plus I think I have your guys for art, fourth period."

I scramble to find my class schedule. "Whoo! Yup, I have you fourth period! It's *so* on."

Yes, the angels are conspiring to help me.

My room is on point and ready to go, but my confidence is still a bipolar swing from *I'm good* to *I'm in over my head.* I am emotionally exhausted. Mr. Davis, Ms. G, and Mr. Young were major guardrails who unwittingly held me up today. This ain't an easy-breezy poetry workshop, and this ain't end-of-the-year summer babysitting fluff. Naw naw naw, this is my class all day, all year. This is measured outcomes, daily lesson plans, frequent testing, daily grading, differentiated learning, teacher evaluations, and mastering multiple subjects. I didn't go to school for this shit. I am walking into uncharted territory. There's no way I can do this.

Once again, I'm beating myself into a tizzy.

Public school teachers are extraordinary. They're godlike. And it's been said they work harder than *you* do no matter *what* you do.

I believe that to be an indisputable truth. They're superheroes. But me? I'm just a poet, a playwright, an actress—who creates art. I'm a nonconformist, truth-telling feather-ruffler who isn't scared to say what I think but has the gift to say it poetically. My art has been referred to as "honey on the blade." Honest, passionate, and biting. My intention is always to uplift, enlighten, and inspire, whether onstage, on the page, or in a poetry class. And here I am at Rikers Island teaching, all day. I signed up for this, and I don't know how long I'll last, what impact I'll have, or what my purpose is for being here, so I just pray for clarity. Everything happens for a reason. I'm strong and resilient like my ancestors. I pride myself on being an artist with the soul of a nightingale and the skin of a rhinoceros, but today, by the time I clock out at 2:35 p.m. on the dismal school floor at Rikers Island, I am nothing but a raw jellyfish.

CHAPTER FOUR

Danny Gunz

Thought for the Day: To have once been a criminal is no disgrace. To remain a criminal is the disgrace.

—MALCOLM X

Every morning I write a Thought for the Day on the corner of the board. I ask the students to give their thoughts on the daily inspirational quotes. Some mornings, it surprisingly elicits a hearty discussion; most mornings, they grumble, grunt, or ignore me. Too damn early for critical thinking—I get it. Until this morning, I wasn't sure if the seeds of consciousness I was attempting to plant were even registering. I forgot to put the Thought for the Day up on the board, which Gerald, a quiet student who is easily overlooked, quickly brings to my attention. "Ms. P, what's good? You forgot the Thought for the Day," he gently says.

I smile as his request affirms that they are in fact watching, they *are* taking it in, and I just might be reaching them after all. "You are so right, Gerald...I got you," I pleasantly reply, and I write a new Thought for the Day in the corner of the board as he diligently copies it into his notebook and grins.

Look at what you've been through and what you've survived. You are a walking, talking miracle. You are so much more than you've been told. —Ms. P

The first week is totally about getting to know the dramatic range of characters who I am working with all day, every day, all year. For some odd reason, the alpha males have decided to sit in the front row, right up in my face. The back row is normally where the cool kids sit, reserved for shit-talking and social-lounge parleying. Like the kitchen, it's the space most comfortable, in the cut where real conversation and saloon talk takes place. Later I would figure out that the leader of this alpha male crew has a crush on me; hence the front row spotlight positioning. They call themselves the Bosses. I call them the Bosses of stink, not because they smell, but because they have stank attitudes, always getting on my nerves. They're fly boys, as fly as one can be in jail, rocking fresh haircuts and spanking new sneakers as they damn sure wouldn't be caught dead in pumpkin seeds. They think those jailhouse bobos are for herbs.* The Bosses get barbershop time on a regular basis and clearly have rank and power back in their housing area. They walk like kings with an air of confidence and subtle intimidation, getting a constant flow of salutation fist bumps and handshakes from guys passing by the class, like lil' hoodlum dons. Me and my Gucci girl crew back in high school thought we were the shit too. Knowing the pecking order in this place is important. Who's the OG,† and who's in his crew. Who's the doja?‡ Who's the

---

*Herb: a cornball; a nerd; a square; usually a nonfighter who is seen as weak.

†OG: Original Gangster; an older street player with experience and rank; the leader of the gang.

‡Doja: synonym for pop-off dummy (POD), a follower in the team or group. The doja (like the POD) is the low man on the totem pole who does the bidding or fighting for others with higher rank in the crew or group.

pop-off dummy?* Knowing who's Blood, who's Crip, and who's food†
is critical information to stay a step ahead of potential tensions and
explosions that might arise. But most important is having peripheral
vision, which is essential for classroom management. The Bosses sit
in the same seats every day, immediately declaring their territory.
They claimed the front row seats on the left-hand side, next to the
door and the window that looks out onto the hallway. Guys who
are on their team,‡ which includes their pop-off dummies, sit close
behind them. The neutrals are guys who stay to themselves, don't
claim a gang or team, and sit in the far back row center of the room.
Those desks are generally up for grabs, since no one has a stronghold
on that section. The Harlem crew has claimed four back-row seats to
the far right, next to the filthy windows that face another of the jail's
brick walls. Nothing to see except hardened pigeon shit, feathers,
and dirt splattered on the window slats.

On the board I write "SWBAT [students will be able to] discuss
the five evolutions of Malcolm X and compare and contrast his evolution to their own."

Then I write, "DO NOW. Write a five-paragraph essay reflecting
upon and answering the following questions: What is your government name (the name your mother gave you)? Who were you in the
street (your nickname and why)? Who are you in jail (your jailhouse
nickname and why)?" And finally, "Look into the future. What type
of man do you see yourself evolving into?"

---

*Pop-off dummy (POD): the kid who fights battles, or "pops off," for a particular set
or team. He is willing to take the blame for the "boss" or "OG" in the group. He does
this for inclusion and to receive fringe benefits from the group, relating possibly to
extra purchase power at the commissary or to obtain heightened protection by the particular set or team from physical harm by others.
†Food: a weak kid who is preyed upon for easy extortion and gets "eaten up" like food
by the stronger members.
‡Team: synonym for "set." The group of homies you roll with and pay allegiance to;
your posse.

I ask the group, "Who knows the five names of Malcolm X?"

"What you talking 'bout, Ms. P? Five names? He was just Malcolm X," Tyquan, one of my more attentive (but hyperactive) students, blurts out.

I respond, "He had a government name—the name he was born with. Then he had a name that he was called when he was running the streets hustling and—"

"Malcolm X was a hustler?" Tyquan interrupts.

"Yeah, nigga, he did time in prison! Right, Ms. P?" Tyrone, the leader of the Bosses, interjects, looking for approval.

"Watch that word. No *niggas*," I say. "But yes, he sure did do time in prison, and when he was in prison he was called something else, and later he changed his name to Malcolm X. Then, after his trip to Mecca, he would change it again to something else. Malcolm X had five names. So what was his first name? What was his government, legal name? What did his momma name him?" I ask, challenging them.

"Oh shit, I should know this," Tyrone says, snapping his fingers, trying desperately to remember. "Spike Lee did a movie on him. Denzel played Malcolm and the nigga—"

I cock my head to the side, prompting Tyrone to correct himself.

"I mean that brotha looked just like him too."

After a moment, he says, "I don't know, Ms. P. I can't call it." Tyrone gives up.

I've held their suspense long enough, and they'll never guess it, so I tell them. "He was born Malcolm Little," and I write the first name on the board.

"So okay, when he was in the street hustling, getting paper, what was the street name he went by?" I continued.

Stunned to learn that Malcolm X had a dark past in the streets, Tyquan asks, "He sold drugs, for real?"

"He did a little bit of everything…Burglary, pimping, number running, gambling, hustling…He was in the street hard-body, just like you. So what was his hustler name?" I ask again. Looking at their bewildered faces and shrugging shoulders, I try to give them a little help: "Part of his name described the color of his hair, and the other part of his name was the city where he was from."

"Harlem!" yells Tyrone, confident that he's right.

"Harlem Heeey!" yell Raheim and Marquis, the two Harlem-ites in the back of the class.

"Harlem got the most snitches!" Shahteik quips from across the room.

Raheim flags him with his hand and sucks his teeth as he shoots back, "Not as many as Brooklyn, I mean Snitchlyn."

"I don't give a fuck about snitches in Brooklyn cuz I ain't from bum-ass Brooklyn," Shahteik responds with a trickster smile, knowing his comment will surely get a rise out of his buddy Tyrone, who's from Brooklyn.

"Yo, watch your mouth, son," Tyrone growls, falling right into Shahteik's trap to stir up drama by any means necessary.

Mekhai, another one of the Bosses who sits next to Tyrone, chuckles like a Muppet.

I have to nip this shit in the bud. "All right, all right. Every borough has snitches, so let's drop it and focus." Being called a snitch is a dis. A dangerous dishonor like the mob calling you a rat.

I immediately reengage Tyrone. "Ty, you're on the right track. Malcolm did eventually wind up hustling in Harlem, but he was not originally *from* Harlem. Good guess, though."

"Damn, Ms. P. I'm stumped. I can't call it." Tyrone shakes his head in defeat.

"He was called Detroit Red, for his reddish brown hair."

"I'da never guess that," admits Tyrone.

"Well now you know. That's how you learn," I reassure him.

"True, true." Tyrone's interest in the lesson seems to corral most of the class. He loves Black history and makes sure to let me know. "I like learning shit like this," he says, jotting the answers down on a sheet of paper. He nods his head and shoots me a friendly, slightly flirty, smile. Ty's skin is the color of blackstrap molasses, flawless, and he has porcelain-white teeth that shine like brand-new piano keys.

Shahteik is determined to be a disruption and pain in my ass today, hell-bent on being the bane of my existence. He's back out of his seat.

"Shahteik, please take your seat," I politely ask.

"Ms. P, I don't care about no Malcolm X. What he ever do for me? Fuck that nigga!"

This boy makes my blood rise. I wanna slap the taste out of his mouth for disrespecting my hero, one of the greatest, most courageous Black leaders, whom I consider a divine miracle for Black people...our Black shining prince. And this raggedy pipsqueak, this ignorant little chicken-bone twerp, is throwing dirt on my sacred gladiator of Black love and truth whose life was spent (and sacrificed) trying to wake the sleeping giants to remember our greatness. Aww, hell to the naw!

"Watch your mouth! Don't you dare disrespect Malcolm X like that! You know what, as a matter of fact, go take a walk, Shahteik. I'm not dealing with you today." With my long arm outstretched, I point to the door, gesturing for him to get out now.

"So if someone asks me why am I in the hallway, I'mma say, 'Ms. P told me I could take a walk,' and it's gonna be more on *you* than *me*, ya heard?" he quips through his slightly crooked, candy-corn-colored teeth. He's not a bad-looking kid. He just needs to see the dentist—and the wizard, for a new attitude.

"Say what you gotta say, Shahteik. Just go take a walk, thank you." My tone dismisses him.

"Your wish is my command, lady," he replies all snarky as he excitedly struts out of class doing his infamous George Jefferson peacock walk, which draws more snickering from Mekhai the Muppet. Shahteik has his very own hype man in Mekhai, who laughs at everything Shahteik says or does, which further prompts Shahteik to cut up.

Shahteik has been locked up for over a year, so he knows all the COs and is able to move around a little more freely than some of the other kids. He has ingratiated himself with a few of the officers by being helpful back in the housing area. This, combined with his jail tenure and smart-alecky personality, has earned him a longer leash with some of the COs. Being caught in the hallway is not going to be a problem for Shahteik, who could slip into a buddy's class or chat up one of his favorite officers. He'll figure it out. It will take a long minute for Shahteik to grow on me. Right now he is a supreme pest, the adversary who plucks my nerves—all day, every day.

Tyquan brings the focus back. "So Ms. P, what was Malcolm's third name when he got knocked?"*

"He was so foulmouthed and mean that they called him Satan," I answer.

"Word?" "Oh snap." "Nigga musta been a beast." Several students blurt out responses in a collision of shock.

"Watch that word…but yes, Malcolm was not to be messed with."

"How long was he locked up?" Tyrone asks.

"He was sentenced to eight to ten years and served six."

"Damn, I ain't know Malcolm put it in like *that*," Tyrone says, leaning back in his seat, looking older than his youth.

Daniel, aka Danny, a five-foot-nine scrawny Black and Puerto Rican kid with eyes shaped like the ancient Egyptian eye of Heru (Horus), has been sitting at his desk all morning with a furrowed brow and clenched teeth, carrying distress all over his gentle baby face. I am well aware that every day these kids are navigating a plethora of legal, emotional, and family issues while also facing the pressure of jail life, dealing with layers of drama back in the housing areas with officers and troublemaking peers. This cocktail of stress makes depression and rage commonplace.

Something about Danny reminded me of Tariq, one of my former students during my early freshman years on the Rock as a teaching artist in C-76, where I eventually became the poet in residence for three years. I was the eager, bubbly, bright-light poetry lady sporting a secondhand green army jacket, camouflage cargos,

---

*Knocked or bagged: to be caught by the police and locked up.

and a tall purple head-wrap/turban-esque crown giving me a warrior queen aesthetic and vibe, smelling like Tunisian frankincense. Tariq was the kid with beautiful long lashes adorning his wide, walnut-shaped sad eyes who never smiled. His thick fuzzy cornrows looked like they were done three months ago and he needed them done badly or cut off or else they'd turn into dreadlocks. He was super-gifted and super-angry. Didn't talk much but still came to class every day, albeit stone-faced. His writing revealed a childhood wound and tremendous pain that evolved into adolescent rage. I marveled at his capacity to articulate it so honestly in his prose and transform it into poetry. A brilliant kid who obtained his GED before getting arrested, he ran the streets desperate for money, desperate for love, haunted by his mother's abandonment at age four. Tariq had been passed around to live with various family members like a rotten hot potato. One cousin hung him out of a housing project high-rise window by his ankles, threatening to drop him, and broke beer bottles over his hand when he was just six years old and still playing with superhero action figures. The keloid battle scar is still there reminding him of a war he was drafted into against his will. He just wanted to watch cartoons, eat sugary cereal, and play. He just wanted his mother's love and a safe lap to crawl into. He would share his story with me, the luminous windows to his soul revealing a wounded baby, now a gorgeous man-child navigating turbulent emotions without a road map or any support.

Tariq smoldered. There was something about this kid, a light, a spark of genius, a flash of great potential I saw in him. "I knew I shouldn't have robbed that man, Sista Liza, but I was hungry and I ain't have no money to eat. All I did was take the cash. I even gave him back his wallet with his credit cards and ID. I had a gun on me but I didn't use it, but that don't matter 'cause now I got a violent felony on my record. I'll never get a job. Seems like my fate is sealed, Sista Liza." Tariq quietly confessed this to me as he let out a deep sigh and put his head down to write, and write and write. Despite this being his first arrest, Tariq was facing five years in an upstate adult prison. Weren't there second-chance programs for kids like this? No one was hurt, no one was killed. Didn't this constitute a crime against poverty? Isn't five years and a permanent felony conviction a little extreme for a kid's first offense? A kid who, just like most of the boys sitting in my class now, still hadn't started growing facial hair yet?

Going to jail is a traumatic experience. Some guys fight to release and snap themselves out of depression. Some sleep a lot to escape. Others dance and joke around. And then there are the instigators, who set up conflicts for entertainment wherever they can. They all have employed various coping mechanisms, which vary from kid to kid and from day to day.

I generally don't let the guys sleep in my class, but I told them if they *must* sleep, if they have been up all night due to a cell search by the officers or couldn't sleep because they're stressed, mind full of doubt, fear, and anxiety, or if they are not feeling good for any number of reasons and need to put their head down for a while, just find a seat in the back row and be as inconspicuous as possible. I explained, "If the assistant principal walks by my class and sees you all sleeping in front of my face, then I have to answer for that."

Danny is sitting in the second row, and halfway through the lesson he puts his head down. I continue talking as I walk the aisle toward his seat and very lightly and gently tap him on his shoulder. Like a rattlesnake ready to attack, he pops up in a wild rage, which shocks me. He spits venomous fire. "Miss, don't touch me! Don't put your hands on me or wake me up for *nothing*!"

I somehow hold it together and remain calm, sensing he just might bite. "Excuse me, but I was not disrespectful to you, and there is no reason to be disrespectful to me when I was only going to tell you to take a seat in the back row if you need to put your head down." With Danny consumed by a rage that has nothing to do with me, I've become the target of his anger as he continues to explode. "I don't want you telling me nothing. And don't fucking touch me!"

He wants to attack and fire off his loaded clip of bottled-up fury, and if it has to land on me, so be it. He is ready to pop off and suffer the consequences. All reason has left his mind. I can feel it. This is not the normal wolf ticket I'm used to. I remember how he first walked into my class: wound tight, brooding, and looking awfully broken.

"Sir, I don't know what happened to you, but it has nothing to do with me, and I am not going to tolerate this level of disrespect," I snap, squeezing a formal response from between my clenched teeth.

"So write me the fuck up. The fuck I care," he growls.

"Thank you, I most certainly will." I see what kind of day this is going to be. "You're gonna have to leave the room, sir. Go take a walk. Think I'm gonna let you sit in my class and disrespect me like that? No *siree*. Take a walk." I have to put him out. He's not testing me; no, this is pure misdirected rage. The tone and cadence differentiate the two. That may be why I have a mustard seed of compassion for him in spite of his outburst. Instincts in this place are a matter of survival as much for the inmates as they are for the teachers and COs.

He walks out of class and stands right outside my door, pouting with eyes on the verge of tears; the kid looks twelve in an instant. Not having jail-time tenure, status, or a cavalry of comrades to visit in another class like Shahteik, he knows he can't just wander the hallway. He's too new. A neophyte. He's been here two, maybe three days max.

No sooner than he leans back against the faded gray wall, an officer roars, "Get out of the hallway and go back to your class. Now!"

With great hesitation, Danny tentatively walks back into my classroom, then pauses. He braces himself for my reaction. He's caught between a rock and a hard place. Just minutes earlier he had torn his drawers with me, but now I have the leverage, and every right, to deny him reentry into my class, sending him back into the grips of the grisly CO monitoring the hallways. He doesn't know how to navigate this terrain; he's too green. Back out in the hallway with the roaring CO means a loud and embarrassing verbal flogging, plus a possible infraction* if the officer inquires why he was kicked out of my classroom. I have the power to inflict more punishment, and we both know it. Briefly I glance at Danny and, in a split-second decision, I grant him a lifeline. He slowly and humbly takes his seat, his shoulders slouched in defeat, the fire in his eyes doused by the tears rising and dancing on the edge of his lower lid without falling. We make a silent truce.

I continue on about Malcolm, not skipping a beat. "And what's so deep about this brotha is that he dropped out of school in the eighth grade, was involved in every kind of criminal activity you can think of, got arrested, sent to prison, and was so mean and grimy that even the other inmates called him Satan. But it was during his incarceration that his most profound transformation began. He didn't go to prison thinking he was going to evolve into a great man and world leader who would touch the lives of millions of Black people. He was just like *you*. But the Creator had a different plan for him. Just like the Creator has a plan for each one of you sitting right here."

The room is focused, hanging on my words, and, with the timing of an annoying gnat that flies in your glass of red wine right before you take a sip, Shahteik pops his head back into the room and bounces over to Mekhai.

"Nigga, lemme git that strawberry Pop-Tart. I know you got it. I'm hungry as shit."

"Shahteik!" I yell.

Mekhai laughs while digging into his pocket, handing over the sugary Pop-Tart to Shahteik as he runs out of the room, but not before turning and winking at me on his way out.

I take an audible deep breath, unable to hide my irritation. Mekhai, a skilled instigator, takes the opportunity to bring attention to the obvious. "He be gitting on your nerves, don't he, Ms. P?" I refuse to

---

*Infraction: a ticket; a recorded incident of an inmate for a violation of a prison rule. An infraction can result in the forfeiting of "good days." If the offense is serious, the infraction can result in a new criminal charge and the inmate being rearrested.

dignify his baited question with a response. Instead, I just roll my eyes at Mekhai, making him giggle even more. I know he wants to get me riled up and the eye roll was enough to satisfy him for the moment.

I continue: "Your moment of transition into greatness could be happening right now. Maybe it will happen tomorrow, next week, next month, next year—you don't know when you will be called for greatness or when your purpose will be revealed, just like Malcolm didn't know he was being called for greatness. He didn't know part of his destiny was going to prison in order to become a great man; just like you're sitting right here and in my class for a reason. Your life is still unfolding, brothas. Who you are now is not who you are going to always be."

Tyquan's eyes are big, water-filled, glassy brown full moons, mesmerized by my every word.

"That's deep, Ms. P," he says, nodding his head. "I like how you put that. I'm feeling that. Word. I'mma be a great man."

Mekhai sucks his teeth, making Tyquan respond in defense, "Ms. P talking that real talk, my man, 'cause part of me still be wilding out but another part of me know I'mma do great things one day; it's like I'm caught between the devil and God," Tyquan exclaims.

"Africa, that's *you* talking like that?" Tyrone says, turning to face Tyquan. The Bosses gave Tyquan the nickname "Africa," referring to his blackberry velvet skin and tribal-looking scar under his left eye. Tyquan is a short and wiry good-looking kid who probably doesn't know it. Kids rich in melanin, kissed deeply by the sun, catch hell from other kids who think *dark* and *ugly* are synonyms. Racism—white supremacy did a number on us and on our self-image. It's been imbedded in our psyche for hundreds of years, passed down from generation to generation, and has been on autopilot for a very long time. Over time, we internalized the lie and now tell it to ourselves. Dark skin. *Ugly.* Nappy hair. *Bad.* Broad nose. *Curse.* Thick lips. *Undesirable.* We've been infected from centuries ago and are still sick with self-hate. There is so much to deprogram and teach the babies.

The Bosses have embraced Tyquan because he's Blood and their pop-off dummy. Tyquan willingly accepted their jailhouse term of endearment: Africa. I love that they call him that. I know they meant it as a dig, so when I first heard it I flipped it back and did alchemy. "Africa is the most mineral-rich continent on the planet. So much beauty comes from the motherland. Black is beautiful and Africa is the cradle of civilization. That's a strong name, Africa."

Tyquan goes on, "Yo, don't sometime you be feeling like, you've been handling your business the way you've handled it for so long that you don't know no other way, but yet and still you know God don't want that from you. That's what I mean between God and the devil, my G."

Tyrone is clearly impressed with Tyquan's interpretation. "Africa, yo, my dude, I'm feeling that. That shit be true. God on one shoulder; the devil on the other."

Tyquan puffs up with pride. "Word up my G, ya feel me?"

I chime in, "I know each and every one of you has a long story to tell. I can look at you and tell that you have climbed the rough side of the mountain and survived a lot. Am I right or wrong?"

The class is all nodding in agreement with a cacophony of: "Word!" "Hell, yeah." "My life is a movie, son." "My shit is a trilogy." "I'm surprised I'm still here."

I continue with the lesson. "So, just like Malcolm had five different evolutions or major phases in his life that were represented by a different name, I want you to think about yourself and what names represent the major phases in your life so far. Who were you at birth and what did your mother name you; who were you when you started running the street and who are you right now in jail... do you have different names? Think about it. You all have a story to tell... so tell it."

"Yo, Ms. P, I'mma need a lot of paper for this one, ya heard!" Tyquan excitedly exclaims.

This lesson seems to engage the entire class. They all have long stories riddled with urban drama, and they all want to tell it. They want to be seen, heard, and recognized.

"Can we curse?" Mekhai asks, totally shocking me because he's always *so* unenthused.

"Within reason, but don't go overboard with it. Profanity should be used like an exclamation point, not randomly used every other word like you talk in the street. And remember where you are, gentlemen; don't write anything that would incriminate you. Keep it real, but be wise."

"Word, don't snitch on yourself, nigga, ya heard, Harlem!" Mekhai says with a smirk on his face. He's stirring the pot.

Raheim, one of the Harlemites in the back, falls for it and quips, "Yo, what? I know that's not missy snitchy over there talking."

"Yeah right," Mekhai shoots back. "Fuck Harlem."

"Fuck Brooklyn!"

"Hey-hey-hey, watch ya mouth when it comes to Brooklyn, ease up," Tyrone chimes in, aiming his comment toward Raheim.

I have to nip it quick. "All right, all right. Stop throwing batteries,* Mekhai. Ignore him, Raheim. Stay focused…Mekhai. Start writing. Please! And all of you *please* watch your mouth; this is not the pool hall or the barbershop."

I walk over to Mekhai to give him the attention he is clearly crying out for. I need to get him focused on the assignment before he finds another target to stir up. He has nothing on his paper.

"Mekhai, you haven't even started."

"I don't know what to say," he says nonchalantly, shrugging his shoulders.

"Well, let's start with: What did your mother name you? Were you the only child? Were you spoiled? What kind of son were you and at what point did you get pulled into the street life? I'm sure what your mother calls you and what your boys in the street call you is not the same, right?"

"Naw, they call me Killa Khai, the wavy one." Even Mekhai has to laugh at his own inflated ego.

---

*Throwing batteries: to instigate someone to get pumped up to fight; to charge someone up with energy and give them courage; getting someone to do something they wouldn't normally do. A battery can have a positive or negative effect, depending on the situation.

I chuckle. "So, write how you went from being Mekhai, the apple of your mother's eye, to Killa Khai, the wavy one. What's your story? What was the journey? Come on, get started."

"I got you, I got you, Ms. P," Mekhai relents as he begins to write, "I was born September 28th, 1991, a bouncing baby boy in Brooklyn…"

I walk up and down the aisle commenting on their stories, encouraging them as they begin to write their mini-autobiographies.

"Can I have a piece of paper?" Danny asks.

Without even looking at him, I calmly reply, "No, you may not."

I'm unwilling to completely let him off the hook for coming out his face and spitting a Molotov cocktail at me earlier, so I choose a mild spank…no paper. I'm not giving him anything he asks me for, especially since I haven't received an apology. Letting him back in my class, rescuing him from the wrath of the CO, was about enough of an olive branch I'm willing to extend.

Danny softly replies, "Miss, I was going to do your work."

I keep walking the aisle.

"I got you, scrap,"* Tyquan says, handing Danny a piece of paper from his personal stack.

"I appreciate that, Tyquan," I comment, recognizing Tyquan's goodwill in a place where kindness can be interpreted as weakness and preyed upon. Tyquan is a loose cannon with a wild look in his eye and at the same time a tender, wounded heart that I will later learn more about. He responds to positive acknowledgment, like most kids who want to feel smart and be recognized for their achievements. The more I point out Tyquan's progress with each assignment, the harder he works. He's a kid who was probably ignored during most of his schooling, like most inner-city kids who attend overcrowded, underserved, failing public schools. On my class roster, he is labeled as "special education," having a learning disability, but while in my class, I observe that his reading and writing ability proves otherwise. And during math, when the math teacher

*Scrap: homeboy; a term of endearment.

pushes his cart into my class to teach, Tyquan is fully focused and does the work finishing the algebra equations with pride.

He, like many special education children, is given that label because of behavior rather than academic proficiency. If a child is deemed special needs, they are eligible for Social Security benefits, and the amount of money a parent receives from Social Security is more than what they'd get from welfare for the child. So rarely do poor, uneducated parents object or investigate the label that erroneously stigmatizes their children. Therapists play a role as well. In some cases, if a therapist hikes up the diagnosis from an adjustment-reaction disorder (a low-level short-term diagnosis) to something more chronic, they get unlimited sessions with a long-term client and pharmaceuticals profit from ongoing prescriptions that can follow a kid well into his adult life and potentially create an unnecessary dependency.

I have witnessed that if you label a child as "slow," they will eventually believe it and live up to the label; they will prove it to you. A label garners attention. A label is an identity; an identity in a world that otherwise deems Black and Latino children to be invisible.

I remember when I was growing up, kids would hide their special education labels for fear of being teased. Nowadays these labels are so commonplace that kids discuss and trade their labels and diagnoses like baseball cards. "I'm ADD." "Yeah, well, I'm bipolar." "I have a learning disability." "I've been in special ed since third grade; I have to have a teacher's aide with me at all times." "I'm dyslexic." "I can't control my temper." "I have a personality disorder." And on and on, casually, like that. The more I encourage Tyquan, the more he works to please me to receive the positive recognition he so desperately craves and clearly never got in school.

As I walk the aisles, reading over my students' shoulders, giving brief feedback and asking questions prompting them to go a little deeper, I pause when I see "The Life and Times of Danny Gunz" written at the top of Danny's paper. He is already at the bottom of the page, writing furiously in a stream of consciousness. I hand him more paper and say, "Wow, Danny, you are really going in. I'm impressed."

Danny responds, "I wrote a book."

"I see. You are certainly on your way."

"No, not this, this ain't nothing," he says. "I wrote a book when I was upstate in juvie.* The counselors said I couldn't write it because it had curses in it so I tore it up. I had two whole notebooks, over five hundred pages."

"Danny, are you serious?" I ask with pointed focus and inquiry designed to engage conversation. We are verbally shaking hands; he is apologizing and I'm accepting, all done through subtext and tone. Like when I used to get spanked by my mother as a child, then soon after she'd come in my room offering *Dinner's ready, ladybug, you hungry, sweetie?* in a truce-like tone.

"You have to write your story again, Danny. You wrote five hundred pages? You're a writer, Mr. Gunz, and I know you have a compelling story to tell." I call him by his street name, Mr. Gunz, to pull a smile from him, and it works.

"Yeah, I guess I should, huh? I been through a lot, miss. When I read *The Coldest Winter Ever* by Sister Souljah, I really liked it and was inspired to write a story like that, but more so what I experienced."

"Everybody has a story to tell," I reply, "but the difference is, not everyone has the gift to write it. Out of all the urban hood books out there, I have yet to see one written by an adolescent from a teenager's perspective. Why can't you be the first, Danny?"

His eyes are intensely fixed on me, deeply contemplating the seed I'm planting, which appears to be resonating in his spirit.

"True, true," he replies.

I think I have activated something in that young man. I go over to my desk and give him a photocopy of several chapters from Hill Harper's book *Letters to a Young Brother: MANifest Your Destiny*

---

*Juvie: juvenile detention.

and tell Danny, "You could write a response, a book called *Letter to an OG.*"

"Word. Thank you, miss. Today's my last day here too; I'm going home tomorrow. I'm not supposed to be here. That's why I was so upset earlier. I apologize for my behavior."

"Apology accepted. And congratulations!" I exclaim with excitement. "Go home and stay home, Danny. You have a book to write and I want to read it. I want to walk into Barnes and Noble one day and see *The Life and Times of Danny Gunz* on the bestseller shelf." Danny laughs and blushes as I hand him a composition book. "Here's a fresh, new notebook to start writing your story in. You are a writer. Never forget that."

"Thank you, thank you, miss! It was nice to meet you," he says, standing taller than when he first walked in. Just then a CO comes in, calling Danny by his last name, and says, "Let's go, Nelson, you're packing up," and gives him a friendly smack on the back of his head like a coach would do to a player done good.

Tyquan yells out to Danny, "Yo, scrap, don't forget."

Danny reassures him. "I got you, son, no doubt."

He clicked his pumpkin seeds three times and is really going home. Danny Gunz and I came full circle, all in a day. I reached him and planted a seed I pray will take root and grow. As I inhale a deep breath of accomplishment and relish in the moment of the joy of teaching, my nemesis pops his head back into the room.

"Ms. P, wait, don't put me out. I'mma do work, *really,* I ain't gonna act up. I wanna learn, Ms. P."

"No, Shahteik! I was born at night, not *last* night. I know a swindle when I hear one!"

Tyrone chimes in: "Yo, Ms. P, you mad funny," and then turns to Shahteik to say, "You gotta respect the Black Nubian queen, son."

Tyrone snatches a smile from me with that one. They're tag-teaming me, hitting me with the cultural reference, my weak spot, wearing me down. They're good.

Taking a cue from Tyrone, Shahteik adds, "I apologize, my Black queen," and he bows, gesturing as if he is rolling out a red carpet for me to walk on. "Want me to dust off your crown?"

I fall for the swindle. "Shahteik, if I have to speak to you *one* time—"

"Not at all, Ms. P. I promise," he says as he does another overexaggerated bow. Then he asks, "Ms. P?"

"*What*, Shahteik?"

"You forgot to tuck one of your lil' nigga naps in the back of your dusty crown."

"Shahteik, get out!" I yell.

The class falls out like hyenas and even I can't hide my laughter. That was a good one. He's going to be a problem *all* year, I can already tell. The boy is rude *and* funny. That's gonna be a tough one to handle.

A CO pops his head inside my class and barks a single-word command, "Bathroom!" All the kids jump up out of their seats and line up in the hallway for their group bathroom trip. If a kid has to go before or after the loosely scheduled field trip to urinate… tough luck. On several occasions, I've had to plead with an officer to make an exception with one of my kids, who would squirm and chair-dance in desperation for me to advocate for him to be granted individual bathroom time. It doesn't sit well with me when a CO denies a kid a trip to the bathroom. Watching him do the pee-pee dance—shaking and hopping from leg to leg—is enough to get me to step in. The male COs are the ones who do bathroom call, so I employ my soft feminine stroking tone to get the officer to relent. *Let the kid pee, for Christ sake* is what I'm thinking, but it comes out more like, "He can't concentrate on the lesson, and he's truly about to pee in his seat. This one is legit, Officer; he really *really* has to go. I wouldn't come out here and call you if it wasn't serious, and Lord knows I don't want to deal with piss on my floor."

That line always works.

CHAPTER FIVE

One, Two, Poof

Thought for the Day: If the mountain was smooth, you wouldn't be able to climb it. Challenges and obstacles are meant to build character and strength.

—Ms. P

The schedule is wearing on me. I'm fatigued... very fatigued. It's raining today and my favorite sneakers, the green patent leather Bathing Apes, are separating at the seam and the pink ones have a tear at the toe. My day-to-day favorite Italian boots have a gaping hole in the sole. I am behind in my bills, student loan officers are calling, rent is due next week, my cell phone is about to get cut off if I don't pay *this* week, my paycheck is already spent before I get it, and I need dental work but don't have health insurance.

I am officially low-income working class, living check to check and one pay stub away from compromising my integrity. Up at 4:30 a.m. every day, I'm busting a huffing, puffing sweat to get to work, doggie-paddling my ass off to keep from financially drowning, but the water is rising faster than my limbs can move. I'm stuck on this hamster wheel of survival. I understand how poverty produces rage, which can trigger violence and be the linchpin for desperate crimes *against* poverty. I get it. Hell, I'm *living* it.

When this rage is turned inward, depression sets in and my body gets heavy, weighted down with sadness, making it difficult to even walk. It feels like the earth's gravitational pull is working against me. I cling to the bed and sleep becomes my refuge. But when there is no more space in my body to contain my pain, when my cup runneth over with frustration and self-hatred and I still have to move throughout the world in order to "earn" my place on the planet, the rage has to be released. Sometimes my rage gets unleashed on a random soul who bumps me, stares too long, jumps in front of me in line at the store, or happens to be the rude bus driver on that day... anyone and any offense will do. I could easily be sitting where my kids are in a split-second act of misdirected fury. I've always been a punch-you-in-the-face, knuckle-rumbling, pretty-tooth chipper from West Philly anyway. So it doesn't take much for me to revert back, like a Black girl's press-and-curl hairdo does in the rain. When I'm angry at myself and circumstance, my dormant *her,* the she-beast, is easily triggered.

I have worked very hard at keeping *her* tucked away in my hornet's nest of around-the-way-girl-fists-of-fury antisocial behavior. I've worked hard at managing *her* and learned how not to stir *her* up. It took years of self-reflection, acknowledging my wounds and my bullshit, along with years of doing various types of holistic, spiritual self-therapy. Iyanla Vanzant books, *Women Who Run with the Wolves* by Clarissa Pinkola Estés, *Your Word Is Your Wand* by Florence Scovel Shinn, *Sacred Woman* by Queen Afua, *A Return to Love* by Marianne Williamson, and *The Secret* by Rhonda Byrne all gave me the tools and language to talk myself out of dark, unhealthy places that I periodically crawled into. They offered me enlightened perspective. I have become much more skilled at tempering my rage toward others than I am at managing my sadness and self-judgment, which can overwhelm me. This morning, like many mornings, I pray myself out of bed, out the house, on the train, and back to jail.

"I am *not* in the mood for y'all's shit today! Git the fuck back in line before I fuck you *up!*" yells Ms. Jouju (pronounced "Ju-Ju"), an older CO with more salt than pepper in her two-toned hair. Standing at five foot three and big-boned, she's a dark brown thick munchkin of a woman with a couple of front teeth missing who walks with a slow, commanding gait. Don't let her height and gray hair fool you; Officer Jouju is sandpaper rough and does not p-l-a-y *play*! A sailor-mouth saloon type of broad with absolutely no filter, she serves it to the kids straight no chaser, rugged and raw. The sharp, symmetrical features of her beautiful face are a stark contrast to her snaggletooth gangster grill and profane tongue. Her densely silver-lined hair has earned her the moniker Grandma.

"Oh shit, Grandma got the belt!" yells a kid named J.J., and damn if he doesn't look like Jimmie Walker from the television show *Good Times,* except with more muscles. Running from Grandma is a game that the kids like to play; it gets their adrenaline flowing and has become a routine of cat and mouse, cops and robbers, inmate and CO, niggaz and Grandma. She doesn't think it's a bit of funny, which makes it that much more fun for the kids and raises the stakes.

"Keep playing with me and see what fucking happens to your ass!" Jouju continues yelling as she slowly strolls toward J.J., swinging her belt. Other kids are egging her on.

"Tear that ass up, Grandma," a signifying rascal yells, trynna get her more hyped. But Ms. Jouju doesn't need any help hyping up her morning show.

"I'mma tear *your* ass up if you don't shut the fuck up!" barks Jouju.

"Damn, Grandma, I'm on your side," the kid whines.

Jouju has her sniper scope fixed on J.J. and, with nowhere else to run but into the hands of another CO at the other end of the hall, J.J. slips into my classroom.

The kids are all laughing, slapping their knees. Everybody's hyped. The drama is on and popping and in *my* class, prompting other kids from the hallway to run into my room behind Ms. Jouju, to see the show, which is now kicking into Act Two. Ms. Jouju strolls into my room. "Excuse me," she says without looking at me, her eyes fixed on J.J. like a hawk.

"Go right ahead, handle your business, Ms. Jouju," I reply while backing up, positioning myself to watch Grandma open up a can of whoop-ass on J.J.

J.J. jumps over several desks as Ms. Jouju is bull-knocking them out of her way, gunning for J.J., slow and steady.

"You know I'mma get your ass sooner or later so you might as well get it over with now and not make it worse for yourself."

"Naw, fuck that, Grandma," J.J. says, scrambling like a rat trapped in the corner, eyes shifting, looking for a clear opening to run past Jouju.

"What! You getting *smart*? I'mma tear that ass up!" Jouju knocks over more desks, going in for the kill. She's closing in on J.J. and he has nowhere else to go except to slip past her or through the brick wall he's cornered himself into.

J.J. starts pleading and nervously laughs. "I'm sorry, Grandma."

Now just one arm's reach away, she goes for the execution and pushes a desk into J.J.'s legs to trap and hold him. Before the desk can meet his thigh, J.J. tries to jump like Jordan over the desk and misses, clumsily slipping between two other desks as Grandma swoops down on him with the belt. Wham! Wham!

J.J. jumps up to run, but Grandma is faster and grabs him by the collar and, with the other hand, twists his ear, like a grandmother would do her badass, foulmouthed grandson. Grandmothers are the only ones who can get away with humiliating a teen-child in front of their peers like that.

"Owww, Grandma, okay okay okay, I'm sorry, I'm sorry! *Owww!*"

Grandma gives his ear one more hard twist along with a verbal "umph" for emphasis and dramatic effect. J.J. wiggles out of her grip and she swats him one more time with her belt as he runs out the class. Wham!

"Now take your ass to your class and don't let me have to speak to you again! I mean what I fucking say!"

I laughed along with the class because it was a straight-up jail-house comedy routine, but Ms. Jouju never cracked a smile, never broke character. Why? 'Cause Ms. Jouju don't p-l-a-y. Today she only has the belt. Some days, she walks up and down the hall swinging a big, black rubber mallet with a wooden handle, her signature tool for monitoring badass teenage bandits on the school floor. Ms. JoJou doles out tough grandma-style love. She's from a generation when a good whooping was meant to rear you right and protect you from a society that fears Black boys and is unforgiving to their rebellious shenanigans. The kids know she cares. She feels familiar, reminding them of someone back home. Grandma.

There is a subtle family dynamic between the youth at Rikers and the Black and Latino correctional officers. A mother/son, father/son, aunt/nephew, uncle/nephew, grandma/grandson, grandfather/grandson dynamic plays out in any given moment, depending on the officer and depending on the student. I was not exempt from this subtextual, extended African village relationship. Some days I was the momma, the aunt, the big sister, and sometimes the crush. I doubt this plays out in the same manner with the adult inmates, but with the kids, our children, they represent our collective future. They remind us of a youngling in our family, reflections of a wayward nephew, brother, son, or grandson we love. They're still impressionable enough to offer us some hope in being able to shape, influence, and guide them in a different direction and turn a productive corner. The stage of adolescence is a crazy time for *all* teenagers. It's a temporary time of insanity where they take wild risks and feel invincible, experimenting with sex and drugs. Their prefrontal cortex in the brain is still developing and doesn't stop growing until approximately age twenty-five. Their hormones are continually shifting and changing, so boundaries are tested, behavior is spontaneous and reckless, authority is challenged, and narcissism is at critical mass. They are experiencing the second phase of separation individuation which occurs during adolescence, where they tend to push their family away and their peers become everything. The first phase of separation individuation is when a child is two years old, aka the terrible twos. During both phases, the child is awkwardly defining their individuality and identity for themselves and will throw frequent tantrums. Black and Latino kids are criminalized for going through this normal adolescent stage of development while white kids get slapped on the wrist, sent to therapy, sternly warned, and given multiple second chances. Reckless and impulsive behavior is universal, but Black and Latino teens are held to a higher standard and treated like adults in the eyes of the law, while most white kids are allowed to be normal crazy teenagers without getting systematically warehoused into prison.

Two white boys walk into my class and sit next to each other either because they're friends who knew each other before they wound up in the den of wayward warriors or because being a white adolescent inmate in this place is so nonexistent that they instinctively gravitate to the familiar in each other. White youth rarely even make it to Rikers Island. Usually, the judges give them programs, probation, and slaps on the wrists. And while 34 percent of Black youth are sent to adult prison, only 5.5 percent of white youth are sent to adult prison. Seeing white kids here means their white privilege didn't work in court because they must have fucked up really bad and the judge's hands were tied, or the judge wanted to teach them a lesson, or they're really, *really* poor (maybe even from the same neighborhood as the Black and Latino kids); perhaps all the above.

The Bosses immediately start calling one of the new boys "white boy" and the other "Wonder Bread." Kenneth, the lanky Gandalf-from-*Lord-of-the-Rings*-looking one, doesn't talk, I sense, out of fear. Head hung low, he looks depressed and in a complete daze like he's shell-shocked. Brandon, the chunky, potato-face white kid, has a little edge to him. He's already talking and challenging the other guys for calling him white boy. "But yo, why I gotta be called white boy? I don't call you Black boy."

"'Cause you white, nigga, that's why. And if you call me 'Black boy,' you gonna get washed,"* Tyquan threatens.

"Well my name is Brandon, my dude."

"Yeah, whatever, white boy…where you from?" Tyquan inquires, winning the short-lived power struggle over Brandon's jailhouse name.

"I'm from Staten Island." Brandon gives up the fight and starts talking about how he knows one of the rappers from Staten Island–based Wu-Tang Clan, which starts a heated debate. Momentarily, he diverts attention away from his whiteness, holds court in the discussion, and even gets support from a couple of Wu-Tang fans and wannabe affiliates in the class. Brandon is gonna be all right; he can hang, looking like a gangster Russian anyway.

Shahteik is quietly sizing them both up to choose his prey. He comes from across the room to take the empty seat next to Kenneth. I sense an extortion is about to go down, so I intervene.

"Shahteik, go take your seat. You have nothing to talk to him about."

"Ms. P…"

"Shahteik, let's go, take your seat, please." I am firm, trying to shield Kenneth from the hunt.

"All right, all right, I don't want no problems with you today, Ms. P." He turns to "Wonder Bread" and says under his breath, "I'mma talk to you about that later, ya heard?"

Kenneth looks at Shahteik and quickly directs his gaze back to the floor. Defeat. He is afraid and weak. I can smell the fear, a mild scent of sweat and mildew seeping from his pores. I can't protect him from being food back in the housing area, but I won't let it happen in my class, not on my watch. I give him a notebook, folder, and pencil and tell him to write in his journal and, if inspired, write a poem about what he sees. He looks at me with distant, sad eyes that say, "Okay," and immediately begins writing with nonstop flow. The pencil is a paddle moving him through the deep river of words

---

*Washed: to get beat up, tossed around, and pummeled, like being in a washing machine.

gushing onto the page as he tries to make sense of this haunted twenty-first-century middle passage boat he's wound up in.

> Dear journal, I see inmates around me. We all want to go home. I see pain in the prisoners' eyes, but they don't want it to show. I dream that their dreams they follow are dreams of a bright tomorrow. I see myself going home one day. I see nasty food. I see depression. I see tears, judges, lawyers. I dream of being free. I dream that I will get a job and my mother will be proud of me. I dream of not breaking the law. I see people who conceal their emotions because they have an image 2 live up 2. They throw up gang signs and find a crew that they can fit into, and their lives are based around the music they listen to. I see kids treat their weapons as friends, and try to live the life of gangsters from the messages rappers send. They hide who they are and all lean on the same image. They do as the rappers do and their emotions are hidden. They all do the same thing, like being unique is forbidden. You have to find new role models and engage your craft, because you can write your future but you can't erase your past.

I keep Kenneth writing every chance I get. It's his prescription to heal and find freedom. He thanks me for giving him the extra work. I like this kid. My spidey-senses detect a wounded soul, a poet.

I'm getting so tired of yelling at Shahteik. I have to come up with something innovative to deal with his badass behavior. Sending him out of class to take a walk isn't sufficient and it doesn't faze him one bit. I want to come up with something that will get under his skin and feel like a pinch. He's driven me to custom-design a "spank," which I believe to be a brilliant strategy: a *ONE, TWO...POOF* composition notebook. In it, I'll keep a record of my verbal warnings to students, primarily Shahteik, of course. First warning will get documented in my book. Second warning will get documented in my book. By the time I get to the third, there will be no warning, just straight, "Poof!"' That means out of my class for good, no coming back, accompanied by an orange infraction slip. Poof is the last straw and my Poof logbook means I will have the transgressions well documented to justify putting Shahteik, I mean, *a student,* out of my class forever, should I be questioned. It's my way of keeping a paper trail of their shenanigans and my ploy to get rug rat #1 out of my space and face once and for all. I'm sure he'll *One… Two… Poof* in one day, *easy.* And Captain Blackwell has literally *just* informed me that there are 350 adolescents in their housing areas but only enough classroom seats for 250 students, which means there are literally a hundred kids waiting in the wings to come up to the school floor. Therefore it's a privilege to be sitting in class, which definitely beats sitting in a cell. This is great leverage for me.

"They wanna cut up and create problems, not do work and distract the kids who want to work and behave? Well, Ms. P, they can simply go. Vamoose! They're taking up a valuable seat for a kid who wants to learn," Captain Blackwell tells me. She's a six-foot-tall, statuesque, very well put together Black woman with immaculate hair worn in a bone-straight bob. Back in Philly we'd call her "shitty sharp," with her manicured nails, shiny black uniform shoes, and Prada glasses that sit on the tip of her nose. All Department of Corrections top brass—captains, deputies, wardens, and chiefs—wear crisp white shirts with a gold badge, decorated with an array of gold stars, stripes, clovers, and eagles on the shirt collar depending on their rank. Their crisp white shirts and shiny ornaments are a sharp contrast to the masses of dark-blue-uniformed, regular-rank correctional officers.

She tells me, "I like working with the adolescents because there's still a chance they might change their life and you never know what kind of a positive influence you could have on them. Some of them are never going to change and will wind up being in and out of prison for the rest of their life. But I believe if you can touch one life then you've done God's work." Captain Blackwell cares. I think she's taken a liking to me partly because I, too, am an Amazon woman she can look eye-to-eye with (which we've joked about), but also because my Ancestor Wall of History resonates with her. During one of her first visits to the school floor, she stopped in my room, studied the details of ancestral majesty posted on my walls, nodded her head in approval, and complimented me on it. She turned to the boys. "Gentlemen, you clearly have a teacher who wants you to learn your history; I hope you realize what an opportunity this is to be in her class." She senses I care about the rug rats and can tell that I want to make a difference. We're on different teams, but on the same page.

She turns to me and says quietly, without whispering, "So remember, the seats in your class are gold, Ms. Peterson. You need a kid out, you just let me know and I'll fill it with a kid who will appreciate it. I usually give them three strikes. You give them two warnings but, by the third time, you send them directly to me." I was already ahead of her and that's all she needed to say. I have her blessing to "Poof" Shahteik. I grab an empty black-and-white composition book and write on the front of it, *Ms. P's ONE, TWO... POOF Book!* It's official.

Even if a kid doesn't want to do schoolwork, they all want to be on the school floor since they get to see their buddies and get out of the housing area they're restricted to all day and night. It gives them something else to do during the day and breaks up the monotony of their confinement.

Shahteik has long positioned himself to be the first casualty of my Poof initiative. He's hell-bent on not doing a lick of work, loves coming to class to gossip and talk shit, loves to instigate and talk more shit, is constantly disruptive, and loves to argue and stir up *conflama* (confusion and drama) in my class all day like it's the barbershop/pool hall. He's a leader, so he sets the tone in class and it's not a good one. I remember what Ms. G said: "The first sign of a troublemaker, make an example out of him ASAP." Shahteik, aka Lil' Rumbles, has got to go.

Shahteik manages to cut up and tear his ass faster than I can write him up, sending him from One straight to Poof (skipping number Two) all in the same day, just as I predicted. But Shahteik is like a bad penny. I Poof him and he comes right back. He seems to have some magical, rug rat–gangster pull with the COs and happens to be a favorite of Ms. Collins, the CO in his housing area, who sits in my classroom from time to time. The first time I Poofed Shahteik, Ms. Collins assured me that she'd have a stern talk with him and I wouldn't have any more problems. For some reason, she adopted motherly nurturing feelings toward him and advocated for him to stay in school and in my class. I give him a pass *only* on the strength of Ms. Collins's favor because she's cool and helpful whenever she sits in my classroom. Once she realized that I was actually demanding the guys do work and pushing them to learn, and because I maintain an unwavering standard of high expectation for the boys, she became engaged in the class and supported me. She helps to keep the guys on task and focused on doing their work. She keeps the chatter to a minimum whereas most other COs couldn't care less. Her classroom participation is a rare exception to the rule.

Getting a student to do their work is not the CO's job; all they're supposed to do is make sure no fights break out and no infractions occur. Their sole focus is safety. Care, custody, and control. Classroom management is the teacher's job. If you suck at your job and your classroom is a zoo, then that chaos is on you. But Ms. Collins is different. She's earned respect from the Bosses and they listen to her because she's fair and balanced in her approach. Ms. Collins gives them rewards and privileges for good behavior, looks out for them in the housing area, and gets them to the barbershop, commissary, and the gym regularly, along with other perks like extra blankets, two mattresses, and extra lockout time that can be easily taken away for the slightest infraction. She looks out for "her boys" and, in return, they give her little to no trouble. Whenever I'm teaching Black history, she chimes in to drop a jewel or two about the subject. The Bosses like when she participates. It's like she's taking a personal interest in what they're learning and, by extension, in them. I almost never have to have a correctional officer stationed in my class, but when I do, I always wind up with the cool ones, like Ms. Collins.

My class is low behavioral management not because they're angels but because I move around the classroom; I stay on my toes and keep the students engaged. I hold it down, making it easier on the officer to not have to babysit. The COs who sit in my class enjoy my weekly vocabulary lists, the poetry assignments (some of them even join in to write poems), and, hands down, they all love my Black history lessons. My class isn't a zoo. Maybe a circus, but not a zoo.

Ms. Collins assures me that Shahteik won't be a problem and will listen from here on out. I give him a mean, hard eye roll and let the bad penny back into my class. Her plea trumps my Poof. It's smart to keep in good graces with the officers because you never know when you might need one. *Battlefield politics.*

Christopher is a light-skinned kid with pink zits blooming on his cheeks like cherry blossoms. The acne snitches on his youth, holding space for a beard that's not quite ready to grow. If it weren't for the missing bottom tooth in the front of his grill, he'd have a Colgate smile with perfectly straight, milky white teeth. He's built like a gladiator, tall and muscular, with broad grown-man shoulders and arms chiseled for the Gods...jailhouse *guns.* He walks with a body builder swagger and an arrogance that takes up too much space. This boy irks me. He never does work and talks all day, much like Shahteik. Barely moving his lips, he makes this strange guttural noise with his throat that sounds like a mangled swamp frog. It's a stupid, aggravating game he likes to play with his voice. A fucking weirdo, this kid.

"Christopher, please, stop making that noise. It's very annoying," I sternly demand.

"I got you, miss," he responds, and three minutes later, I hear him making that ugly sound just to grate my nerves and defy me.

Nasty girl taught me all the lingo / While mama play bingo, she ride Mandingo… All of the kids are singing LL Cool J's new song and keep repeating the word *Mandingo,* proud that they have learned a new word for dick and getting a kick out of saying it in front of me, thinking I have no idea what it means. About the third time I hear it, I have to let them know I know what it means and ask them to stop saying that word in front of me, out of respect. Telling them not to do something is, of course, registering in their rug rat brains to *do it*. Christopher keeps saying "Mandingo" over and over again in that weirdo frog voice, while pleading with the guys to tell him what *Mandingo* actually means. The Bosses get a kick out of him saying a word he doesn't know the meaning of and making me mad for saying it.

"Miss, what's that word mean? Why you tripping over that word?" Christopher innocently asks.

I hand him a dictionary and have him look it up.

"Oh, that word's in the dictionary? I thought it was slang," he says, quickly flipping through the dictionary to relieve his suspense. The guys are cracking up as he spells the word aloud as he searches the dictionary.

"Man, m-a-n…dingo" he says, sounding it out.

"Miss, how you spell *dingo*?"

The Bosses are on the floor, tears rolling down their face from laughing.

"All right, all right, it's not that funny, guys. He asked a legitimate question and that's how you learn," I say in my very Ms. Crabtree, teacherlike voice. I have to be extra clinical with this slippery slope of dick jokes.

I continue, "That word has a historical literal meaning *and* a metaphorical meaning. So, once Christopher finds the literal meaning, then I'mma tell you the slang meaning."

I have Christopher read aloud the dictionary definition for *Mandingo:* a member of any of a number of peoples forming an extensive linguistic group in western Africa, inhabiting a large area of the upper Niger River valley.

Then I tell him how it's used as slang to imply a man's large-sized reproductive anatomy.

I may as well have said "dick," the way they are snickering and carrying on as if they're ten years old.

"So, now that you know what it means and how it's being used, please don't use that word around me again."

"Okay, I got you, Ms. P," Christopher says, leaning back in his desk, nodding his head in agreement just to get me out of his face. Two seconds later, when I turn my back, I hear "Mandingo" in that frog voice I hate, again! He's testing me to see what I'll do. He's challenging me to a duel. He's calling thug mama out for a fair one. He's rubbing the genie in my lamp. I feel *her* stirring.

I draw a line in the sand. "Christopher, I asked you not to say that. Do not use that word around me—it's vulgar and disrespectful! Stop it right now. And stop doing that thing with your voice. It's creepy!"

He shakes his head in a dismissive chin-up nod that reads like, "Fuck you, miss," making me want to slap him. My chest rises and falls slowly with the long, measured breath I take to keep my pressure from spiking. I turn my back to write on the board, and I hear "Mandingo."

I swing around in slow motion, a Neo-in-*The-Matrix*, full-body whirl, with my neck being the last thing to snap into alignment. It is a knee-jerk reflex that flings my thug mama genie out the lamp into a full-octave, West Philly, all-up-in-your-face, carazaay woman verbal fury. I am full throttle: extremely loud, intense, and temporarily unhinged. *"I am sick and tired of your disrespect. I asked you five times—five times, Christopher—and I am not having this foolishness in my class. You haven't done any work since you came to my class. You just run your mouth, make annoying noises like Kermit the damn Frog, and now you're being totally disrespectful. You think you're slick and you think I'm stupid, but don't get it twisted, son! I am not stupid and I don't play games with kids. You got to go—believe that! You gots to get up out of here, son. I am sick of your crap. Poof, poof, poof! Get him out of here now!"* As I am screaming like a wild banshee, standing over him like a giant possessed mother, he cowers in his seat, stunned by my beast. He's the incredible shrinking thug.

I'm spraying him with electric shocks of Poof like a theatrical magician doing a magic trick, throwing invisible talcum powder from both of my hands with each "Poof" I shout. The CO next door runs into my room to assist, but when he sees me standing over Christopher with the wild look of homicide in my eye, he pauses to momentarily watch me deliver the spank before swiftly removing Christopher out of my class and from the jaws of *her.* Another CO approaches me. He asks if I need to take a minute, to go to the bathroom and calm down.

"*No,* I don't need to go to the damn bathroom!" I snap. I am still in my crazy thug mama trance. No filter. I stunned him, and the shocked look on his face reels me back into my body as I dial it back, quick.

"Excuse me for that, officer. I'm good, thank you. Now that he's out of my class, I'm good. He took it too far and I just snapped. I'm okay now, honest and truly, I'm okay. Thank you." I'm slightly out of breath but deliver my response honey-toned with steam still seeping out from my nostrils.

And then, like a scene from *Sybil,* without skipping a beat, I continue teaching the class like nothing happened. I do a 180-degree change of tone on them and go right into my Ms. Crabtree: "Now open your books to page forty-seven to verb tenses. A verb, as you remember, shows action or a state of being." I'm speaking just as calmly as can be, but my vibe is layered with hot ice.

I walk the aisles, making sure everyone is on task. As I walk past Tyquan, I pause, noticing he is not on the correct page. Sternly, I demand through clenched teeth, "Turn to page forty-seven, Tyquan; *everyone* should be on page forty-seven; let's get this work in, gentlemen, that's what we're here for." Quickly, Tyquan turns to page 47 as he shakes his head with a perplexed look on his face and says in a whisper, "Ms. P, you went extreme—I ain't never see you get like that. Your eyes got real big and crazy-looking. You put on a show, Ms. P—that was a sure-nuff show. I ain't messing with you. You kinda type throwed off."

Then Tyquan turns to his buddy, William. "Ms. P said turn to page 47, I'm turning to page 47, nigga, *ya heard*? Ms. P makes it cali-ente,* son!" His comment draws some chuckles and a few remarks like, "Word, son, Ms. P is kinda MO.† She turns it up." Without looking at Tyquan or raising my voice, I address him in a slow, low monotone growl, "There are no niggas in my class, thank you. Maybe some fools, but no niggas." I am still carrying the thug mama don't-mess-with-me-today veneer and wielding it as I walk the aisles, demanding work.

"My bad, Ms. P," Tyquan says as he sits up straight, overexagger-ating his compliance like an obedient soldier.

I laugh to myself because that's exactly what it was, a show. And that was exactly my point, to go overboard and get crazy in the eyes so they see I'm a little nuts and will flip on their asses. Mission accom-plished. Shahteik may have been the first Poof I doled out, albeit unsuccessfully, but even his Poof couldn't be matched by the one I just served. Today will go down in "The Legend of Ms. P's Poof."

This should last a good few months. God willing, I can ride on this show until the end of the semester and keep thug mama genie tucked away in the lamp.

After lunch, I don't have my usual band of rug rats but, instead, there are fifteen new kids sitting in my room. I am clearly confused and I ask the strange group of students, "Excuse me, I don't mean to be rude, but what are you gentlemen doing in my room?"

"We 'bout to sign out," says a Latino kid with frizzy cornrows in desperate need of being rebraided.

Just then, Captain Blackwell walks in. "Hi, Ms. Peterson. We

---

*Cali or caliente: Spanish for "making it hot," bringing unnecessary attention to a sit-uation, usually from an authority figure.
†MO: inmates at Rikers under mental observation; synonym for crazy.

need to use your classroom to let the kids who don't want to be here officially sign out of school. So, *gentlemen*"—she turns to address the small group of too-cool-for-school hooligans—"Ms. Peterson will hand out pencils and a yellow form for you to fill out. I will return to collect them and you will no longer be on the school floor, as you wished."

A few grumbles can be heard, prompting Captain Blackwell to bark, "Excuse me? Is there a problem? Because as I recall each one of you made it very clear that you didn't want to be bothered with this school, either verbally or by your actions, so I should hear *no* complaints! Do I make myself clear, gentlemen?"

The room is silent.

"I asked a question! *Do I* make myself clear?" Captain Blackwell spikes the volume with agitated authority.

"Yes, ma'am," a few kids respond in unison, enough to satisfy the captain.

Captain Blackwell goes on, "And if Ms. Peterson has to call me for *anything,* it's going to be problems; I will make your life miserable, so let's not play. Out of school is what you want, so out of school is what you get. Now, is there anyone in here who does not want to sign out, who has second thoughts?"

There's silence again.

"Ms. Peterson, after they fill out the forms, can you collect them? I will be back in about twenty minutes to get the forms and take the guys back to their housing area, so the regular scheduled classes can continue."

"No problem, Captain Blackwell," I assure her.

Out of all the classes to be the "holding pen" for the sign-outs, why *my* class? Maybe word spread about my major Poof this morning, so my classroom seemed fitting to facilitate the official group Poof. I hand out the forms and sit at my desk as they quietly fill them out. An unfamiliar Latino CO enters my class and decides to address the group. "You guys had an opportunity for an education and you're throwing your lives away; you're really stupid for doing that."

I cringe because that word *stupid* makes me uncomfortable. Aside from *nigger, stupid* is the other word I don't allow to be used in my class. I yell at my guys all the time, whenever I hear that word being thrown around, saying, "Nobody in here is stupid! You might be lazy but not stupid." The term is condescending and affirms what they've been told for far too long. Deep down beneath the skin of indifference, that word has clipped many a sprouting wing. It's a hammer to their spirit and debilitating. It's a crippling mantra that plays on repeat in their subconscious. Too many of them believe it. I try to interrupt that tape as much as possible.

As strongly as I feel about that word, I choose not to challenge his authority. Learning to pick your battles in this place is essential.

The frizzy cornrowed Spanish kid passionately blurts out, "I got three felonies! What kind of job can I get? What's the point of getting my GED when I got three felonies and can't even get a city job?"

I jump up out of my seat and leap to my feet like an evangelist catching the Holy Ghost, ready to run to the altar and testify. "That's not true at all! You can have a full life and obtain employment even *with* felonies. My homeboy just came home from doing thirteen years upstate and got a good job, with benefits, working full-time supporting his family. And I have a former student of mine who was right here at Rikers as an adolescent just like you, and he did five years upstate for a gun charge in an adult penitentiary. He has a felony and just got hired. I have another friend of mine who just got a job teaching part-time and he has a felony too! So don't tell me you can't get a job with a felony when I *personally* know people who have felonies and are gainfully employed, brother. Don't you believe that lie."

The Spanish CO chimes in, "My brother-in-law has his own cooling and heating business and makes forty-five dollars an hour and his son is eighteen years old working under him, making fifteen dollars an hour and doesn't have his GED. He learned a trade, has a good business mind, and makes good money, my friend...good money."

The kid looks stunned. The room is quiet as the CO and I have their full, focused attention. Still on a roll, I continue, "My dear friend, my homie and mentor, a straight-up OG poet, Abiodun from the legendary Last Poets"—I grab his book from my desk, hold it up, and point to his picture—"this brother right here is a great writer, thinker, and revolutionary. When it comes to telling the raw truth about history, loving Black people, and writing poems about it, it doesn't get much realer than this man. Years ago, he was sentenced to twelve years in prison for robbing and kidnapping a member of the Ku Klux Klan down South and did a quarter of his sentence. Who in here knows math? If he was sentenced to twelve years and did a quarter of his sentence, how many years did he actually do?"

I have their minds working.

A chubby dark-skinned kid with a tailored goatee and immaculate geometric cornrows yells out, "A quarter is four parts, so twelve divided by four is three. He did three years?"

"You better know your math, son!" I exclaim, boosting his confidence. "Yes, he did three years. So sometimes it doesn't matter what the judge says or what the lawyer says, because the Creator can change and adjust your life at any moment, if you believe." I grab a marker and write a new Thought for the Day on the board, something that I am inspired to share in this heightened moment of what feels like church. I read it aloud:

It's never too late to become who you dream of becoming. All break-downs are always followed by a breakthrough.

"You can decide to change your life *any* second. Your breakthrough to greatness could happen in the next hour, the next day, the next week, next month, next year. Who knows?"

I decide to lean on Malcolm again. "Look at Malcolm X. He said, 'To have once been a criminal is no disgrace. To remain a criminal is the disgrace.' He went to prison an ignorant man. He went in a criminal and his breakthrough happened right in the belly of the beast. He self-educated himself and became a great man of tremendous power and influence. You have *no* idea what the Creator has in store for you! Malcolm had *no* idea what the Creator had in store for him when he was locked up. God started working on him when he was in total darkness at his lowest point, just like you. How you know God didn't put you here for a reason, maybe to save your life, maybe to get you to slow down and get still and think about your future differently? Maybe to put you on a different path, just like what happened to Malcolm. You could be on the verge of your breakthrough right here, right in Rikers Island. God ain't done with you yet! And my brother, when you do break through into your greatness, you have a responsibility to encourage someone else and to share your story—tell people how you did it, how you made it out of the cave, out of mental slavery!"

Passionately I'm pointing and perspiring as I walk back and forth in front of the class like a preacher delivering the sermon. The kids are leaning forward with laser-focused attention. Their body language encourages me. I start to feel lightheaded and am suddenly aware of energy moving quickly through my body. It's an electric sensation. I am *catching the spirit*. One kid is leaning so far on the edge of his seat, it's a wonder he doesn't slip onto the floor. He has tears in his eyes as he embraces my words, shaking his head affirmatively as I speak. I am in a zone and he is riding the wave with me. He yells out from the congregation, "Nelson Mandela was in prison too. How many years did he do?"

"He did twenty-seven years…twenty-seven years in prison! And once he was released, he became the president of South Africa, one of the most diabolical, racist countries on the planet next to America! So don't tell me change can't happen; don't you sit up here talking to me about a damn felony when great men and great minds have come out of prison! Read *The Autobiography of Malcolm X.* That is mandatory reading for each and every one of you brothers sitting in here. That is your assignment from Ms. P, ya hear me?"

Just then, Captain Blackwell returns and the guys are lined

up to be escorted out. This is the last time they'll be on this school floor. Several of them thank me and say they are going to read the book I assigned. The chubby dark-skinned kid with the fancy corn-rows laments, "Damn, miss, I wish you was my teacher."

I tell him and the others as they walk out, "Just because you are signing out of school don't sign off on your education. You don't have to be sitting in a classroom to educate yourself. Don't sign off on your life. Educate yourself and get that book."

Within a matter of seconds, they are out of my classroom and Poofed off the school floor for good. Captain Blackwell doubles back to say, "Ms. Peterson, I had to hurry up and get those guys out of your class before they changed their mind and demanded to be back in school...you were about to cause a mutiny."

We share a laugh. "Maybe they'll pick up a book in their housing area and appreciate the value of school and not take opportunities for granted. Make 'em think about their actions and their life. That's good for their asses."

I planted strong seeds of consciousness today. I pray they take root. And though I may not ever witness the sprouting, I'm pretty confident I touched at least one student.

CHAPTER SIX

Rug Rat Roll Call

Thought for the Day: Believe while others doubt. Plan while others play. Study while others sleep. Begin while others procrastinate. Save while others waste. Listen while others talk. Prepare while others daydream. Persist while others quit.

—AUTHOR UNKNOWN

They've grown on me, these dusty boys. They work my nerves and make me laugh in spite of myself all in a day. They test my patience every moment they get, and sometimes I slip and get weak, letting them get me flustered. Today is one of those days. It starts out like any other, with mumbles and grumbles early in the morning that quickly turn into the foulmouthed barbershop/pool hall, with Shahteik leading the charge, making me nuts.

"Shahteik, will you *please* sit down and stop all that talking and do some work? Will you? Just for a change, why don't you try something different, like doing some work for the sake of switching up your routine, *you know*, doing something different, for a change, why don't ya, huh?" I'm being sarcastic and he knows it. Some of the Bosses laugh at my snarky attitude, prompting Shahteik to ignore me and continue talking to his buddies. Plucking my nerves at 8:30 a.m., I yell, "Shahteik!"

He snaps, "Ms. P! Yo, relax! The hell is wrong with you, damn!"

In a split second, quickly reading my *oh-no-you-didn't* look on my face, accompanied by the universal Black mama neck swivel and head lean, he shifts gears and follows up with a playful tone: "Ms. P, you know you love me. You like saying my name, don't you? Matter fact, you prob'ly tell your husband, 'Baby, I'm so tired of dealing with them kids all day, especially that boy Shahteik.' I bet you talk about me so much that your husband prob'ly say, 'If I hear that Shahteik Jackson's name one more time, I'm leaving you.' That's prob'ly what he be saying while he's rubbing your feet, right, Ms. P?"

He has the class's attention, making them laugh as they look at me for the comeback. I'm in his crosshairs; it's showtime. But it's too damn early for a fight and all I can come up with is, "You know what? Don't play with me today. Y'all are getting on my nerves already, acting like a bunch of…" I pause, quickly searching my mind for the perfect noun. They pause laughing and momentarily stare, wondering what insult I am about to hurl. Their faces ask, "Will it be fun or a fight?" Then I blurt out, "…a bunch of rug rats!"

They fall out in hysterics, exploding with laughter, whooping and hollering, pounding desks, keeling over, caught off guard at the absurdity of my Nickelodeon reference, part tickled at the term of endearment, part relieved I didn't hurl insulting fighting words like they're used to receiving.

"Yo, Ms. P, you crazy!" Tyquan says, wiping the tears from his eyes, nudging Mekhai. "Yo, son, she straight called us rug rats!"

Tyrone leans back in his seat and cocks his head to the side, slowly rubbing his chin and grinning, flashing his perfect pearly whites. "But I'm your favorite rug rat, right, Ms. P?" I know this boy isn't trynna mack?

I suck my teeth and roll my eyes, making him laugh loud. "Yeah, see that, son, I'm her favorite rug rat; she just can't admit it in front of y'all fools."

"Nigga shut up, you muthafucking Stewey-looking-ass nigga," Shahteik quips. The class is officially comedy central and in a good mood. I let it rock for a little bit, since they could use some laughter therapy. Hell, so could I.

"Watch that word," I say with my back turned as I'm writing on the board.

"*Aight,* I got you, Ms. P, my bad," Shahteik agrees, to my surprise. My term of endearment must have definitely won him over for the moment. I'll take it, moment to moment.

My rug rat roll call reads like a ghetto farce and a cruel joke on me. I have three "Day-shawns," each one spelled differently—Deshawn, Dayshawn, Daeshaun. Also a Dayquan, a Jaquan, a Naquan, a Sean, and an Antoine. One student, Joey, I nicknamed Peanut. He's a short, skinny kid, the runt of the crew, with a Mr. Peanut–shaped head and beady eyes that are too small for his face. He's constantly bouncing around superhyper and *never* sits still, always dancing, always moving, like a jumping bean. The boy reminds me of that Duracell toy monkey with the cymbals that plays frantically, nonstop. Joey needs recess to run around and wear himself out.

One morning, frustrated at his dancing antics in the middle of a lesson, I blurted out, "Peanut!" yelling at him to sit down. The name just jumped in my head and out of my mouth right at that moment, and it stuck. Even the other kids call him that now. Despite the fact that Peanut does absolutely *no* work at all, I like the kid—there's something endearing about his hyper little ass. Maybe it's because when I yell at him to do work, he smiles at me sheepishly and responds with, "Yes, my Black queen sister…I'mma do my work, my Nubian queen," forcing a smile from me. He's such a swindler and I fall for it every time. Today he walks into class with two white plastic forks from lunch sticking out of his short, cropped afro. He takes one fork and begins picking his hair. "See what jail do to you, Ms. P? I gotta use a fork to comb my hair. Ain't that a damn shame?"

"What's a damn shame is you flicking your nappy little peas all on my floor. Sit down, Peanut," I say jokingly.

"Aww, Ms. P, wait till I go to the barbershop. You gonna see my waves then, I'mma be spinning,* watch." And he does the Harlem shake, a popular dance that resembles syncopated stylized rhythmic convulsions, before he sits in his seat to do no work.

"Boy, sit down!" I say through a smile, shaking my head. Peanut tickles me and knows how to melt my icy front.

Then there's Antoine. This lil' sucka is a bona fide comedian with an old soul. Reminds me of Huggy Bear from *Starsky & Hutch*, the way he walks and talks like a corny 1970s dusty pimp. He's got a high-pitched nasal voice and does this exaggerated, slow-motion, slide-dip walk. One arm strokes the wind like a boat paddle to the rhythm of his strut, helping him glide. He's a clown, putting on a show without even opening his mouth. But when he does, everything is *fo'sheezy this, fo'sheezy that.* Walking into class making an entrance with his Funkadelic cat-daddy playa stroll, Antoine declares in his Alvin and the Chipmunks/Michael Jackson voice, "Fo'sheezy, Ms. P, check this out. When I get back on the town, I wanna take my girl to restaurants where you have to dress up, where you have to wear tuxedoes and the tablecloths be pressed linen, ya heard? I'mma expose her to a high quality of life 'cause I'mma different kinda nigga, Ms. P... fo'sheezy!"

"Watch that word, Antoine."

"Fo'sheezy!"

Walking the rows, passing out work, I ear-hustle Shahteik whispering to Mekhai, "Yo, Khai, don't she look a lil' thicker today? You can see her shape more... she look more thicker."

Then Shahteik proceeds to ask me, "Ms. P, you ever heard of a restaurant called Junior's in Brooklyn?"

"Yes, Shahteik," I respond with a tone of annoyance because he always gets on my nerves, even when he's just breathing.

He continues. "You ever eat there?"

---

*Spinning: when your hair displays visible waves.

"No, I don't eat there, Shahteik. Their food is too greasy. What's with the twenty questions about Junior's?"

"Naw, it just look like you went to Junior's over the weekend and had some of that cheesecake."

I totally didn't see that one coming. Nice setup. One for him. His annoying comment draws a bunch of snickering from Mekhai and a couple other rug rats in earshot. I really can't stand Shahteik, aka Lil' Rumbles (his jailhouse name). He irks me and is hell-bent on fucking with me every damn day he sees me. It's sport to him. The observant, big-mouthed, dusty rascal rug rat supreme was right. He noticed that my jeans were in fact just a *tad* bit more snug than normal because I did laundry last night, making my otherwise loose-fitting jeans hug me a little tighter. Moments later, I catch him staring at me with a glazed look in his eye. I shudder to think what he was envisioning. My nemesis is crushing, which can only make matters worse. Lord, why me?

Mekhai wants to keep the drama going and has the nerve to try to break on me for wearing the same jeans every day.

"Ms. P, you wear the same jeans every day. You don't have no other jeans—what's up with that? They not paying you?"

"Mekhai, unlike some of you who feel the need to floss and wear fresh gear in jail, impressing *who*...I have no idea. I, on the other hand, have no desire whatsoever to impress *anybody* in j-a-i-l. Why? Because it's j-a-i-l; not an office, not a club, but *what*? J-a-i-l, jail!"

I shut him down and he still tries to cut me and defend his position.

"I'm just saying, Ms. P, you can wear another pair of jeans. You been wearing the same jeans since I been here. I'm not calling you a bum, but that's kinda bumlike. No disrespect, I'm just saying," he says, snickering along with Shahteik, who revels in any joke or dis at my expense.

Tyrone, who prides himself on being my self-appointed favorite rug rat, comes to my defense. "Yo, son, she wearing them G-Star Raw jeans. They mad expensive, son. They got a boutique in SoHo, nigga. You can't get them in no department store. Right, Ms. P? You got them jeans in SoHo, didn't you?"

"Yes, Tyrone, but it doesn't matter what kind of jeans I wear or how much they cost, or what I wear, because I am here to teach. I'm not here for a fashion show."

"I know you be wavy on the town, Ms. P. I saw you rocking your Gucci ballerina slippers in here the other day, and your Italian leather boots, rocking your Polo rugbies every other day, you feel me? I know you got the *wave*. You don't have to dress up every day, but just one day? Just to show these fools, for me, Ms. P? Get flossy just one day, Ms. P." Tyrone is pleading for me to turn it up with my outfits so he doesn't have to defend my fashion honor. He has been clocking my attire the entire time, and had clearly ventured out beyond his Brooklyn comfort zone to shop in SoHo.

Then there's Miguel, a quiet Mexican kid with porcupine black hair—the Bosses call him Mexico. He sits in the back row on the same side as the Bosses. Always pleasant and polite, Miguel struggles with English and does work only when I push him, and still winds up giving me minimum effort. He's low literacy, just skating by, and was most likely a product of social promotion, in some overcrowded urban school, even though he wasn't ready to move to the next grade level…I know for a fact he could benefit from ESL (English as a second language) classes, which may be the barrier to his learning. Miguel isn't the least bit disruptive and is actually quite pleasant, but he's easily influenced by the Bosses, who love putting a battery in his back, encouraging Mexico to say slick shit to me in his thick Spanish accent. Nothing he says is actually funny but his heavy drawl, which sounds like a stereotypical Hollywood Mexican gangster, makes any hood slang they have him say sound absurd. They think it's the funniest thing. He's their entertainment…at my expense.

"Esophagus," pronounced "'sophagus," is jailhouse terminology for "shut up or swallow it." It takes me a minute to figure out what it means and when I ask the Bosses, they refuse to tell me, getting a kick out of having a secret over me and talking in code, like boys in a stinky clubhouse with no girls allowed. They get him to say, "Ms. P, 'sophagus," in his thick Spanish drawl. Even though I haven't quite figured it out, I know it's a dis and they're making me the brunt of an inside joke, using Miguel.

I cut my eye at Miguel. "Don't let them put a battery in your back, Miguel. Don't go there with me, I don't play that." Mexico clasps his hands as if in prayer and slightly bows his head, shrugging his shoulders with a coy grin on his face. "I'm sorry, Ms. P." His schoolboy smile, accompanied by him shrinking into his seat, always earns him a pass from me. I yell at the Bosses instead. "Y'all stop throwing batteries in Miguel's back because you're going to get him in trouble." Then I turn to Mexico. "You heard, Miguel?"

"Yes, Ms. P, I'm sorry," he whispers in his thick accent. "It won't happen again."

The Bosses are rolling in laughter.

Most of the kids don't claim any particular religion and if they do it's usually indicated on their ID. Protestant, Catholic, Jewish, Muslim, and Other are the categories to choose from. Aside from the occasional plastic rosary beads some of the Christian kids get from Catholic services, religious affiliation is not that big a deal, except for Samuel, who comes to class carrying a large Koran under his arm and donning a white crocheted kufi on his head. The Muslims have a strong alliance in jail and are untouchable for reasons unbeknownst to me. Once you convert to Islam in Rikers you become part of a very strong group that protects its members. Though they're not a gang by any stretch of the imagination, they wield ganglike power, offering protection, influence, and a sense of family. Their reputation supersedes Rikers as they have an almost impenetrable force field that is recognized in prisons upstate and even across the country.

Samuel recently converted to Islam while at Rikers, much to the chagrin of the Bosses, who hate this kid and were plotting on getting at him. But once he came to class donning his kufi and a Koran, he automatically had the protection of the Muslim jailhouse brotherhood and the most they could do was insult him and sell wolf tickets. "Nigga, you been a Muslim for two hours. Shut the fuck up! You know you became a Muslim 'cause you was about to get washed, nigga, and you know it too, you pork-eating doja!"

Samuel rarely comes to class because he's the object of continuous verbal assaults as soon as he steps in the room. There is clearly some serious housing-area drama or gang politics with this kid that I know nothing about, and it has the Bosses ready to pop off on him, but he's saved by his kufi and Koran. Samuel loves vocabulary and, taking a cue from Malcom X, who learned every word in the dictionary while he was in prison, Samuel always carries a dictionary with him. When the class plays Jeopardy based on lessons they recently learned, Samuel stays with the vocabulary category, bringing a victory to his team *every* time. The few times Samuel has ventured to class, he has always been extremely respectful and once, out of the clear blue, said to me, "Ms. P, I appreciate your presence."

It was on a day I needed to hear it, a day I needed to be reminded, a day when I felt totally inadequate, doubting if I was making a difference, doubting that I was actually teaching the right things the right way. It was on a day I was feeling unnecessary and pointless. It's funny how the children will randomly remind me of my significance, in divine time, as if the Creator is talking through them. It gives me just enough light to hold on to and continue on this bizarre journey in such a dark place. Like the time when Lawrence, whom the kids call Lips because he has a huge pair, looks up at me with beautiful, big saucer eyes as I'm standing over him to reexplain the lesson. As I patiently stood there making him read the question out loud to me, I helped him sound out the words he couldn't pronounce. I took just a little extra time to help him find the answer to the question that was staring him right in the face.

With a mix of frustration and compassion, I gently blurted out, "Lord have mercy, chile! The answer is right here in front of your face. Take your time and read the paragraph. The answer is right there, Lawrence. Find it. You know how to do this, just focus."

Looking up at me, he beamed and softly said, "Ms. P, you sound like a mother. You're a good mother."

Moments like that make me feel needed and necessary and affirm my maternal resonance despite not having children of my own. "Thank you, baby. Now do the rest of the questions on your own and I'mma come back and check on you." A little attention and compassion go a long way with a kid who's been ignored throughout his years in school and probably even at home. All kids want to be seen, heard, and encouraged, even the most thuggish of thug.

Raheim and Marquis are two Harlemites who sit in the back row near the pigeon-shit windows. They're respectful rascals but hella chatty. They were buddies who lived in the same hood before they got locked up, but now they're in different housing areas in jail so the only time they get to see each other is when they come to class. Schoolwork be damned—it's their time to catch up with each other, trade housing-area war stories, and fill each other in on the latest drama and neighborhood updates from phone calls and letters. It's Harlem ghetto politicking nonstop with these two. Raheim is a very intelligent kid, above par in every academic subject. He should be in the GED class, not my pre-GED one.

He got placed in my class probably because he was too tired when he took the orientation TABE (the test that evaluates your academic level and determines what class you're in) and didn't take the test seriously, placing him in a lower-functioning class. Now, his homie Marquis is, by contrast, dim-witted and lazy. He's the total antithesis of Raheim and I often wondered why Raheim even entertains him; it's such a mismatched odd-couple friendship I just don't get. Maybe Marquis is funny and a good shit-talker. But to talk shit, you have to be witty and swift. Marquis is neither. By himself, Raheim is an absolute joy to have in my class. He finishes all of his assignments and goes beyond what I assign. The boy stays on task and is driven. But as soon as Marquis comes to class, Raheim is instantly distracted and gets tied up in the back-row Harlem pool hall or barbershop cypher. I call them Ernie and Bert: "All day it's the same two, Ernie and Bert, running y'all mouth. Raheim, don't let him pull your focus; come on now! You're gonna make me split you two up, Ernie and Bert!"

Marquis responds with a smooth, laid-back grown-man tone, "Naw, Ms. P, we more like Bonnie and Clyde." He leans back in his chair like he just hit me with a dope comeback analogy.

He thinks he's saying something cool.

"Oh really? So which one of y'all is Bonnie?"

Pregnant pause from the Harlem pretty boy then. "I mean we more like Clyde and Clyde."

Marquis is slow but Shahteik isn't. Picking up on Marquis's Freudian slip, Lil' Rumbles quips, "Yo! Harlem be on that homo shit!"

Marquis shakes his head, "Aww, naw, Ms. P, you got me confused with that Ernie and Bert shit!"

"Watch your mouth," I laugh and say. "Ummhmm, see that's just what you get...talking too damn much. Now do some work, Marquis!"

I have quite a spirited group of drama kings, court jesters, flyboy gangsters, tricksters, and wannabe pimps all in my charge, all up in my face, to educate. Corralling this motley crew of bad-news bears to do any lesson is like running boot camp for hyperactive gremlins. I have to be consistent, alert, firm, witty, fearless, and demanding, and most important, I have to have a strong command of the subject I'm teaching. English and social studies are my forte, my strength. But science? Ha! Out in the battlefield armed with science I'm vulnerable and weak; scared. There's no push-in teacher for this? No, goddammit, *I'm* required to teach science. I *hate* science. Shit. They're gonna eat me alive this period. I decide to teach something I have a little familiarity with—the digestive system. Since I cleanse periodically by juicing and eating live-raw foods (salads, fruits, and unsalted nuts) and because I also get colonics several times a year, I have a general knowledge about the digestive system and should be able to teach the lesson with some semblance of authority. I talk about an unhealthy colon versus a healthy one, which leads to discussing what we eat and how it travels from the mouth, down the esophagus, through the small and large intestine, finally exiting through the anus. Well, saying the word *anus* gets a rise from the peanut gallery of Barnum and Bailey rug rats. These immature adolescent boys are tickled pink and entertained every time I say "anus." This lesson is giggle-filled.

Shahteik thinks he's setting me up when he asks, "Ms. P, did you know your anus could stretch up to twelve inches?" He tries to sound serious, but his sarcasm is so transparent. Mekhai clenches his lips to swallow his laughter but snickers so hard, he blows a snot bubble out his nose. He wipes it with his sleeve. Nasty little sucker.

I ignore Shahteik, which amps him up even more, thinking he has me in his trap, "Ms. P, I'm not trying to be funny, I'm being dead serious—did you know your anus could stretch up to twelve inches?"

He manages to keep a straight face but his hype man, Mekhai the Muppet and snicker king, can't control his amusement and bursts out laughing. All eyes are on me for a reaction.

Calmly I ask, "Shahteik, now how would you know something like *that*?" The rest of the class catches on to my subliminal jab and falls into raucous hysterics. Shahteik is confused, slow to pick up on the subtext.

Mekhai says, "Ooooh, Ms. P, that was a good one, I gotta give credit where credit's due, son," as he leans over to Shahteik and fills him in on the joke that's on him.

Finally catching on, Shahteik nods his head and squints his eyes at me as if he's a snake. "Oh snap. It's like that, Ms. P. Word? Okay, I'mma git you." He is outdone. I stung him good. I throw my head back and laugh a loud, gutbucket-belly saloon laugh along with the class as I revel in this small victory. This is the last period before the end of the day, so it is a delicious and perfect finale. As the COs round up my students and walk out, Shahteik, crumpled and embarrassed, yells, "Ms. P, anus…anus, Ms. P!" It falls flat. One for me. I won that match, royally.

CHAPTER SEVEN

Africa Prince tha Don

Tyquan, aka Africa, greets me with a cheerful salutation every morning. In a place where fools rule and apathy is the norm, Tyquan has an uncanny zeal for learning and is academically bright—I adore this kid. He seeped further into my heart the day he shared his childhood wound during a class presentation, triggering my propensity to nurture, amplifying my desire to see him soar beyond his circumstances and win. But Tyquan is needy. He craves attention from me and, like a parent who spoils their wayward child, I give it to him because it keeps him motivated and on task. He's the teacher's pet who vehemently guards his self-appointed role, competing with anyone who grabs my attention for too long. When Tyquan's not in a good mood, he'll tell me, "Ms. P, I need to sit in the back and get my mind right, lay my head down for a minute, *aight*? It was mad drama in the house last night. I ain't get *no* sleep." I always oblige him.

Some mornings I'll put brainteasers on the board, and *every* time I do Tyquan excitedly jumps at the 7:55 a.m. challenge, quickly figuring out the most obscure and difficult mind benders, loudly exclaiming, "Ms. P, come on, I told you I'm smart. I read all that Grimm fairy-tale shit back in kindergarten, son!" Once he got so wound up, I witnessed him slip into a psychotic zone, which I believe explains his special ed classification. It was a bizarre emotional outburst that might have otherwise scared me if I didn't know him. In that moment it became crystal clear: Tyquan is disturbed, a little throwed-off and crazy as cat shit, but still my favorite baby rug rat, nonetheless. I am convinced that when painful childhood experiences and multiple complex traumas are not acknowledged, interrupted development will occur and the child will have great difficulty self-regulating their emotions, which manifest as behavioral problems—specifically, emotional outbursts. A lot of kids don't need meds; they need the elephant in the room, their trauma and source of pain, to be unearthed and properly addressed. Inner-city schools are already overcrowded, understaffed, and without the resources to handle a child who needs extra attention, so the "difficult" kid gets placed in a smaller classroom setting labeled Special Education/Special Needs.

All the kids in my class eat raw, powdered Kool-Aid straight from the small paper packet like it's candy, turning their tongues into bright cherry and grape Popsicles from the synthetic food coloring. This powdered crack gives them the shakes and has them transforming into ADD gremlins at warp speed. I forbid the guys to eat it in my class, but they still sneak it in, frantically licking their hands for one last granule, just like crackheads. Their red- and purple-stained palms, lips, and tongues incriminate them every time. For Tyquan, this shit is kryptonite, launching his already hyper ass into the stratosphere of *red alert*. Ring the alarm and get the straitjacket on deck cause he's about to turn up.

Tyquan popped a pack before he came to class this morning and walks in high, already beaming up, up, and away into a galaxy of madness. He is having a sure-enough crack attack. I think it must have been a bad batch or he overdosed because suddenly his eyes begin to jump around like my cat when I give him too much catnip.

Already excited about figuring out *all* the answers to the brainteasers, he proceeds to go into a manic victory rant, turning to the class, not speaking to anyone in particular, and blurts out,

"What, nigga? What? You can't touch me! Ain't nobody on my level, Ms. P! I'm not even human. I'm from Prince tha Don World!"

"Tyquan sit down, please," I calmly ask like a nurse dealing with a beloved patient.

"Naw, Ms. P, fuck that. I don't feel like doing no work today."

Tyquan turns to his buddy Fred and demands, "Yo, nigga, gimme some of that honey bun I see you got in your pocket!"

Like an ethical bartender who refuses to serve the drunk at the bar any more liquor, Fred calmly refuses to give Tyquan more sugar-crack. "Naw, you buggin', son. Yo, why you coming at me like that, son? Relax."

Tyquan gets more agitated and belligerent. "*What,* nigga? Yo, son, you know I will make it hot. I don't give a fuck. I will turn it up! It's about to be a problem, my nigga! Gimme that fucking honey bun, son!"

"Tyquan!" I yell.

"Yo, Ms. P, you might as well get that mutherfucking orange slip out now because I'm 'bout to catch a fucking infraction this morning, I don't give a fuck! I got bodies,* ya heard, fuck I care about an orange slip! I shoot niggas! I make 'em leak and meet their maker!"

Thank God Fred didn't fall into his trap but instead took the high road, just shaking his head in disgust, ignoring Tyquan's exaggerated empty threats. *Whew.* A young Jedi move; Fred is a quiet storm who walks with strength in his aura.

During one of my lessons on the Black Panthers, Fred took copious notes, paying attention more than I've ever seen from him. I praised his focus and he shared his personal connection to the history. Fred's grandmother's brother is the late Geronimo Pratt, the well-known Black Panther and political prisoner. I told him he carries a mighty legacy. He told me he wants to live up to it. I did a little praise dance in the aisle, making him open a smile and share a giggle.

---

*Catch a body/have bodies: to be incarcerated for murder; to have murdered someone.

My spidey-senses detect it's more than the Kool-Aid spiking Tyquan. It's not so much *how* he's acting, but what he's saying. He is talking so erratically, looking wild in the eyes, and becoming *so* unhinged he's diving off an emotional cliff and it scares me. I'm not scared for my personal safety but scared for him; he's unraveling into a pain I can't yet identify. My mind races trying to assess what is going on. A few weeks ago, I remember he told me that he was getting closer to his date to be transferred up top* to serve his sentence in an adult prison. He is noticeably terrified and perhaps this is his way of pumping himself up, convincing himself how gangster he is, inflating his courage and pounding his scrawny chest, practicing a roar that he can believe.

Tyquan is *fighting*. He's swinging at a haunting only he can see, the ghost of what could be, nightmares of unsolicited sodomy. It's a coping mechanism to help him walk toward the unknown, horrifying fire he's imagined. He continues ranting, confirming my theory. "When I go up top, I'm going straight to the bing,† ya heard? Ain't no nigga gonna take my peanut butter.‡ I'mma wild out, knock niggas out—*bam*! And go straight to the box, nigga *what*! Ain't no nigga touching me!"

Tyquan is consumed with fear and shaken to the core. I understand where it's coming from, but for now Tyquan has to go.

I shout, "Tyquan!" But he doesn't hear me. I have to climb two octaves higher to reach him at the ledge of the beanstalk to pierce through his frenzy. "Tyquan! Go take a walk, right now! You crossed the line, go take a walk."

Tyquan isn't budging. I need help. He won't sit down, he won't leave, and he won't calm down. I poke my head out the class and call my buddy, Officer King.

---

*Up top: refers to the plethora of prisons located out of the city limits, in upstate New York.

†Bing/the bing: punitive segregation or solitary confinement at Rikers Island; also called the hole or the box.

‡Taking your peanut butter: to be raped by a man; forced sodomy.

King comes to my rescue and asks with concern, "What you need, sis? What's the problem?"

"Tyquan won't calm down and he's totally out of character, being extremely disruptive and disrespectful. Please take him out of my class; he needs a lil' time-out behind the gate to calm down. I'm not putting up with his behavior this morning. It's causing chaos and we're about to have a guest speaker next period and I'm not having it." I turn to address Tyquan. "Tyquan, you know I give credit where credit's due—you're one of my *best* students—but today, I don't know what's going on with you...Actually, I have a feeling what it is, but I won't go into that right now and don't have time to address it this morning."

Officer King barks at Tyquan, calling him by his last name like they do in the military. "Jefferson, let's go!"

Tyquan leaves without a struggle and surprisingly no back lip. He wanted to be rescued, shaken out of his self-induced hell-trance. He had to walk it out.

The *gate* is an open cage—a visible mini holding pen on the school floor that is situated at the end of the hallway. The gate looks out onto the school floor, and on the other side of the gate is an iron-clad door that leads back to the main jail area. In between the bars leading to the school and the iron door leading back to their cells are two rickety benches for the daily incorrigibles to sit on. The gate is for kids who "cut up" enough to be put out of class but not enough to be taken off the school floor for the day; it's the time-out pen.

When the kids come up from their housing areas in the morning, escorted by COs, they all pass through the gate and walk through the metal detector where an officer's desk is stationed. My classroom is four rooms down from the gate.

Today we have a guest coming to present a life skills workshop and I really wanted Tyquan to be present for it, especially now. Mr. Kenny is my boy and former coworker from Friends of Island Academy. Now he works for Corrections in the social services department. We're both up in the belly of the beast on a daily.

The day we first ran into each other in the hallway, speed-walking to our respective chambers within the dungeons at Rikers, we jumped for joy. We're comrades, light workers in a dark house. Kenny is a man who, during his adolescence, served time at Rikers and eventually wound up going upstate. After his bid up top, he got involved with Friends of Island Academy and became a youth leader in the program, dedicating his time and energy to helping other young adults in the program stay "Alive and Free" and out of the grips of incarceration. He is a dynamic and powerful speaker with a gripping story that contrasts with his well-manicured, preppy appearance and command of the King's English.

Kenny is the bomb. He's a great group facilitator and leader. When I told him I was teaching full-time on the school floor, he immediately asked if he could run a pilot project with my class and conduct an eight-week life skills workshop. "Damn skippy, you can," I said. It wasn't even a second thought. I've seen him in action, running groups and working with wayward warriors. He knows how to reach, teach, drop jewels, and get the young'uns to think critically. He was once just like them—an incarcerated adolescent sitting in Rikers Island with gangster dreams and tales of life-threatening escapades in the street. He speaks their language. I am so psyched to have a comrade on the Rock whose heart, like mine, is aligned with helping our children to consider options beyond street culture. Me and Kenny are on the same team. Team Wake-the-Sleeping-Giants. Team Alive and Free. Team Teach the Babies. "Hell yeah, Kenny, let's get it popping. You've got an open-door policy in my class. They need to hear what you've got to give them. Shit, can you start today?" I wasn't joking.

Kenny looks like a hood-nerd. He strolls into my class donning an argyle sweater over a crisp, button-down periwinkle-colored shirt, soft leather loafers with a classy buckle on the side, fresh Caesar haircut, and gold wire-framed glasses on his flawless, mocha-brown face. Kenny walks in holding a Dunkin' Donuts extra-large coffee cup and the guys immediately start sizing him up. His style throws them off; they think he's a square or an herb with *nothing* to possibly tell them that they'd be the least bit interested in. Even his tone is calm, smooth, and measured. The kids are yawning in his face. Then he drops his story at the precise moment they've decided he's a chump and he sucker-punches them. "When I did my first jux before I got knocked, I was straight 'bout the business of multiplication. Multiplying my weight, my money, my power, and putting fear in your heart. My motto was 'fuck it,' everybody got a date with death so might as well *do me to the fullest*. Consequences, *fuck it*. Jail, *fuck it*. Death, *fuck it*. My crew was always scheming."

His hands move like a boxer as he spits the scenario. The hood creeps out, transforming his Clark Kent façade into K Boogz from around the way. He starts speaking another language: their language. The class sits up, side conversations cease, and the murmurs begin. "Oh shit, son is wilding, he talking that real shit, son…" "Word, that's how it be." "Yo, where you be at?"

He rocks them every time. I love watching Kenny get at 'em and kick the funky bo-bo, ninja-style. The guys look forward to him coming, except for Shahteik, who walks out each time he comes. After Kenny shut him down like a closed window at the post office—*no clown stamps here, son*—Shahteik decided it was wiser to leave rather than attempt to disrupt the workshop and get embarrassed by Mr. Kenny, again.

"Hey, Ms. P!" Kenny greets me cheerfully, then says under his breath, "Prince tha Don, you know, Tyquan, was calling me from behind the *gate* when he saw me walking down the hallway towards your class. He begged me to let him back in class and I told him I'd come ask you."

"Well, Mr. Prince tha Don was cutting up this morning, I mean cutting the monkey-ass fool. What he ask you?" I have my hands on my hips, lips curled.

"He was like, 'Mister, ask Ms. P to let me take your class, *please* just ask her.' He was straight begging, reaching through the bars. I'm not trynna interfere and you know I have no problem going back out there and telling him he's deaded today. You know how we rock, Sista Liza, that's not a problem. Just give me the word."

I suck my teeth. "Only 'cause it's you, Kenny, and he needs to get all he can right now. His act-out this morning was just him crying out for help. He's about to go up top and he's scared shitless, covering it with fake gangsta." I sigh in defeat and continue, "I know… I'm soft, right?"

"Naw, sis, you far from soft, you just care."

I roll my eyes at Kenny, knowing I wasn't going to deny food for his consciousness to a hungry student, and Kenny knows it too. We both laugh at my pretend attitude. I head toward the gate at the end of the hallway and see Tyquan hanging on the bars: "Ms. P, Ms. P! Mr. Kenny's here—I wanna take his class, I like what he be saying. Can I come to the class, Ms. P? I promise I'mma be good, I just needed a little time-out. Please don't let him start the talk without me. I probably need to hear what he's gonna say. I'mma be good, Ms. P. I promise."

Tyquan knows exactly how to wear me down and wiggle back into my good graces.

I squint my eyes and speak through clenched teeth. "Tyquan, if I have to talk to you one time, you hear me, one time, it's a wrap," I growl. I ask the officer if he can let Tyquan back in my class since we have a guest speaker that he needs to hear. The disengaged officer barely looks up and unlocks the gate, letting Prince tha Don out the cage and back into my care, but not without shooting Tyquan a mean ice-grill.

Midway through the workshop, Kenny calls Tyquan up to the front of the class for a role-play demonstration. Tyquan's personal truth begins to seep out during the role-play to reveal his wounded soul, right in front of the class. He begins talking in a stream of consciousness with no inhibition or filter. The class is transfixed on Tyquan as he draws us into his painful reality, speaking passionately with fire shooting from between his teeth.

"Can't nobody tell me nothing! I do me! My biological mother put me in the tub to give me and my brother a bath when I was six months old and turned the water on and it began to get hot. She runs to answer the phone and forgets about me and my brother in the tub while she's running her fucking, *excuse me,* running her mouth on the phone. She's having a conversation, never came back to check on us and we burning in the tub; I got second- and third-degree burns all over. My foster mother told us what happened years later when I asked why my foster brother has a different last name than me. That's when she sat me and my biological brother down and told us."

Tyquan has command of the floor and no one interrupts.

"So, if my own mother who gave birth to me left me in the tub, then…okay, I can see you go answer the phone, but you come right back. You don't just *leave* me. I'm your son! I'm a baby! So that tells me that her conversation was more important than her baby; I'm her son." He repeats *I'm her son* over and over like a sacred mantra, a prayer he needs God and his mother to hear to make her repent.

"Now if she can do *me* like that, and that's my mother and I'm her son! How I think *you* gonna do me? And I don't know you, you not even family. I don't trust nobody! Okay, we might be friends and you might be my dude, or like my brother, we might be like family and all, but if your own mother…"

Tyquan drifts back to the memory of his mother, uncorking a pain that has been tearing through his soul, and he bears it to us, offering up a bruised peach.

"If it wasn't for my foster mother…she's seventy-two years old, she took me and my brother since we was babies. I love that woman. If something was to happen to her, God forbid, 'cause she's old, so you never know. And I'm going upstate for two and a half to three years…"

He stops at the thought of his aging foster mother dying while he's incarcerated. It brings the river to his eyes, but the river never flows; he wouldn't dare allow a tear to drop. His eyes glisten like beautiful brown crystal marbles.

"Word to everything I love, if something happens to her while I'm up top, I ain't gonna make it...I ain't gonna make it, son."

Tyquan, aka Africa, aka Prince tha Don, is standing vulnerable, spirit prostrate, at the altar of God in front of his peers in hell. He's peeling his scabs, tearing his skin, blood and pus oozing from his heart. It is painful and necessary. He is brave. He is Black, beautiful, and courageous. He is exposed and raw. He is in Rikers, naked in front of the class, many of whom prey on the weak.

But Tyquan is not weak. He is extraordinary. His testimony has silenced the room, revealing the truth of his humanity, laying down a shield he's carried for seventeen years, too heavy to hold any longer. His wounds and fears resonate with the entire class, all of whom I am sure have childhood traumas of their own buried deep in their hearts, hiding beneath gangster tattoos. I'm proud of Tyquan for being a lionhearted warrior. I'm proud of the class for being compassionate soldiers who didn't strike but held him up with affirming nods. He took a valiant step toward his healing and I pray it continues. Silently I lift Tyquan in prayer. May his growth blossom daily. May he forgive his mother and learn to love himself fiercely. May God and the archangels of Light protect him and cover him during his journey in prison. May he discover comfort and joy. May his divine purpose be revealed unto him. May the ancestors guide him. I pray he wins. I pray he soars. Mother Father God, hear my prayer.

When hearing stories like Tyquan's, and some that are worse, the challenge is to not get caught up and stuck in their *woundology*. I had to learn how to acknowledge the pain without coddling it. I had to learn to let the wound breathe by discussing it, but not giving it absolute power by lounging in the trauma. I won't allow their wound to become their identity. I look for their strengths, I recognize their gifts, I remind them of their resilience, and I find the good and praise it. It's a balance indeed.

Kenny gets it and goes straight to Tyquan's strength. "You're stronger than you think, my man; you're still here, still standing strong, my dude. You got contributions to make. And besides, you can't make it in the hood and be from where you're from and not be strong—you got a leader personality. You're what they call an 'alpha male.' Whatever you put your mind to, both good and bad, you make it happen. Your will is strong."

Nodding his head in agreement, Tyquan revels in the compliment. "Word...word."

Like a commercial interrupting a powerful scene in a made-for-TV after-school special, the CO barks, "Walking out!" signaling the guys to line up in the hallway for lunch.

It's a presidential election year, and quite a historic one, with the first African-American citizen nominated to be the Democratic candidate. The country is less than a month away from possibly moving the first Black family into the White House. Electing a Black *president*? A Black commander in chief? It's trippy. The energy is unprecedented. America is on the brink of experiencing a national miracle, a colossal shift, a psychological breakdown and breakthrough. It's a new perspective and brand-new fucking day. The adrenaline is loaded. Barack Obama is *the man* and almost every Black person's *main man*. Black folks on buses and in barbershops, on street corners and in beauty salons, by the water cooler and in saloons, in checkout lines and the food stamp office, at the bank and the chicken spot, at church and coffee shops, *everybody, everywhere* is pouring the tea, philosophizing, psychoanalyzing, and prophesying about the meaning of it all. What *if* he actually wins? Will America really let that happen? Will they assassinate him if he gets too close to winning? Is he a puppet? Is he a Tom? Is he a brotha or a fraud? And we *all* have something to say about his wife, Michelle, whose presence and essence speaks volumes. Hands down by unanimous decision, he is with a Black queen, a sistah from the South Side of Chicago, a statuesque, dark brown mocha-skinned 'round-the-way sistah girl with a phat booty...and she's brilliant. Word on the street, on the underground low, is she validated his

Blackness and authenticated his *brotha* status by helping him pass the Black-enough-for-Black-folks litmus test.

Some of us are still not sure how he'll lean, having a white momma and all. It could go either way. He could do a Clarence Thomas and flip the script and go *Whiteyville* on us. He could be one of the "I'm not one of *them*" self-loathing sucka types who try to prove they're whiter than white folks to be accepted and appear safe enough for white folks to like. My daddy calls them Oreos, Black on the outside but white on the inside of their heart, mind, and spirit. The hood is buzzing with theories. And if having a very Black, indisputably superbad sista for his wife wasn't enough to clutch the pearls, he also has two beautiful Black baby girls twirling gorgeous natural hair with cornrows, twists, and afro puffs, looking like my cousins and me. It is just so much to take in, the enormity of it all. I'm convinced it's visual kryptonite for racist white folks, triggering a self-imploding, terrifying shock to their psyche. But for the vast majority of the 'groid crunktastic brothas and sistas, it's a refreshing reminder of Black superpotential. It's a phenomenon so stunning on multiple levels that I can actually see Black folks walking a little taller this season. I do believe the sleeping giants are stirring.

I bring into class the red, white, and blue November issue of *VIBE* magazine with Obama on the cover. In a strategic effort to reach out to young, urban Black voters, Barack has written an open letter to the magazine's readers. He goes hip-hop. It's a brilliant strategy. Inside the issue, there are ninety-nine different celebrity-artists commenting about Barack Obama and what his nomination and potential election means to them. It's a genius endorsement campaign from hip-hop luminaries like Jay-Z, Nas, Ludacris, Young Jeezy, Q-Tip, CeeLo, Plies, Common, Lil Boosie, Russell Simmons, Bun B, Fat Joe, Scarface, Dead Prez, and more. It is an amazing, powerful chess move on Obama's part and, damn, it's sure delicious to watch him eat up the crusty old white pieces for lunch by gaining youth power, getting up-and-coming generations galvanized, and changing the game. Barack is like turbo Pac-Man. I bring my enthusiasm to the class and develop several lesson plans using Obama for the social studies curriculum. For starters, I read Obama's open letter to generate a dialogue about this historic candidacy and I work in some vocabulary words from the article. Some of my students listen intently, some talk, and some are falling asleep. Shahteik just stares at me, not listening a lick. He's daydreaming. I can tell by the glazed look. Lord, *please* don't let it be about me. My feminine wiles and spidey-senses tell me this dusty rug rat is fantasizing. It's making me uncomfortable. I clap my hands two times to snap him out of it. "Shahteik, pay attention!"

I instruct the guys to copy the vocabulary words from the board and write a sentence for each word. Tyquan finishes first and barrels up to my desk.

"What's up, scrap!" he says to me.

Sarcastically, I look behind me, then to the right and left of me, looking for the person he could be talking to. I try to ignore him but he persists: "Scrap, what's up, you ignoring me?"

"Tyquan, I am not a scrap of anything, so please don't refer to me as that."

"Aww, Ms. P, scrap is good. That means you like one of the homies, you down. Scrap ain't for everybody, but you my peoples, so, you *scrap*," he says, turning to his buddy Fred. "Yo, scrap, tell Ms. P scrap is a compliment. She think I'm swindling."

Raheim chimes in, "Scrap mean you cool, Ms. P. It's hood talk."

Fred adds, "That means you good, Ms. P, you scrap...you good."

"I appreciate the compliment, but I'd rather not be called scrap; Ms. P is just fine."

Tyquan is slightly disappointed. "Aww, scrap, I mean Ms. P...I got you, *I got you*. But Ms. P, can I read that *VIBE* magazine? I finished my vocabulary. You know me. I do my work and finish first all the time, Ms. P, you know that."

Tyquan is right. But I know good and damn well that if I give him the magazine, the Bosses will confiscate it from Tyquan before he can even sit down, guaranteeing they won't even attempt to do work. I have a quid pro quo policy in my class. If they want something *from me,* they have to give something *to me* in return. It's my own way of negotiating extra classwork out of them.

"Tyquan, you know how it goes, quid pro quo. I'll let you read the magazine on two conditions."

"Anything, Ms. P, you know I got you. I do my work anyway, so it ain't nothing. What's the deal?"

"First, you are *not* to let *anyone* else read it because I know the other guys are going to be all over you once I give you the magazine."

"Ms. P, I'mma move my seat. I'm not even going to sit near them. *I got you.* I'mma sit in the back all by myself."

Magazines are a commodity in jail. They're a cheap thrill, full of pictures, especially *VIBE,* with the big-booty vixens and sexy advertisements in the back. And it's like CNN for the hood, with all the latest hip-hop celebrity news, including breakups, hookups, and beefs. It's the closest thing they have to cable and it plugs them back into the world they've been disconnected from since their arrest.

"And the second stipulation is you have to read Barack Obama's letter and write a short paragraph summarizing in your own words what you think Senator Obama is saying to voters."

Tyquan chirps, "That's all? Shoot, that ain't nothing. I got you, scrap."

Before I can open my mouth, Tyquan blurts out, "Psyche, *psyche,* Ms. P, my beautiful Black queen."

I curl my lips. "I want my paragraph, Tyquan, don't play. I know a swindle when I hear it."

Tyquan struts to the back of the room like a kid who just won a prize at the Coney Island arcade. Chest poked out. The Bosses inquire why he moved his seat away from them and they motion for him to bring the magazine over to their station. I cut my eye at Tyquan and he replies diplomatically, "Naw, scrap, Ms. P got me doing an assignment. She got me over here writing; this ain't leisure time, scrap, believe that."

I expect to get a half-ass, get-this-lady-out-of-my-face rushed and raggedy paragraph from Tyquan. I figure he'll write a simple line or two so he can hurry up and get to the pictures and read the tabloid junk. Fuck it, as long as he's reading, occupied, and not acting up, then anything he writes will suffice for today. It's a 180 from earlier, so this is also my subtle way of rewarding him for better behavior and giving him a treat to soothe his rough morning. A visual lollipop.

Tyquan hands in more than I expected. And this is why I spoil him. What he wrote is so heartfelt that I beam with pride and ask him to write a longer letter so I can send it to the editor, because it is that damn good. I give him a couple of notes, telling him to include more of his personal feelings about the potential of having the first Black president. I also tell him to reflect on what this presidency means to a kid from the inner city who's currently in jail. Tyquan is filled with confidence and a sense of duty. He writes down my notes with a furrowed brow, salutes me like a general, and marches off on the mission to complete the assignment. I push and he climbs.

Darnel, a quiet new student who sits alone, asks if he can read the magazine after Tyquan finishes. I give him the same assignment and again, to my surprise, like Tyquan, Darnel far surpasses my expectation. I overestimated their apathy toward the significance of this election and, in turn, they humbled me. I stand corrected—the rascals *do* give a damn about Obama.

Darnel makes it a point to separate himself from the riffraff by telling me he's from a stable two-parent middle-class household and has enough high school credits to graduate. "I already took my SATs for college, miss. I really want to go to Howard. I pray everything works out. My dad got me a paid lawyer. It's in God's hands, I guess." Darnel's been at Rikers for two weeks and is waiting to be bailed out any day now. But, for the time he's with me, I have the kid writing every chance I get, holding him to a higher standard, because he can handle it…and he'll definitely need it going into college.

My impromptu lesson has me feeling bubbly. I'm so excited about the success of the assignment, I want to skip through the halls and proclaim, "My boys give a damn about Obama! They like him, they like him!" I'm on a roll and get other students involved with the assignment. I tell the guys I can't guarantee anything, but their voices are strong enough to warrant publishing, so, with their permission, I will submit their letters to the editor at *VIBE* magazine. I'mma roll the dice for my rug rats. Their voices matter.

Student Letters to Obama

From watching campaigns and reading newspapers and articles out of magazines, to my understanding the world is a disaster. The only way to make a difference in this world would be to vote for a president, a good president we can count on. This world needs a president who is going to change the way things run and make life better, not a president who's going to make things worse. I think Obama should be elected as president because he's a very intelligent man and he knows what's best for our country. He seems like he cares and makes a lot of sense in what he says in his campaigns. It's about time we see something different and live the life we're supposed to live as human beings. As an adolescent being in and out of jail since 14, it makes me proud to see a Black man running for president. I think this is what African Americans were waiting for, over centuries, and our people deserve to get a chance to see how Obama will make the world better. Come November 4, when Obama gets elected, that's when he'll show the world a better way.

I would like to thank Obama because he showed me that I can be anything I want to be no matter the circumstances. I always thought jail would set me back and there would never be another chance to get on track, but seeing Obama run for president makes me more proud and makes me more confident to come home and follow my goals.

Timothy (17 years old)

Hi my name is Tyquan from Brooklyn NY. I live in the projects in Crown Heights, but currently I'm on Rikers Island C-74 adolescent building. I read almost every VIBE magazine and I came across the VIBE magazine with Barack Obama on the cover and I was very inspired by his letter to the people in our nation and I feel that Blacks, whites and Hispanics should take interest in his letter. After I read the letter, I came to the conclusion that Barack Obama is trying to open Black, white and hispanic eyes so that they can see the bigger picture, which is our nation is at its worse and he's trying to change things around for the better, for Black people's communities and to help Black people live a better life than the one we live today. The main point that he's trying to get across is before anything can be changed, we as people have to go out and vote and support and believe in a strong Black leader. Seeing Barack Obama about to be elected for president inspires me, an inmate at Rikers Island, to believe that I can achieve anything that I set my mind to because Obama set the way by showing a good example for Black Americans. As a child I believed that it wasn't possible to have a Black President until Obama came on the scene and has a chance to make history, so I support him 100%. Obama changed my thoughts about Black people because all you see on the news is the negative images of Black people shooting, killing, and abusing other people, and people believe what the media tries to make us out to be, but Obama is encouraging Black people to believe that we can become someone in life.

P.S. I hope everybody that's eligible to vote goes out November 4th, 2008 and votes, because I am. Tyquan 4 Obama.

I'll holla.

Prince Tha Don, the wavy one

Tyquan (18 years old)

The Barack Obama letter is deep. Obama is right; he can't change this crucial world alone. He needs our help, the people of America. Together we can make a change and let everything bad that happened in the past stay in the past. Obama will affect the world in a great way. He says he can't do it alone, but together we can change the economy. The Obama letter leads me to believe that we can make the impossible, possible.

Lynard (16 years old)

Barack Obama, how are you doing sir? I read your letter in the VIBE magazine November 2008 issue and I'm 100% all the way with you. This is the most important election in the history of the United States. I do believe that you can turn this country around. I am only seventeen, a young Black male growing up in Harlem, New York, and even though I'm not registered to vote until next year, my father, great-grandmother and family are by your side. I can't believe that I'm here at this point in time where I see history being made. When I look back at this, ten to fifteen years from now, I can tell my kids I was there to see you become president. It's not even that you're going to be the first Black president, but you want change and that's what we've been waiting for. I am hoping you can change the economic, jail, educational and health systems. Also, I am hoping you can put an end to the war in Iraq. Right now Mr. Obama I am incarcerated on Rikers Island in New York City. I am not a bad kid at all and I am about to go home. I will be home to see the elections on television. I have been jailed for something I didn't do but I've only been here for two weeks and I learned a deep lesson to stay out of trouble. I have always been interested in politics but your way of it has had me focused deeper on it. Even though I messed up by hanging with the wrong crowds, I have learned from my mistakes. So November 4th we need everybody to come together so we can bring change. By the way, my name is Darnel and I pray to God you win Tuesday night November 4th.

Darnel (17 years old)

This presidential campaign really caught my attention because if Obama was to win, this would make history. I made my housing area in C-74 Rikers Island watch the debate because I feel that people should know about what's happening in the world. Listening to the debate I feel like McCain is addressing personal issues instead of addressing issues about America. I feel that McCain will do or say anything to win the election but Obama is more consistent because he says the same thing in every debate. This election is going to make those who never believe, believe that they can succeed and be anything they want to be, mostly we young African Americans. It makes me feel good to see another brother make it because it doesn't happen too often.

William (18 years old)

A Dream We Always Wanted

In my opinion this whole election is strange and makes sense. The strange part of it is I'm about to witness history; a Black American in office fighting for us. The debate I saw today with John McCain and Barack Obama was like a fight but with words. Obama is focusing on giving. John is focusing on taking away. Their facial expressions, especially on John McCains face was more like hate. Obamas face was more like "I'm making sense." Obama just sat back and laughed at this guy who wants to take away from us. This election is so important to me because I'm witnessing history. I hear people talking about "I don't care what happens with the president" but they should, especially African Americans because of the things we've been through; we had to fight for our rights. Now we have a chance for a Black man to make history and become the president of the United States of America. We need change!

Jason (18 years old)

CHAPTER EIGHT

King Down

Thought for the Day: African people introduced civilization to the planet. We were scientists, astronomers, philosophers, master masons, kings and queens, a mighty people long before we became slaves in America. Know thyself. If we did it once, we can do it again. Remember the ancestors.

—Ms. P

My desk sits facing the class on the far right side of the room, in front of the Harlemites' declared territory of seats. In order to create distance between my desk and the filthy pigeon-shit-splattered windows, I placed two tall, metal file cabinets side by side in a line directly next to the nasty view, and have them strategically flanked tightly next to my desk. Zero room to squeeze through. The formation of the cabinets lined up between my desk and the window creates a small man-made rectangle-shaped alcove behind my desk, about three feet wide. For extra precaution, I keep a combination padlock on the cabinet that holds my coat, plastic see-through tote bag, CDs, DVDs, Febreze, frankincense, snacks for the boys, and other personal belongings. The doors to the file cabinets are only accessible by coming behind my desk and walking into the tight alcove I created. I remembered Ms. G's advice to not let any students sit at my desk. To my surprise, this rule isn't difficult to enforce. I've only had to say it once at the beginning of the semester and just a few times after that to new students who weren't given the heads-up by the veteran rug rats.

"Ah, ah, ah…get from behind my desk, please. No one but me sits at my desk. I don't play that. And I definitely don't want you in the area behind my desk. There is nothing there for you. If anything turns up missing from the file cabinets or my desk, you don't want me pointing the finger at you, since you were the only one in my lil' alleyway. This rule is to protect you, my brother. Protects you from being tempted to rummage through grown folks' business and it protects you from being wrongly accused, should anything disappear."

"Oh, *aight,* miss, my bad. Damn," scoffs Rashid. Revealing his frustration as he hisses like a snake, sounding like air slowly seeping out of a punctured tire. He's new and hasn't developed a rapport with me yet. He feels embarrassed over being called out in front of his peers. He's a runt like Peanut and has a lot of attitude, this kid.

"No problem. That's how you learn and now you know. Welcome to my class, brother…" I quickly scan the roster to find the name of this pipsqueak. "…brother Rashid," I say cheerfully in an attempt to soften his awkward moment.

"You can call me Leaky, miss."

"Leaky?" I'm perplexed and not amused. I scrunch my face.

"Yeah, Leaky, 'cause I leave niggas leaking," he says, laughing, giving Tyquan a pound.

"Watch that word; no niggas in this class, Rashid. You're a Nubian king." I tried to pull a smile from him and did.

"Damn, she go hard body, son," he says to Tyquan.

"Yo, scrap, Ms. P cool, but she don't play. She be on that Poof shit, my man," Tyquan warns the new rug rat, who is unaware of my classroom rules. "And she like her row of desks neat too, my nigga…"

"Watch that word," I quip without looking up.

"See what I mean," Tyquan exclaims.

"Give me my rows. I want my rows neat, just how you found them, my Black Nubian brothas…or else Poof, Poof, Poof!" Malik yells from the back of the class, imitating my voice.

"That's right. You better know it too!" I declare. "Hmph, I take time every morning before y'all come in here lining my desks up neat, and that's how I want to see them when I leave. Y'all see some of those other classrooms, looking a hot mess. Not in here, no *siree*. I like a neat classroom. Helps you think better. Feng shui, my brothas." I laugh, enjoying that joke by myself, knowing they have no idea what I am talking about. Mekhai rolls his eyes at me, like a grumpy old man.

"Yo, scrap, I got some shit I gotta tell you," Tyquan says, motioning Rashid to sit in the empty desk next to him.

"Malik, put that Pop-Tart away!" I yell as I catch Malik breaking off pieces to the Bosses seated in front of him. "And Shahteik, take your seat…Lord Jesus, please let this be a good day."

"Who you?" Malik tries to sneak and say, sounding like he just inhaled helium. I've become quite good at locating the ventriloquist. "Who you" is a high-pitched, owl-like hoot the kids can say without moving their lips, making it impossible for a scolding teacher or a yelling CO to figure out who's saying it. When COs come into the housing area, barking at the kids for this and that, it's usually followed by several smart alecks hooting "who you, who you," which *always* ticks the COs off, and the kids know it. Oftentimes the officer will punish the entire housing area since it's impossible to locate the "who you" culprit. The kids play this hooting-owl game even though it gets them in trouble. They derive great satisfaction from ruffling the feathers of anyone in authority. It's a cheap score and the payoff is worth it in their lil' rascal, hooligan brains.

"You already *know* who I am, so don't play, Malik!" I snap.

Malik tries to play innocent mixed with righteous indignation. "Ms. P, that wasn't even me! How you gonna blame me for something I ain't even do. That's not fair, Ms. P!"

Shahteik tries to bait me as he turns to Malik and says slightly under his breath but loud enough for me to hear, "Man, don't pay that woman no mind. She yell 'cause she probly ain't got nobody at home to love her—she ain't getting no love at home, so she come in here getting on *our* nerves, like we need that."

"Word," chimes Mekhai the Muppet, as he snickers and gives Shahteik a soul-pound.

Ouch. That shit pierced me like a dart but I *refuse* to acknowledge he pricked me and pretend I don't hear him. I will sidestep Shahteik's trap today. He's just too damn exhausting, so I choose an easier battle.

"Don't let me see that Pop-Tart again, Malik. And where's my poem you said you were working on?" I ask, quickly diverting attention from the sugary snack.

"I got you, Ms. P, I'mma finish it now. I gotta get some inspiration from my son, though." Malik reaches for the humongous-sized complete works of Langston Hughes. Malik sits behind the Bosses in the last seat in the corner next to the short bookshelf. He immediately took a liking to Langston's work since the first day of class. Abiodun from the Last Poets is his other favorite. This fills my spirit like nobody's business. The kid loves classic revolutionary poetry, earning him a permanent soft spot with me. When Malik is in a defiant nonworking mood, I can always negotiate with him by using a poetry assignment that involves Langston Hughes or the Last Poets as bargaining chips. If the class is doing science or math and he's being disruptive, because, like me, he hates both of those subjects, I can always get Malik to read and write some poetry. How can I refuse *that*? Poetry is my weakness, and he knows it. I have to get stronger, start putting my foot down with him and push him past his comfort zone.

Most days I walk up and down my rows to keep students on task and break up barbershop/pool hall gossip huddles. These boys run their mouths *all* day like radio hosts, reporting on drama from their hood and housing area, reenacting fights, instigating shit-talking, debating athletes, and critiquing rappers. Constantly walking my rows enables me to justify demanding that my aisles stay straight so I can easily pass through while simultaneously intercepting the chatty cyphers.

I keep a chair next to my desk for one-on-one conferences with my students. Initially when I would call a student up to my desk and ask them to sit down in the seat next to me, they immediately assumed they had done something wrong. Sometimes that was the case, making it the "oooh-you-in-trouble" hot seat, but most times I used it to talk to the boys privately about their progress, or lack thereof. I highlighted their improvements and challenged them to push through the areas of weakness and to focus more. One-on-one time helps with building relationships. Now the boys look forward to getting called up to my desk to get a dose of real talk, one-on-one, special attention with Ms. P. This is also a great tool in classroom management. Instead of yelling, I just wait for the right moment and call the disruptive rug rat up to my desk to address their transgression in private and get them to give me their word to improve their behavior. I get more compliance by not embarrassing them publicly. Their skin might be full of tattoos and battle scars, but their egos are fragile and raw.

Tyquan scoots into my private conference seat even though I haven't called for him.

"Yes, Tyquan?"

"What's good, Ms. P?"

I clasp my hands and look at him with annoyance. He is interrupting me grading a vocabulary test. And he's such an attention seeker. Boy, go *somewhere.*

"Ms. P, I got two bodies on me. Word up, I got two bodies," he confesses and blurts this disturbing information from out of nowhere. I don't want to deal with this. He's giving me that "aww, come, on, really?" moment like when a bird poops on you, fucking up your vibe for a good minute. Regardless of what you were doing, you gotta pause to clean the shit.

"You killed two people, is that what you're telling me?" I ask with grave concern. He has my full attention now.

"Well, I wouldn't exactly say it so blunt, but let's just say two people ain't breathing no more," he boasts.

He could very well be telling the truth, but somehow I get the sense Tyquan is still trying to psyche himself up to believe he is a killer, trying his myth out on me. He's trying to elicit a shocked reaction, but I refuse to give him that satisfaction and instead I go reverse psychology on his needy ass. I'mma spank his spirit.

"That's nothing to brag about, actually, and it's definitely nothing to be proud of. And for you to come up here and tell me something like that as if it's an accomplishment means you still have a lot of inner spiritual work and cleansing to do. God made you…*you,* Tyquan—God made you unique, special and rare, one of a kind. And *nobody* has a right to take you off this planet and end your life. End what God made? Nobody but God has that right to take you away from your mother, your son, and your brother." I serve spank number one.

Tyquan relaxes his shoulders. He looks deflated. He wanna come up to my desk talking crazy, talking about murder? Well, he's gonna get the sho' nuff Pentecostal-priestess whooping from me. I continue, "And you don't have that right, no right at all, to take anybody off this planet, unless you are defending your life. That right is reserved for God, not you. Killing someone doesn't make you special or tough, it makes you pathetic and cowardly and you *will* pay a spiritual price for that. So, if what you are telling me is true, my brotha, you have to begin the very long process of praying and asking God for forgiveness and you're gonna have to do a lot of spiritual soul-searching to come up out of that very heavy burden hanging over your head. Your spirit is sick and needs healing if what you're bragging about is true. Your soul is out of alignment, Tyquan, and it will only bring you a lifetime of chaos and confusion in every area of your life." Serving spank number two.

Tyquan squirms in his seat. "You know, I want to be a motivational speaker, Ms. P. You think I could do that?"

I lay down my belt and put on the velvet glove. "Baby, it's never too late to become who you dream of becoming," I say, quoting a Thought for the Day. "I truly believe if you commit to doing inner work on yourself, to grow and heal and take responsibility for your actions, I most certainly believe you have what it takes to be a powerful motivational speaker and to help younger kids not go down the path that landed you here."

Before I can shoo Tyquan out of my special conference seat so I can finish grading, Officer King pops his head in. "Bathroom!" In ten seconds my room empties out nearly as fast as a shoot-out at a block party.

Officer King is my buddy, always checking in on me throughout the day during his shift, offering me a pleasant salutation: "Good morning, sis. You good? They behaving okay?"

"So far, so good. They're doing great work, actually. We just had a vocabulary quiz and most of them did well. I'm impressed. We're off to a good start."

"That's good, that's good. See, you guys have a good teacher who cares," he says, addressing the class.

"You let me know if *any* of these guys give you a problem!" he barks as he surveys the room with a menacing look. A couple of the Bosses elbow each other and snicker, picking up on King's not-so-inconspicuous flirtation with me.

"Yo, King, I see you, son... you funny," Malik says, trynna blow King up on the low.

"What, what you see, huh? A righteous Black man checking in on a righteous sister. What's so funny about that? Watch and learn something, my brother." King cracks a smile, making the Bosses chuckle and shake their heads.

"Lemme find out you a G and be macking on the town," says Tyrone with a sly smile.

"I think my age and experience qualifies me as an OG, son,"

King shoots back, making the class fall back in unison and holla like he just landed a three-pointer, all net.

"Oh snap, yo, son is funny. He wilding, son. King you got it… you got it."

King laughs. "Have a good day, gentlemen. Keep up the good work and don't let Ms. Peterson have to come and get me. Ms. Peterson…" King gives me a gentleman's nod and heads out the doorway.

"Thank you, King. I appreciate that," I reply, flashing a coy smile, treating him to a little coquettishness. One of the rug rats tries to mimic my lady voice: "Thank you, King, I appreciate that," but winds up sounding like squeaky Minnie Mouse. Damn rascals, get on my nerves.

King is tough but reasonable. He's the alpha male who walks the hallways with dominion, keeping order simply by his presence, providing a sense of security and calm whenever he's on duty. He cuts the air with a slow, authoritative stride like a heavyweight champ who knows his skin is really covering iron. Puppies yelp, dogs bark, but King roars with a tenor that commands attention. He can restore order in my class by simply poking his head in without saying a word. He's papa bear for sure and the guys yield to his power and respect his position in the animal kingdom hierarchy, rarely, if ever, testing him. When a kid is cutting the fool acting up, I've seen King reason with him and maybe deny him a privilege (like gym time, commissary, or the barbershop). He might even opt to rough 'em up a bit, slap 'em upside the head and dole out a mild spanking *instead* of giving the kid an infraction, which could lead to the lil' bandit losing good days,* prolonging their stay at Rikers. Adolescent boys, *especially* these boys, many of whom have never had a father figure or positive male role model in their life, need discipline and clear boundaries that have consequences if crossed. Their reckless behavior is a cry for attention but is also an indication that

---

*Good days: the ten-day reduction in the duration of an inmate's actual sentence for every thirty days served.

their foundation is weak and basic principles of respect are missing. Though they resist it and challenge it, there is a subconscious need to hear the bark (and sometimes feel the bite) of an alpha male lest they get a false sense of impulsively doing and saying what the hell they want in a world poised to crush their Black bodies. Navigating between the iron fist and the velvet glove with these wayward warriors is a tricky balancing act but I suspect King has finessed it. I've never actually seen King rough a kid up, but based on their contrite behavior when they returned to the school floor after having a "little talk" with him, I got the sense that either his iron fist or the threat of his wrath combined with his king-of-the-jungle tongue-lashing roar may have played a role.

There was a time when one of my other disruptive rug rats, William (Shahteik's best buddy, of course), acted out so bad I had to sic King on him. Most of the time when I see kids sleeping in class I use the huge silver stone ring I wear on my index finger to tap ever so lightly but continuously on the desk until the snoozing gremlin wakes up. Sometimes, when William is sleeping I let him nap because on the days he actually decides to come to school (which is rare), he's worse than Shahteik, with nonstop disruptions. And it makes matter worse that he and Shahteik are best buddies; together they are the Tasmanian devil terror duo, like two little Chucky demon dolls. It's sheer pandemonium. So I let him sleep. Sleep, my little pretty, *sleep*.

After Shahteik told me that William is facing a fifteen-year sentence, I tried my best to cut him some slack and give him a compassion coupon. I tried talking to him privately; maybe I can reason with him, negotiate with him, connect with him, anything. He'd "yes, ma'am" me to death and "I'mma get it together, miss" and "I'mma do my work, miss." Not once has he ever called me Ms. P, just "miss"—a slightly underhanded but slick way of minimizing me by not fully acknowledging me. I was on to him. Immediately after getting up from our umpteenth one-on-one conference, he'd be back at his desk carrying on like he was at the honeycomb hideout trap house, talking 'bout nothing, wheeling and dealing, running the spot like I bet he did back on the town. He's a ringleader who corrals the Bosses in gossip, blatant vulgarity, and manipulation schemes. He runs the crew when he's here, so he's the one I have to pop. He the bad seed; the weed in my wild garden. Today is the final straw. I am officially done. Done talking to him, done asking him to take his feet off the desk, done letting him sleep, done sending him out of class for the day, done asking him to keep his voice down, done asking him to watch his mouth. Done. He is up out of his seat, *again,* and commences to lean his dusty ass in the doorway like he's leaning on a Cadillac Escalade kicking game to some chick, arms and feet crossed, talking shit, talking loud, holding court, disrupting my class in the most brass-balls, audacious manner. Homie is *t-to-the-ri-double-p . . . tripping*!

"William, please get out the doorway and take your seat." *One.* He gives me a contemptuous nod and continues his conversation, shamelessly ignoring me. "William, I'm not going to ask you again. Get out of the doorway and take your seat!" *Two.* My octave is escalating toward going banshee.

William turns from talking to his buddies, locks venomous eyes with me, and spits, "Yo, who the hell you talking to?"

My head rears back. I feel the acceleration of *her,* a whirling dervish of thug mamma flying out the lamp with nunchuks. "Who the hell are *you* talking to like that?! You clearly have it twisted, son! I am an adult; I give respect and demand respect! And you are way out of line!" *Three. She* explodes out the lamp. A shouting match ensues.

"Look, *miss,* I don't fucking care or wanna hear what you have to say. Really, I don't! So go somewhere with all that noise, *miss.*"

"Oh *really*; okay, I got something for you!" I yell as I stomp back to my desk and pull out the infamous orange infraction slip.

"You think I give a damn about that? You ain't doing nothing!"

Unbeknownst to William, as he is popping mad shit to me in the doorway, Captain Blackwell is standing behind him the whole time, letting him twist himself up into a guaranteed infraction. Then, with the timing of an eagle swooping down on a flapping fish, she snatches him up by the collar and whirls him around. William's eyes nearly pop out his head. All the kids sit up straight in military attention and murmur, "Oh shit, oh snap, I ain't even see her there, yo, captain 'bout to make it hot."

"Captain Blackwell! I'm sorry, Ms. P—" William starts stuttering and folding.

Captain Blackwell crumples his bravado like a paper ball. "Ms. P nothing! I heard your disrespectful mouth. Come with me!" Captain Blackwell asks me if I want him out of class for the day or for good. "I can sign him out for good if you want me to, Ms. P."

I hesitate and cough. Sign the kid out *for good*? As angry as I am in this moment, I still can't bring myself to take away his learning for good. Maybe for a day, even for a week, but not for good. I'm a punk with wolf tickets. I choke. Captain Blackwell picks up on my trepidation and graciously leaves me a way out. "Think about it and let me know what you want to do. In the meantime, fill out the infraction report and give it to Officer King." At this point, King is in the room standing with his arms akimbo, scowling at William, who is in a state of puppy-eyed surrender, eyes begging for mercy, transformed from his grown-man pomp faster than the magic click of Dorothy's ruby slippers. Good. As the old folks say, "That'll learn him."

The class was in the midst of a social studies assignment just before William turned it up. We were studying the Middle Passage, and William interfered with my Black history flow, which pissed me off even more. "Y'all answer the questions on the handout and we'll go over the answers together in a minute," I say, sitting at my desk filling out the orange spank-slip on William.

The rug rats are quiet and doing their work, or at least looking like they are. They know the temperature is hot and Captain Blackwell's on the floor. Shahteik gets up and slides into the conference seat next to me. He's up to something.

"Hey, Ms. P, can I sit here and keep you company?"

"No, Shahteik, go back to your seat."

"Okay, no problem, I just...Ms. P, you gonna really write William up? You know you don't *really* have to do that, right?"

"Shahteik—" He cuts me off, jumps out of his seat, and runs to grab a piece of paper from his desk before barreling back over to me holding out a piece of evidence.

"Look, Ms. P, see, William did his work, look."

I look at the worksheet, which has a few questions answered but no name on it.

"Shahteik, just because there's no name on the paper doesn't mean I can't tell it's your handwriting and your work!"

"Okay, okay, Ms. P, you got me, but I'm saying, don't write him up. Please, Ms. P, lemme talk to him. I can fix this." Shahteik is working hard to throw a lifeline for his friend. I'm impressed by the brotherly love, actually.

"Shahteik, I appreciate you advocating for William. You're a true friend. But it's too late, I already started the process. The form *is* being filled out...you see me, right?"

"But Ms. P, you can fill it out, but you don't *have to* turn it in." Shahteik knows the loopholes and ropes around this place better than me, and he is not letting it go. He's negotiating relentlessly for his comrade, trying to pull me to his will. I dig my heels in.

"Shahteik, I have given William chance after chance. I gave him a time-out last week and you told me *back then* that you were going to talk to him, so obviously your little talking didn't work. Sometimes people and things just don't mix no matter what. Roaches don't mix with Raid, milk don't mix with vinegar, perfume don't mix with funk, and William and I just don't mix; it happens and that's okay. But I have a job to do, and my job is to teach, and *anybody* who gets in the way of what I have to do, they gotta go."

I feel my pastor-preachah-deaconess ready to raise her finger in the air and thump with the good word again. "And just because you're in jail doesn't mean you can't learn, and it's my job to teach. I don't see you all as criminals. I see young men who made a mistake and still have a chance to turn your life around. And my job is to bring knowledge. I show you *all* respect, and he thinks he can come in here and come out his face and disrespect me like that? Oh no, no, no no, no *siree*, no baby, he's got it twisted, and I'm not a pretzel," I fuss, sounding like my auntie Julia. "Everybody has their breaking point when enough is enough, and today is my breaking point. Enough. Done. *Finito.* A wrap. Closed for business. Liquidation. Everything must go. *Nada.* No more. Marshal's at the door. Bye. *Bye.* My cup runneth over. That's it on that. Like the setting sun. Scratch the needle on the record. Party's over, son. I'm sure you understand that, don't you?" His tongue's too short to box with a pissed-off poet. I keep my clip loaded.

"All right all right all right, damn, Ms. P, I hear you. I tried, Lord knows I tried to help my boy out." Shahteik humbly offers defeat. "But, yo, you did that straight off the dome like that? You kinda nice wit' it, Ms. P. Lemme find out you can freestyle. Word."

For lunch I usually convene in the teachers' lounge with other staff to watch whatever blood-curdling scary movie Mr. Wilcox, aka Trinidad, has brought in for lunchtime entertainment. It's *always* a horror movie. Always. Crazy how we all seem to unwind by watching the goriest, bloodiest, most heinous chop-'em-up flicks in a place filled with darkness and violence. We sit around the table with just the sunlight beaming through the windows, slightly illuminating the dismal gray room. We scream and yell and talk back to the TV screen like we're at the movies. It's twisted and fun.

Today I've skipped the *Night of the Living Dead* movie feature to have some quiet time and sit at my desk to eat lunch, alone. I unwrap my peanut butter and jelly sandwich and squeeze a pack of honey into my hot tea.

Officer King pops his head in. "Ms. P, no scary movie today?"

"No, not today, King. I need to clear my mind and be still for a minute."

"We all need that every now and then," he says as he approaches my desk. "I see you had a rough time with William today."

My mouth is full of peanut butter and jelly so I just "mmhmm" him.

"Why you ain't come get me? I told you let me know anytime any one of them gives you a problem. And then when I saw it was William—that's my favorite knucklehead, right there—I was like, man, why she ain't just come get *me*? I had to give him the business last year, so he knows what time it is with me. Me and him have an understanding and I can reason with that kid. You should have called me, I coulda fixed it." It felt like King must have said "me" about ten times. I think he's a little upset I didn't ring my damsel-in-distress bell for him to come save me and fix the problem. My older sister once told me that alpha males like to play the role of rescuer and fixer-upper.

I hand King the orange slip. "Lemme see what this jughead did," King says as he reads out loud what I wrote on the report. "'Who the hell you talking to?'" King gives me a blank stare that makes me feel like the incredible shrinking woman. It sounds petty now. "*That's* what he said to you?" King asks a simple question, but the subtext, mixed with the dumb look he gives me, is more like, "You're writing him up for this trivial bullshit? *Really?* You can't be serious."

I feel silly. I try to put it in context for him. "I know that's not a big deal and it's hardly a threat, and it probably sounds like I'm being dramatic, but King, this boy *never* does work and whenever he actually comes here, he disturbs the class *all* the time, *all day,* worse than Shahteik. If you can even imagine *anybody* worse than Shahteik…it's William. And today was the last straw for me. It's not so much *what* he said but *how* he said it. His tone was so cocky and in-your-face with it, it was too much." I'm trying to convince King the offense was more egregious than what I wrote.

He puts the orange slip in his pocket. "I'mma talk to him, Ms. P. You won't have no more problems out of him."

I'm sure that slip will be shredded in the trash.

"Please talk to him because the next step is I'm going to have him signed out for good. I don't want to do that, but he's pushing me."

"I got you, sis. I'mma get him straightened out. That's my son."

King is Houdini. Whatever he said to William works like magic. Badass comes back to class eating humble pie.

"Ms. P, can I talk to you for a minute out in the hallway, in private?"

The Bosses look as surprised as I do. "Of course, William," I calmly reply.

We stand right outside the doorway for some semblance of privacy, but I know the Bosses, who sit near the door anyway, are ear-hustling like a mug. William looks me in the eye, then shifts his gaze to the floor, then back up at me. This is uncomfortable for him. "I truly apologize for my behavior and for disrespecting you yesterday. You didn't deserve that. I was just really angry about a lot of things going on in my life right now and I took it out on you and that wasn't fair. I know you probably still mad and all, but I am truly sorry and hope someday you will accept my apology."

King is a wizard too. He gave that boy a heart.

"William, I accept your apology and thank you for coming to me like this. Today is a new slate."

William smiles a sincere smile. "Thank you, Ms. P."

Hmph, ain't that something. Today I'm Ms. P, not just "miss." And, just like that, William comes back into class, buries his head in the workbook, and *does* work, quiet as a church mouse. King's methodology, whatever it was, worked like a charm and saved William from receiving an infraction.

This isn't the first time King has come to a kid's defense and managed to sway me, like the time when he intercepted one of my many multiple attempts to Poof Shahteik. And then it dawned on me—of course the adult alpha would know how to corral and connect with the alpha rug rats.

"Ms. P, you fucking irking me! You stay irking me... Why don't you Poof your damn self? I can't stand this lady, son. Everybody in here talking, but *who* name she call out? Mine!" Shahteik's having a tantrum.

"Because your voice was the one heard over top of everyone, meaning you were being the most obnoxious and the loudest, Shahteik!" I yell back as I walk over to my desk to get the orange slip.

"Go 'head and write me up. You think I give a fuck?"

They always bluff, pretending like they don't care, but deep down they know that enough of those orange slips could take away their good days, and *none* of them want that. They *all* want to go home sooner than later. Infractions hurt. Shahteik is fronting; he does give a fuck.

I shift gears, ending the yelling match, and serve him a snarky pleasantry.

"Shahteik, *abracadabra.*"

Upon hearing the commotion coming from my room, King pops his head in to check on me. "Ay yo, Officer King, will you *please* put me behind the *gate*. I gotta get out of here. I'm asking you *please,* 'cause I already know what kind of mood I'm in and I don't want to make it worse with this lady. *Please,* Officer King, put me behind the *gate* now, I'm begging you!" Shahteik's half-pleading, half-commanding.

By now I am sitting behind my desk, calmly humming to myself in an effort to keep my veneer of being unaffected while I write up Shahteik's orange slip.

King motions for Shahteik to follow him, calling him by his last name, "Come on, Jackson, let's go." He escorts him out of my room, down the hall, and behind the gate. Moments later, Officer King pops back in and asks to speak with me, motioning for me to step outside the classroom and out of earshot from nosy rug rats who love to ear-hustle. I leave the rug rats briefly unattended. They know better than to cut up and act a fool with King standing right outside the door, and besides, he's got supersonic hearing and they know it. I have the orange slip already filled out in one hand, with the other hand resting on my hip. All attitude.

King starts in. "You know if you go through with the infraction, he might get some good days taken away from him and be permanently removed from your class. It's totally your call, Ms. P. You really want me to go through with it?" He's totally using some reverse-Jedi mind-trick psychology on me and knows I bark like a Rottweiler with no teeth. I'm soft.

Shahteik pisses me off and gets on my fucking nerves worse than a buzzing mosquito in my face when I'm trying to sleep. But do I loathe him enough to add suffering to his incarceration? He's a pest, not a creep like Christopher, the frog boy. And if I'm really honest with myself, Lil' Rumbles and I have our good days and he has been helpful in the class at times, so I really don't want him out altogether.

King presses me. "You want me to give this ticket to the captain? 'Cause if you say yes, I will, Ms. P."

I cross my arms, suck my teeth, and let out a deep sigh of defeat. "No."

I'm such a sucker. As mad as the rug rats get me, the thought of putting them out for good never sits well with me and I almost always fold.

King chuckles and reaches for the orange slip. "Let me get rid of that for you. I'll straighten out Shahteik. He just needs a lil' time-out with me."

Officer King is smooth. I appreciate his compassion. Watching him intervene on behalf of yet another one of my foulmouthed rug rats, intercepting another infraction, is refreshing; I see him as their protective big brother, their understanding uncle, and loving father. He's great at what he does. He might have a heavy hand, which is needed with adolescent boys in jail, but he definitely doesn't have a mean spirit and the guys respect him for it.

A new teacher came on staff a couple of weeks ago and teaches in the classroom two doors down from me. She doesn't look any older than twenty-two or twenty-three, fresh out of college. Her skin is pale and creamy like a perfect Lladró figurine. She's a timid, mousy-looking lady; I get a really bad vibe from her. She walks with her chin way up, with an air of superiority. She has to pass by my classroom every morning to get to hers but she never speaks or says, "Good morning." I have an unnaturally strong aversion to this woman and don't know why. So what, she doesn't speak to me. Not every teacher on the school floor speaks to me, and it's not because they're being rude; it's because they're preoccupied with a host of bureaucratic bullshit on their minds. But with her, it's the energy she emanates.

She makes the hairs on the back of my neck stand up, my spidey-senses tingle; my intuition says she's a dangerous and treacherous woman. I don't know why and I have no rational explanation for it. The woman has triggered some genetic memory in me. I once got a vision of her that dropped into my spirit. I saw a lady of gallantry, a white heifer in the post-Reconstruction South who lusted after Black men and would cry rape if they rejected her advances or if she got caught with her bustle up. Then she'd fan herself while sipping a mint julep as her Black buck was being lynched in front of a bloodthirsty cheering mob of savages for sport.

I snap myself out of the vision. This is crazy, nutty, and totally irrational. I know I'm bugging, but I can't shake the visceral sense that my rug rats (and all of them on the school floor) aren't safe around her. My protective spirit for the boys is on high alert and my aversion toward her is so palpable that every time I see her I get a momentous urge to slap her fucking face. This definitely has to be some past-life shit for real, because on face value it makes absolutely *no* sense why I despise this woman, who has done *nothing* to me. And it's not because she's white. There are several other white teachers on the school floor who hold it down in their classrooms and are good educators. Hell, they have more rank than me and I've sought advice from them on more than one occasion; they're cool people. But this Little Miss Muffet trollop—I'm having none of her. I know this allergy and absurd abhorrence I have toward her, based on absolutely *nothing* she's said or done, is unhealthy. Killa is the only one I feel comfortable enough to divulge my unfounded, secret hatred of this woman to. Maybe he can shed some light on her since he teaches art in her third-period class. Maybe she's really nice and just supershy because she's new and happens to be just a little scared. I mean, it *is* jail. Bring it down a notch, Liza. But naw, fuck that, you coming up in Rikers to teach, you better have some swag somewhere in your spirit.

I confess to Killa during lunch. "Killa, I don't know why I don't like that new teacher, Little Miss fucking Muffet, down the hall. She hasn't done anything to me, but I get a bad vibe from her and I can't stand her and *I don't know why*. She doesn't speak, she be wearing high-heeled gold disco pumps and leopard blouses and shit. What she trynna do, turn the boys on purposefully? Killa, I don't know why I don't like this little strumpet … please tell me, is it me, am I buggin'?"

Killa takes a deep breath. "Sis, you know I like everybody. I'm that *one* dude that will give an asshole the benefit of the doubt even if *everybody* else hates him. But, sis, I don't like that bitch either, and you know I don't even use the B-word to refer to women, so that should tell you something. She's stuck-up and thinks she's better than everybody. Won't speak, won't even look at me. She wears these weird little outfits. Too seductive, if you ask me. I don't know, for the life of me, why they hired her."

I feel affirmed. "I am so glad you said that because I was thinking I was tripping. I had to do a self-inventory to check my own shit." I share my past-life theory with Killa, 'cause if anybody would get it, he would. "Yo, Killa, sometimes I get the vibe that she was one of them cracka bitches back in Reconstruction and the Jim Crow era who lusted after Black men but would be quick to cry rape and have no qualms seeing them lynched."

"Sis, you're picking up a strong energy from her. Maybe y'all had beef in a past life and you remember some foul shit she did. Genetic memory is real, and the soul's energy never dies; it recycles into a different clay suit in a different time and space."

Killa is my boy! He speaks my language. He gets *my crazy*. Real recognize real.

I keep a small stash of CDs in my locker to play music for the guys. Nas, Mos Def, James Brown, Dead Prez, Al Green, Aretha Franklin, Jay-Z, Ray Charles, and Ghostface Killah. I even relented and copped two Lil Wayne CDs specifically for my lil' rascal rug rats since Weezy is the best leverage for getting the gremlins to work. Sometimes I play music during the last period of the day when the guys have worked hard. I let them have open game time and play cards or various board games like checkers, chess, dominoes, or Connect 4. And sometimes I rock music as a method to squeeze more work out of them by using it as my quid pro quo strategy: You do my work and I'll let the radio rock, but as soon as the work stops, the CD player goes off. That always makes 'em mad, but keeps 'em quiet and working because they *love* listening to music. Music for them is the sound of home, the sound of being back on the town, the sound of when they were emancipated, the sound of being teleported back to memories before jail. Some housing areas don't have a radio, some do. Some COs play music, some don't. So music is a high commodity.

My two absolute rules with the boom box are:

1. Don't touch the radio, because *I'm* the DJ.
2. Absolutely no radio station music because I don't want to hear the mediocre garbage that's played on constant rotation. (Plus, the radio station reception in the classroom is so bad that the kids don't want to hear it either.)

Still, it's a constant fight when it comes to the boom box, especially with Rashid. The CD player is *my* magic box. Some mornings, after anointing the desks with frankincense oil, I put on James Brown as they're walking into class. This morning I'm snapping my fingers, doing a little two-step soul-bop as I write the morning assignment on the board, rocking Al Green. "Good morning," I cheerfully chirp to the students entering class. Instead of being greeted by grumbles and grunts, I get a barrage of:

"Aww, come on with that music, Ms. P, really?"

"Damn, you killing me with that early this morning."

"That's the kind of music my grandmother be playing."

"Yo, Ms. P, put Lil Wayne on!"

"Naw, I'm tired of hearing Weezy, son. I wanna hear that new Hova; play that, Ms. P!"

One kid notices the aroma-scented therapy that I've anointed the class with.

"Mmmm, it smells like Habibi's incense shop, Ms. P."

This prompts another rug rat to belt out, "Allahu Akbar, nig-gaaaah, what?"

"It do smell good though."

"You gonna play Lil Wayne, Ms. P?"

One passerby stops in his tracks. "Yo, that lady's room sound like my aunt's house. She be listening to that old-school soul. I wish that was my class, son, *word*." The escorting CO pushes him along to his appropriate class down the hall.

Unbeknownst to me, Rashid, quick as a roach, has made his way over to my desk and pushes stop on the boom box, making me snap, "Boy, I know you done lost your mind...don't touch my radio!" The nerve of this rascal. "You know I don't play that. *I'm* the DJ. And I was just about to put some Lil Wayne on, but now you done messed up." This elicits a cacophony of whining from the entire class.

"Yo, my nigga, get away from the radio, *please*. You making it hot!" yells Tyquan.

"Aw, come on, Ms. P, don't punish all of us because of *that* nigga," cries Malik.

"Watch that word," I quip.

Malik adjusts. "My bad, but for real, Ms. P, don't make us suffer 'cause of him."

The class is whipping him. Rashid holds his hands up in surrender. "My bad, Ms. P. I shouldn't have touched your radio, it's just that music was killing me."

I'm more incensed that the knuckleheads couldn't appreciate Al Green than I am at Rashid touching my radio. "Y'all need to hear good music in your ears from time to time, be reminded of your soul music roots."

"Damn, you sound like my grandmoms, Ms. P, real talk," Marquis says with a cool Harlem drawl.

Raheim agrees. "Word, son. I ain't gonna front, tho—I *do* like some of that shit. But can we be reminded another day, Ms. P? I'm just saying, some Weezy would chill us out and I *know* you'd like that."

I know Raheim is working me, but hearing him say he likes old-school soul music warms my heart. I throw him a sunny smile and approving nod.

Peanut is out of his seat, dancing and singing some made-up a cappella lyrics, snapping his fingers to music that's in his head. *"Let's, let's stay together. Ooooh, baby, Ms. P, please play that Weezy, 'cause I'm still in love with you, oooh oooh."*

The class cracks up and Peanut's original number wins me over. I fake-roll my eyes, pull out Jay-Z and Lil Wayne, and take requests, writing the songs down, creating a mini-playlist. I begin with two albums I want to hear first. Ghostface Killah's *Fishscale* then Jay-Z's *The Blueprint²*. Why? 'Cause *I'm* the DJ and get served first. The kids get a kick out of seeing me shoulder-shake and head-nod to Jay-Z.

"Ms. P, you crazy!"

"Yeah, she prob'ly be in the club getting light.* Lemme find out Ms. P get light," Peanut says, prompting him to do the Harlem shake and get light. The kids know Peanut can dance his ass off and urge him to get light. As soon as they start doing the universal get-light

---

*Get light: a specific Harlem shake dance routine where the shoulders move in a syncopated rhythm; it's a frenzied tribal-like praise dance that has a specific accompanying handclap done by the audience/onlookers.

handclap (one-two/one-two-three, one-two/one-two-three), Peanut is off and shaking. The class chants, "Yo, yo, go Peanut, go Peanut!" The audience is just as important as the dancer. It's a rhythmic handclap call-and-dance response. A hood ritual. An ancient conversation. Stolen people's history lost but not all forgotten. Cellular memory.

It's getting loud, so I end the hip-hop praise-dance ceremony. "All right, all right, Peanut, sit your butt down. It's getting too loud and y'all making it hot. I don't want no COs coming in here 'cause then I'mma have to dead the radio altogether."

"Word, we don't want that, so chill. *Chill*, Peanut," Mekhai says as he shushes the class.

I turn the volume down just a tad and start writing categories on the board.

"Word, we playing Jeopardy, Ms. P?" Malik asks. He loves playing Jeopardy. Vocabulary and Black history subjects are his favorite.

"Yup, so get your folders out and start reviewing your worksheets." I write: Vocabulary, Black History, Social Studies, Grammar, and Science. I draw columns with ten questions per category. The guys have as much excitement with Jeopardy as I do. And it's a fun way to review material. They get so competitive, huddling and whispering among themselves before declaring their team's final answer. And the exhilaration when one team is able to make a steal by answering correctly what the other team got wrong is priceless.

We're midway through the game and suddenly I hear loud cheering from another classroom down the hall. There's a lot of thumping, desks scraping across the floor, commotion, and a "whoah!" Then, like a sudden flash of lightning that dances with thunder, the town crier sprints down the hallway yelling, "Niggas is turning it up, son! Niggaz is fighting a CO!"

My entire class jumps out of their seats and runs to the door, spilling out into the hall, only to be greeted by Officer Collins, who barks in a tone I've never heard her use before.

She's in the bowels of her belly with a ferocious mama bear

growl, yelling, "Get in the room *now!*" as she runs down the hall toward the pandemonium. The kids scoot back in my classroom momentarily and, as soon as Officer Collins is out of range, they try to run back out into the hall, but I'm faster. I quickly close the door and stand in front of it.

It was pure reflex. My heart is a drum, pounding furiously with anxiety and adrenaline.

The fight has spilled out into the hallway and makes its way directly in front of my door. Thank God the door is closed and thank God I'm standing in front of it. As I peer out of the door's small seven-by-seven-square-inch window, I see Officer King being jumped by two kids! Oh my God! They're hurting my friend! My heart leaps in my throat and snatches my breath. The drum pounds louder, shaking my rib cage. I tremble.

Shahteik runs toward me and I am face-to-face with a testosterone-pumped adolescent ready to move me out of the way with brute force. His eyes glow like the mouth of a volcano ready to erupt and his nostrils expand, transforming him into an angry bull. He's ready to attack. As he charges toward me, Mekhai the Muppet grabs Shahteik's arm with warp speed and says, "Yo, son, don't touch the teacher...don't put your hands on her, man. Don't push her."

Shahteik pauses briefly, glaring at me with hot steam coming out of every orifice on his face, fuming like the old children's Claymation character Heat Miser. He gives it a split-second thought before running over to the bigger window that peers out into the hallway. He aggressively pushes the dojas, PODs, and other underlings out of his way to secure a front-row spot. My students are all piled on top of each other in a huge football-tackle mound of bodies, their sweaty faces mushed against the window, watching the gladiator brawl take place directly in front of us. Lord, let the glass hold up.

I peek through the much smaller square window in the door. Officer King is swinging wildly with atomic force. The two kids are power windmills punching with unhinged rage. All of a sudden, King loses his footing and slips, landing on his back! His assailants swoop down on him. The two younger lions go in for the death bite. It's vicious, violent, and painful to see, but I watch. I am transfixed with shock, horror, and fear. My kids are spectators in a coliseum, screaming and cheering in a wild frenzy. I can smell their adrenaline. It's metallic. One Simba has flipped on top of King and is pummeling my friend with iron paws. My breathing is staccato. I'm unconsciously holding my breath until my lungs are forced to gasp for air. I cover my mouth to muffle a shriek—it's a kid I recognize and know.

Simba #1 is Jason. He is towering at six foot four, long, muscular, and lanky; the kids call him Slim. He stopped by my class on several occasions to talk with Marquis and Raheim, who are his buddies from Harlem. Slim's cool with the Bosses as well and, though he briefly politicks with them, it's Raheim who he really comes to see. Slim has always been respectful to me. Once he asked if he could sit in my class and work because his class was too noisy and said it was an unproductive environment for him to concentrate. I gave him a one-time-only free-trial pass and the kid actually sat down and did some work.

By now, Ms. Collins and another female CO are screaming and pepper-spraying Slim and Simba #2. An army of turtles* has arrived, running into battle swinging batons and knocking anyone without a blue uniform down like bowling pins. The hallway is a sea of turtles, rug rats, and *blood*. It's scary, it's real, and it's right outside my room. They rescue Officer King after what seemed like an eternity but lasted no more than five minutes. Both Simbas are in handcuffs being hauled off. The spectators who were stupid enough to run out into the hallway to watch the melee are now on their knees facing the gray brick wall with their hands clasped behind their heads.

I see Captain Blackwell and some other white-shirt officials

---

*Turtles: the riot squad at Rikers Island. The correctional officers' riot gear resembles the paraphernalia of the Teenage Mutant Ninja Turtles characters from the iconic children's television show, with all-black helmets and armored vests.

with shiny gold badges and stars, probably the warden, in the hall-way. This is a *huge* deal. The kids see them too and scramble back into their seats, clumsily bumping into each other like circus clowns. I begin passing out English workbooks.

"Ms. P, are you serious. I know you don't expect us to do work?" Tyquan shoots me a perplexed look.

"No, but I want y'all looking busy."

"Word, word, pass me a book, son!"

Just then, Captain Blackwell swings my door open with such force that it slams against the wall, causing the metal frame to ring. She is piping mad and on the warpath. "Ms. Peterson, which kids were out in the hallway?"

"None at all, Captain Blackwell," I earnestly reply.

She looks me squarely in the eye, searching my face for any hint of a lie. "Are you sure?" she demands.

I am emphatic. "I closed the door and stood directly in front of it the entire time, Captain. I didn't want them mixed up in it at all." It's the truth and I am able to say it with confidence and pride. My boys are clean.

Captain Blackwell glares at the class. "Thank you," she says, sharp and curt, slamming the door behind her, making the window shake.

Mekhai looks up. "Good looking out, Ms. P. You had our back. I respects that."

"Well, I told the truth."

Shahteik nods his head in agreement, knowing I saved him from a legal bullet. The kids are wired, frantically recounting the fight in a hushed volume among each other, speaking in rapid, col-liding sentences. Tyrone quietly walks over to me and hands me his black military-style G-Shock watch. It's fancy without being flashy. I'm sure he paid some coins for it. "Ms. P, can you hold my watch, keep it in your locker for me? I already know the COs are gonna turn it up later on tonight in the house. They gonna search all of us and it's gonna be bad, I know it."

I'm sure I could get into trouble for doing it, but I discreetly take his watch and put it in my locker. I look at him with fierce purpose and laser-beam intensity meant to pierce through any irrational thoughts he might have, and I speak to his higher self. "Ty, you have ten days left until you go home…ten! No matter what they say or what they do, keep your cool and keep the number, *ten days,* in the front of your mind, do you hear me?" I sound like a concerned mother warning her hardheaded son before he slips off into the night toward random danger that lingers in every hood on any corner under broken streetlights. All a mother can do is pray with anointed words to cover her sons with a sacred veil. "No matter how hot the COs make it, you fall back and go home when you're supposed to, in ten days. Everybody already knows how you rock, so you have nothing to prove. Be strategic and wise. Swallow your ego. You're too close to the finish line, Tyrone. Stay in the light, baby. God bless you."

The pending wrath back in the housing areas tonight is imminent.

Tyrone nods his head affirmatively. "I will, Ms. P. I wanna get the fuck out of here. Ten days can't come fast enough. That boy who jumped King only had three months left. Now he's gonna prob'ly get an additional five years for assaulting an officer. Shit is fucking crazy." Tyrone shakes his head in disbelief.

Another officer comes into my room and shouts like it's boot camp. "Everybody line up, no talking at all! If I hear your voice, it's gonna be problems! And right about now, you don't want it to be any more problems, 'cause it ain't gonna be pretty. So line the fuck up and shut the fuck up!"

One of the boys sucks his teeth. The grisly officer prowls the line, stopping in front of Tyrone, who's at the end. I silently hail Mary. He turns away from Tyrone and spits acid at no one in particular: "Did I fucking hear something? Somebody got a goddamn problem? Whoever wants to be the big guy, speak now or, like I said, shut the fuck up!" He's daring them, baiting a wise guy. Nobody squeaks or peeps. Church mice.

The kids file out in height order, hands clasped behind their backs; they already know the drill without having to be told. I collapse into my chair, sitting at my desk, dumbfounded and in a daze. My solar plexus is throbbing. I witnessed pure savagery, bloody pandemonium, and *mayhem*. I work in a jungle. I'm in shock and too shook to cry. I remember my first funeral when I was seventeen years old—it was my mother's. I stood in front of the open casket and froze. I didn't cry, I didn't move, I didn't breathe. I was a petrified tree. Paralyzed like I am now. I probably need smelling salts like they gave me then.

Killa walks by my room with his noisy cart and pokes his head in. "You okay, sis?"

I shake my head "no" and whimper, "What. Happened?"

Killa steps in and whispers the scoop. "I was teaching in the room right next door to the altercation. You know whose room it was, don't you?"

"No, who?"

"Your friend, Little Miss Muffet," he says as he tilts his head, looking at me sideways. I can't even muster a reply; I just shake my head in pain and disgust. He goes on. "She can't control her class and the guys don't respect her. So she apparently told the principal, because he comes to her class to lecture the guys about respecting her—"

I cut him off. "The principal? Why the fuck she call the principal? Isn't that what the officers are here for? The fuck can the principal do?"

"I know, sis, who *you* telling? But she doesn't talk to nobody, not even the officers, so I guess she figured she'd go to Mr. White Man who hired her. She didn't want to deal with the officers."

Rage is boiling inside me. "Yeah, but you *have* to deal with the officers. And you *better* develop some type of rapport with the COs, 'cause this is *their* house. Oooh, now I really wanna fight her. I told you I ain't like that bitch!"

"I feel you, sis. So the principal is lecturing the kids in her class about respecting her and one of the guys pops off at the mouth, disrespecting Phil. So King, who happened to be in the class, goes to pull the kid out of class and the kid swings on King, talking 'bout, 'Don't fucking touch me.' He just went off on King for no reason. It was so strange, so out of character."

Just then, an officer we know walks by and tells Killa he can't keep his cart in the hallway. Even though there aren't any kids on the school floor at this point, everybody is on edge. Killa obliges; he bounces out of my room with the quickness. "I'll talk to you later, Ms. P. Hold your head and try not to let this place get to you. You're an artist first, remember that."

As I hear his cart squeak down the hall, I lean back in my seat, taking deep breaths in through my nose, out through my mouth, to slow my heart rate and try not to cry. I fight it but the salt water wins, spilling out against my will, and a stream of hot tears races down my face.

CHAPTER NINE

This Is Some Bullshit

Thought for the Day: What you focus on expands. Your thoughts become things, so choose the good ones. In order to achieve it, you first have to see it. Again, what you focus on expands, so *focus* on your dreams!

—Author Unknown

I pray myself out of bed, again. *"Mother Father God, Infinite Great Spirit NTR, and guardian angels of Light, show me what to teach, show me how to reach these children today. Protect my boys. Open the way for the divine design of my life to reveal itself to me. I'm ready for change. I need a breakthrough. Show me what I need to do. Thank you for abundant blessings and for my divine perfect health. Tua NTR, Amen."* This too-early-in-the-goddamn-morning work schedule is wearing me down like a pencil with no more point, burning me out, sucking the creative marrow from my bones, draining my spirit dry, slurping the corners to get every drop of creative juice, leaving nothing but an empty cup. My tank is on E. It's only been two months, Halloween is just around the bend, but I don't know how much longer I can do this.

When I arrive on the dismal school floor, there is an eerie quiet that hovers over it. All of the teachers are walking with their noses buried in what appears to be some memo. No conversations, no morning chitchat, nobody's talking. I feel a vibe. Something's up, but I'm too absorbed in my own schleprock-funky cloud of rain that's following me to give a rat's ass or be interested in any bureaucratic drama.

I clock in and check my mailbox. In my thin stack of papers are unimportant memos, random notices, and my daily roster, which informs me of any new students added to my class. There's also a small photocopy of a New York *Daily News* article, no longer than two paragraphs, with a headline that reads: TEEN FOUND DEAD IN RIKERS CELL. My heart jumps, then sinks. A lump drops in my gut. I begin speed-reading to search for the student's name. Please, God, not one of my boys. And if it is, God, I quit. I will resign today 'cause it's only but so much that my little heart can take.

The article finally reveals a name I don't recognize. It's no consolation: *Body found face up, bruised and bloody, beat to death in his cell.* Was it a CO taking revenge for Officer King's attack last week? I wonder. Or was it at the hands of several adolescent inmates who jumped him in his cell, settling some beef, and it went too far? The article didn't say. The only definite news is that a child is dead! Jesus. I imagine his mother's pain. Womb amputated, throbbing, and numb. But I *don't* know. How could I know what his mother feels? I'm a woman who is acquainted with pain, but not *that* pain. I think of the boy, his fear, him wanting to go home, his loved ones flashing in his mind, his final thoughts—his final cry as his last breath exhales with his spirit leaving his eighteen-year-old lifeless body lying limp on a green plastic mattress in a dingy cell with water bugs and mice. *Dear God.* I look up at the ceiling and take a deep breath in through my nose for five counts, then release it out through my mouth. Repeat. In through my nose five counts, then out through the mouth. I *really* have tumbled down the rabbit hole into a bizarre warped world of altered reality...and I signed up for it. Repeat.

I need today to go smoothly. I run through the morning agenda in my head to momentarily take my mind off the murder. *Murder.*

Shake it. I give my head a sharp, quick shake to fling away the thought. I try to stuff it down. Okay, first I'll get my students ready for next Monday's vocabulary quiz. After the review, I'll do another lesson on the Middle Passage. We'll read the chapter together from their African-American history book and then they can work individually and answer the questions I've prepared on a separate handout. *The boy is dead. Murdered.* Shake it. Fling the thought. After they finish that, I'll play two tracks from Nas's album *Nigger* and have a group discussion about the lyrics and the iconic album cover that shows Nas's bullwhipped and keloid-covered back. I'll have them compare it to the source photo, a historical image of a nineteenth-century slave's scarred back, which inspired Nas's cover. It's important that my boys are informed of their history. It amazes me how much they don't know, how much they haven't been taught, how disconnected they are from the truth, and how culturally mal-nourished they are. I try to feed them as much as I can, whenever I can. I just plant the seeds and pray they take root and sprout. A tree without roots can't grow. My boys have to grow. Someone dropped the ball on their cultural education and spiritual development but dammit someone's got to pick it up because they matter.

I don't know how I'm going to make it through the day with mur-der hovering over my spirit and in the air but I know I have to find a way to connect them back to their humanity. I have to get them to see their value and understand they come from a powerful, meaning-ful, worthy people. They matter. We need them. They have to know that. They have to know how valuable they are so death won't be a goal and murder won't come so easily. They aren't disposable. They have to see that. There is a reason why Black and Brown people are in the condition that we are today. God didn't create niggers, America did. It was a systematic process. They have to see the bigger picture. Savage is not who we are. I want to scream. There is so much I want to shove into their teenage minds. My heart is pounding, my inten-tions are righteous but far-reaching. I'm all over the place. Thinking of that dead boy, murdered, has my mind racing. How can I fix this?

Where do I begin? I remember the saying, "How do you eat an elephant?...One bite at a time." Nas's music will be their bite-sized lesson and definitely my balm. Music has always been medicine for me. We need a healing today. Come on, Nas, help me out.

I want the boys to be exposed to bold artists and intellectuals who are unafraid to speak about the rich legacy of Black culture in a creative, informative way. I believe it can stir the dormant warrior inside them and activate their higher potential for enlightenment. Exposure to righteous information and creative inspiration can wake a sleeping giant when you least expect it. But our children are fed so much poison in the music that when they hear something healthy and uplifting, they think it's bad, corny, and irrelevant. Even popular mainstream artists trying to make a difference are quickly drowned out by the overwhelming loud pollution of toxic ignorance being peddled and marketed for profit. Poisoning the music is like drinking contaminated water. It's by design. Keep the masses dumbed down in order to keep them easily controlled and operating on the lowest frequency possible: no critical thinking, no positive inspiration, no forward movement. Reward the lowest of who we are and celebrate mediocrity, denigration, destruction, and murder. Package it and sell it to our children, play it all day on rotation like a mantra of death, and watch them imitate the diamond-studded, stacks-of-money-flashing, material-driven, gun-toting, misogynistic pied-piper minstrels. Our babies are suffocating from false images and dying from layers of lies. America has been feeding off and been propped up by Black folks for five hundred years. Our blood is in the soil. Slavery is the rotten root, foundation, and engine of America. Prison is the remix, and music is one tool to fuel it. Infect the psyche of our children with poison on a funky beat until it becomes a meditation and mantra. It's like a death sentence for our future that we dance to. I believe in certain conspiracies. These are strange times and dangerous times.

The rug rats shuffle and grumble into class, some of them sucking their teeth at the assignment I've written on the board. They suck their teeth at everything I write on the board, like cranky old men who just like to complain about *everything*.

"You nasty, stinking-ass nigga!" one of the boys blurts out. "Yo! That's fucking disrespectful, nigga!"

I spin around from writing on the board. "Watch that—oh my God!" I am immediately smacked in the face with pure funk, concentrated stink, garbage vapors. It's beyond obnoxious; it's downright abusive.

"See, Ms. P, throw that stinking-ass nigga out. Shit is like police brutality!" Malik yells.

"Watch that word," I say, while covering my mouth with my hand. It's a smell I can taste. Sweet baby Jesus! I need a mint. I run to my locker and grab my Altoids and the air freshener. I hate when they fart in class. Dookey boys letting loose in the room is always brutal. And right now, it's fucking lethal. Oh my God! I *can't*.

"Thank you, Ms. P! Get the spray and hose his nasty ass down," Mekhai yells, hiding half his face underneath his shirt.

"My bad, yo," Peanut embarrassingly admits to the rank-stank, funky offense.

"Yo, my dude, farting and letting some disgusting-ass shit seep out your ass like that need to be a felony, my nigga!" Raheim makes the class laugh.

Peanut moves to stand by the window. "Oh, no! No, no, no. Peanut, if you're still farting, step outside," I snap while spraying the room down with a wintergreen scent. "Don't do that in class, *please*. Those little windows won't hardly help."

"Naw, I'm good, Ms. P, I'm just standing over here to air out. I'm sorry. I ain't mean it. It won't happen again."

"Better not or I'mma have my son, Africa, wash you up," Mekhai says as he kisses his fingers to the sky to emphasize his fake threat.

"I ain't touching farty boy. Fuck that. I got my limits, my dude," Tyquan says, laughing at his buddy, Peanut, who's a good sport. As usual, he just waves his pals off. They seem to be in a good mood. Regular shenanigans. Nothing to indicate the dead boy and his murder. They gossip about *everything* so it's strange that no one has mentioned it at all. Maybe they're keeping it hush for a reason; maybe they're avoiding it like me. I'm relieved they're not talking about it. I'll get the scoop from Killa later.

Finally the boys settle down and I finish writing the vocabulary words on the board: *belligerent, cliché, colossal, obsolete, tremendous, plethora, obstacle, excruciating, liberation, toil.*

Tyrone walks in and apologizes for being late. He's such a gentleman and has an edge of maturity above the rest of the guys. Either he has a close relationship with his father, comes from a stable home, or dates older women. Someone is schooling him in the art of carrying himself like a respectful grown man. It's a specific kind of swag. "Sorry for coming in late, Ms. P; I was on duty last night and had to talk to one of the officers about something this morning." Tyrone works in the housing area and is assigned to suicide watch. He has to monitor the cells and make sure no one hangs up and has to talk to guys who are depressed, helping the COs check on them throughout the night, reporting any strange behavior or emotional deterioration. I can always tell when Tyrone has had "watch duty" because he's visibly tired from staying up so late making the rounds. On those days, I let him put his head down and take a nap in the back row.

Today he doesn't go sit in the back like he usually does. Instead, despite his obvious fatigue this morning, Tyrone wants to do work. He takes his regular Boss seat in the front row. It must be the lessons he sees written on the board. Along with Black history, which is his favorite subject, Tyrone likes learning vocabulary because he says it helps him with his "honey-macking skills with the older ladies." Bless his heart. Not long into the lesson he has slowly slid down in his seat, giving me the classic dope fiend nod: spine curled forward, head landed on the desk, limbs Jell-O, mouth slightly agape, knocked out cold, fast asleep. Before I can wake him up, I notice Marquis out of his seat.

"Marquis, sit down now!" I say through clenched teeth. He gets on my royal nerves because he does absolutely no work, and I mean *no* work. He only comes to class to talk to Raheim. I've warned him for weeks that he's on a banana peel with me and half a Pop-Tart away from being Poofed out my class for good.

Raheim tries to deflect attention away from Marquis by singing loudly and off-key, in a bizarre, Tourette's-like fit, "I love to love you baby! I-I-I…love-love-love…"

"Raheim, will you stop that! It's so annoying, *please*! Lawrence, turn around. Tyquan, sit down *now*. Guys, it's too much talking, way too much talking! Get your feet off the desk. Malik, get your hands out your pants. Mexico, put that Pop-Tart away!" They've got me in a tizzy, putting out small fires, and Lil' Rumbles is steady winking at me. "Shahteik, don't play with me!"

And then, in a fit of temporary insanity, Marquis decides to treat the class to a special musical number, using one of the metal file cabinets as a drum, and begins fist-pounding a hip-hop beat, making me shriek, "Marquis, have you lost your damn mind? What in God's name is wrong with you!"

At this point Tyrone pops his head up like a jack-in-the-box and growls with grown-man confidence, "Ms. P, will you stop all that damn yelling!" And then, as if his indignation needed a touch of emphasis, he adds, "Dammit!" totally pissed that I have interrupted his peaceful right-to-sleep-in-class in front of my face.

I work in an insane asylum. My crazy hood-genie in the lamp has been summoned again and whirls out with rattlesnake speed. I spray the entire class with thug mama venom. Everybody's getting it today, starting with Tyrone.

My neck swivels back into alignment after having completed a 360-degree snake war-move and I aim right between his big, shiny black forehead. "Get out! Get out of my class right now! How dare you fall asleep, in front of my face, in class, and have the nerve to yell at *me* because your self-appointed nap time was disturbed? Well, I got news for you, this ain't kindergarten! And it damn sure isn't Romper Room! You must think I'm Mr. Rogers, but I'm not, son!

Oh, no, no, not in here, not with me, you won't speak to *me* like that!"

I brace myself for his defensive alpha bark, but Tyrone gives me no back talk and just mumbles under his breath to no one in particular, "Yo, I'm out, son," and stands in the doorway, waving for an officer to come and get him out of class. And within seconds, Tyrone is gone. I continue spanking the crazies with my vocal octave rising to an alarming decibel that has two officers running to my door. Once they realize the boys aren't fighting and I am not in any danger, they pause, just like the last time, to watch my show...and I give 'em one. 'Cause that's what I do is perform. I employ my theater training to make my voice boom from the bottom of my diaphragm and hit the back wall in the room, all while flinging my arms with a strong controlled gesture, letting my intense evil eye land on each face gazing back at me.

"I am *not* having this nonsense today! *All* of y'all! I'm sick and tired of repeating myself, tired of the disrespectful behavior, tired of the foolishness." I start calling names: "Tyquan, Raheim, Marquis, Shahteik, Malik—" Shahteik tries in vain to protest, but I cut him off. "Everybody!"

Malik tries to butt in. "Ms. P, you going crazy, yo!"

I whip my head in his direction. "That's right, *know that... you better know that!*" Then I continue wielding my belt made of words and tone. "I am *not* the one! Some of y'all got it twisted!" I see some of the rug rats getting annoyed, taking it personally, rolling their eyes and shifting in their seat. I change gears and throw a little honey on my blade. My voice is still loud and stern. "This is a smart class, *nobody* in here is stupid; ya might be lazy, but you damn sure are *not* stupid! Y'all've been doing good work lately and it's my job to make sure you continue...but not in chaos! Not like this! Not with disrespect! No sir, no *siree*. I respect each and every one of you and expect the same in return! I'm here to teach and y'all are here to learn and *that's* what we're gonna do today!" I pump the brakes and bring my volume down to a sane level, speaking as if nothing ever happened in my Ms. Crabtree voice, showcasing my vocal range, from 'round-the-way banshee to little red schoolhouse teacher. "Now, let's start with the vocabulary. Someone choose a word, give the definition, and then use it in a sentence."

The guys look perplexed. Some are shaking their heads. The officers chuckle and walk off. Malik raises his hand. I nod and he says, "*Belligerent,* means to be rude and to speak angry-like, with a nasty attitude. My sentence is: 'Ms. P was very belligerent today in class, yelling and catching an attitude, making it hot.' Belligerent."

This makes the class laugh and loosen up. It *was* funny but I can't laugh lest I break character. I keep a stern face and clinical tone. "Excellent. And your sentence let me understand the meaning of the word. Very good. Someone else. Yes, Raheim."

"*Excruciating* means painful or extreme pain. 'I have an excruciating headache after Ms. P screamed with tremendous volume.' *Tremendous*, mean a lot or huge. I just did two words in one sentence 'cause I'm nice like that."

I smile and nod. "I'm impressed. That's what I'm talking about, fellas; let's get this work in. Who's next?"

Peanut raises his hand. I'm shocked he's participating to do work. "Peanut? All right now, let's have it."

"Can you play the radio?" he innocently asks with a sincere straight face.

I furrow my brow with indignation. "No, I most certainly will not. I'm not playing *anything.* You all made me very angry today and I'm not feeling anybody right about now. Maybe tomorrow—a new day, a new attitude. Now, pick a word, Peanut." Peanut shrugs his shoulders. "Pick a word, just try, even if you get it wrong. That's how you learn. And you might just get it right. *Just try.*"

Peanut picks *plethora*. He can't pronounce it. I help him with the pronunciation and ask him what it means. He shrugs his shoulders, again.

"Somebody help brother Peanut out. What does *plethora* mean?" I ask the class.

Tyquan has his hand up. "Don't it mean 'a lot,' like to have a lot of something?"

"Very, *very* close, Tyquan. It means to have an excess in quantity, a superabundance of something."

Tyquan gives it some thought, rubbing his chin, and then he says, "Oh. Yeah, like I have *plethora* of hoes on the track. I got an excess in quantity, ya heard?"

The class cracks up, and I smirk, slightly breaking character. I want to laugh but refuse to give them total surrender. Within one period the class went from being in an unhinged whirling-devil maniac state of turbulence, to normal, mildly chatty students. Tyrone slips back into class and slides into his seat. He volunteers to help me pass out the African-American history books, which is his subtle, nonverbal way of apologizing. The guys are working independently on the Black Panthers handout with questions based on the chapter they just read. I sit at my desk to do what I rarely do. Just sit. I am exhausted, feeling postperformance fatigue as the adrenaline wanes. Malik comes to sit next to me in the teacher-student conference seat.

"Yes, Malik?"

"Ms. P, no disrespect but when you get belligerent with us, you look cute. I'm mean you get real crazy belligerent-like, then you get real calm and talk like nothing happened…that's kinda cute."

Belligerent is now Malik's favorite word. At least he learned something today. Since he's in my seat, I take the opportunity to talk with him about his academic strengths and weaknesses. I point out his progress in social studies, particularly Black history, but his need for more focus with English, a subject he always resists since he's most challenged by grammar. Malik likes to get special attention and enjoys one-on-one time with me. As I'm talking with him, I'm ear-hustling some of the students talking about me, recapping my theatrical routine.

"Yo, son, she probably be yelling like that at her man, going crazy, calling the police and shit."

Mission accomplished. It's been a while since I've had to sum-mon *her* and they were in need of a tune-up. I think they get a kick out of seeing thug mama anyway. Probably reminds them of that woman in their life who doesn't play and keeps her foot up their ass...because she cares. Usually when they pluck my nerves, instead of yelling I play the exact opposite and give them "icy-clinical," or sometimes I serve up the silent treatment or whip 'em with sarcastic wit to embarrass them into shutting the fuck up. I relish in foiling them, not giving them the reaction they wanted since they love try-ing to get me riled up and seeing my feathers ruffled. I have to par-cel thug mama out sparingly so she won't lose her potent effect. If I don't ration *her,* I'll wind up screaming all day, sounding like static on dead radio stations—useless. Even though components of vol-ume, tone, and theatrical range are important when I explode, the most effective element is "surprise-fool," not knowing when she's gonna show up. Timing is everything.

Today's lunchtime movie matinee in the teacher's lounge is *The Texas Chainsaw Massacre: The Beginning.* Oooh, classic blood, guts, and gore, and yelling at the TV screen. Fun. I have officially watched more horror movies at Rikers Island than I have in my entire life, including when I used to do dumb shit like watch *The Devil's Rain, Carrie,* and *The Omen* in one sitting with my cousin Terri.

Every afternoon we gather in the teachers' lounge to partici-pate in this gruesome screamfest, with me leading the charge, being the main spectator yelling at the stupid lady walking into obvious danger. "Why!? Stupid dumb bitch! Why you gonna walk your silly ass into the dark barn, alone, with just a flashlight 'cause you heard some fucking noise? Hope your ass gets chopped the fuck up for being a goddamn investigative dingbat and if you run I know you gonna fall, *watch.*" Seeing this always manages to piss me off and conjures colorful words I hurl at the actress, making the other teachers laugh. A big-mouth punk, I watch the entire movie peek-ing through my fingers covering my face, steady talking shit. I hate that I enjoy the barbarity of it all. But what I hate most is having my bloodcurdling horror-joy cut short because of an idiotic staff development meeting, which is mandatory for all teachers.

I meet up with Ms. G in the hallway and walk with her to the dumb meeting. I ask about the dead child. "Girl, I know you heard about that adolescent that was murdered here. He died in his cell." The word *murder* feels heavy in my mouth.

Ms. G looks back at an officer sitting at his post and speaks in a hushed tone. "Yeah, girl, keep your voice down and don't talk about it in front of the officers or the kids. The higher-ups at the Board of Ed don't like us talking about anything involving DOC issues, especially something as serious as this. The less we know the better. Since it didn't happen on our watch on the school floor then we won't be investigated. No questions, no drama. That's DOC's mess. BOE wants no parts of it."

I'm confused and clearly haven't been in the trenches long enough to understand the bureaucratic politics. "What drama could it possibly cause the Board of Ed?"

Ms. G pulls me inside her classroom, which is next door to the meeting. She's still speaking in a hushed tone. It's clearly some secretive and sensitive information she's about to drop on me.

"Girl, when something major, like a murder, happens it's now a criminal investigation. This building is going to be swarming with investigators. Once you start talking about what you heard then you're leaving yourself open to be questioned by investigators and could be called in to make an official statement to be used in a court of law. And since no one truly knows anything, because it happened after school hours and off the school floor, why bring potential unnecessary attention to yourself? Besides, even though we're with the Board of Ed, we're still in DOC's house. We're visitors, not the host."

"But who was the boy? Did you know him and what happened? The news clipping didn't say hardly anything."

Ms. G is so patient with me, entertaining my naïveté and barrage of questions.

"A kid named Christopher. He was rarely on the school floor

because he was in the bing all the time, you know, one of the bing babies. He was registered in the school out in the sprungs but because he moved around from house to house so much he wound up here on the main school floor a few times. He was never in my class, but I remember him."

Ms. G goes on to tell me that she heard the kid was giving the officers in his housing area a lot of problems being really disrespectful and unruly, so as punishment they packed him up and moved him to a house where a rival gang lived to put him in a hot situation and teach him a lesson. They thought he'd just get beat up a little bit and humbled. They never thought he'd be beat to death and murdered. Even the goon squad who beat him up never intended to intentionally kill him. He died hours later in the hospital and several adolescents from that house are going down for murder; some COs are going down too. All the kids, like the teachers, want nothing to do with being investigated so everybody's mute.

"Why would the officers go down? Fights happen all the time. They didn't know he would be beat to death. They didn't beat him, did they?"

"Girl, I know you heard about 'the Program'?" Ms. G asks me as if I should know the obvious, making my freshman green status evident.

"The Program? No, what's that?'

"The Program has been around long before I even started working here, girl. It's a system some COs have set up to keep their house in line. Makes their job easier."

I look so perplexed.

"Some COs look at it, like, instead of getting into battle all the time with the strong leaders of the house, making their shift hell every day, they make a pact with them. The leaders make sure the house is run a certain way keeping their 'team' in line and in return the COs turn a blind eye when the new jacks get extorted for their commissary and phone calls and other stuff. Kids that aren't *with it* get beat up while the CO *isn't looking*."

"That's crazy. I hear the kids in here talking about being *with it* all the time, 'oh, he's with it, or he better be with it,' but I had no idea 'with it' was a real operation going on." I shake my head in disbelief. I am getting schooled.

Ms. G continues, "Girl, I know. It's real trip. And this is what I've heard from the kids themselves. The officers work the leader's power in their favor and in exchange they give the leaders certain privileges like letting them lock in late, smoke cigarettes, which is contraband, and they let the 'team' run their little extortion ring, taking the weak kids' PIN numbers for phone calls and commissary. I feel bad for some of the kids. That's why I bring in snacks from time to time because I know a lot of their commissary is being extorted."

Ms. G grabs a notebook from her desk. "Girl, come on, we gotta go to this lady's meeting."

I follow out after Ms. G. I am stunned to learn about a dark underworld that goes on in the housing area. Being on the school floor affords me, and other teachers, the opportunity to see kids in a positive learning environment, albeit jail. But seeing them in their jailhouse living room, in their housing area where they eat, sleep, shit, shower, talk on the phone, watch TV, commune, and play, is clearly a wildly different setting I hadn't given much thought about until now. I wonder if my buddy King ran a house like that.

As we walk out of Ms. G's room I whisper, "Do you think King ran the Program in his house?"

"King had seniority so he didn't work in the housing areas; he was just on the school floor. But I heard he could be pretty brutal when he wanted to be. I never saw it but one of the other teachers told me he was known to smack kids in their face in the hallway."

Ouch. No, not King. I didn't like hearing that. My perception of my buddy was being smudged. I immediately wondered if the two kids who jumped him were adolescent vigilantes seizing an opportunity for revenge that was lying dormant until that fateful day. No, not King, I kept thinking. But then again, I really don't know.

"Whatever happened to him? Do you think he's coming back?" I ask, pausing in the doorway.

"I heard he got bruised up pretty bad and he's not coming back to the school. He'll probably get transferred to another post or he just might retire. I think he had enough years in to get his full pension. I'm not sure."

Ms. G just gave me a speed course education and glimpse into the dungeon where my rug rats are housed, giving me a deeper understanding of what they're navigating when they leave my class. She also made real the duality and flaws of my friend.

As we walk to the next class my mind keeps picturing King slapping a kid in the hallway. Once you know, you can't unknow no matter how much you try to push it out your mind. Damn.

I'm all for staff development to learn something new and brainstorm better ways to improve lesson plans but I can't stand *these* meetings, with *this* assistant principal, which are centered on some new stupid system of lesson planning we've been suddenly mandated to implement. I find them to be a waste of time, totally irrelevant, unnecessary, and draining. I. Don't. Give. A. Fuck. About. These. Meetings. *Ever.*

These staff development meetings feel like I'm sitting in an episode of *Charlie Brown* when the grown-ups talk. All I hear coming out of the mouth of the assistant principal is "*whah whah whah whah, whah whah.*" I don't like this woman. It's not even personal, but I loathe what she represents and defends like a dutiful mechanical puppet. I find her to be cold. She doesn't smile and isn't the most cheerful cyborg on the plantation. She should have taken the officer's test and been a CO. She and I have never clashed, but it's her military-like adherence to procedure and rules, rules, rules that grates at the independent thinker, artist-rebel spirit in me. We don't mix. Clone drone versus rogue artist woman. Even Phil, who's the principal and her boss, has more creative flexibility than this brownnosing, ridiculous zombie. Even he understands the necessity of using the arts to enhance literacy and will bend the rules from time to time, giving teachers some semblance of freedom in the classroom. But with her, *hmph*. Hardly. I think maybe she's gunning to be principal or maybe she has her sights set on an upper, *upper* administrative position, because how else could this woman be standing in front of us, in this yawning-for-the-gods stupid meeting, telling us with such stern, unwavering, absolute authority some horse-dog-cow bullshit that makes no fucking sense. She's a classic case study in humans who are obedient, digitally programmed robots, loyal to the Matrix. Just like in the movie, she's a *blue pill* broad.

A new set of unrealistic lesson plans and laughable teaching mandates has come down from the superintendent's office and this 'droid is arguing the case for it despite loud, valid protests from *all* the teachers in the room. We're the ones on the front line, in the *actual* classroom, and she should have our back. At least hear us out and let us know you identify with our concerns. Show some compassion, let us know that *you know* what the superintendent is asking of us is supremely dumb and makes no sense. Help us to push back and get around this nonsense. Administrate. Problem solve. Discuss ways to accommodate some sort of middle ground; give us some leeway to get us out of this new straitjacket the superintendent is telling us we have to wear in the classroom. Let us know you are on *our* side. But no, this remote-controlled Stepford bobblehead keeps repeating the program, saying, "This is what the superintendent is saying you have to do, so that's what is expected of you. I don't make the rules, I just enforce them." This bitch is whack. And the superintendent, Cami Anderson, is even worse; she's an out-of-touch numbskull with no insight into the real needs of urban public education.

To add insult to injury, our teacher evaluations will be based on how well we adhere to this asinine, restrictive, loony lesson-plan farce. What they expect of us is a joke. Based on this new lesson-plan initiative, straight from the bowels of the superintendent's orifice, I mean *office,* a typical forty-five-minute class period is now supposed to look like this: The first ten minutes are for preassessment. Given that the students have all arrived on time and are settled down in their seats and focused, we have to assess *in ten minutes* what the students know or don't know about the lesson we are about to teach. Well, you might ask, how will we know what they know or don't know about the lesson they have not yet learned? Oh, that's easy. We simply pass out a preassessment questionnaire on the subject that asks: *What do you know about this subject? Is this your first time learning this material? If so, what do you think it's about?* We have to get the students to fill out this assessment form, collect it, and *then* start the lesson. The next ten minutes we're supposed to talk about the lesson and give instructions. And then, for the next fifteen minutes, students are expected to work independently. With the last ten minutes left in the period, we should use five minutes for sharing and five minutes for postassessment to determine if they learned anything.

Now, after the students have dutifully finished their work within that structured format, we have to grade them using some new rubric system. What the hell a rubric system is, I don't even freaking know, but we are expected to hand out rubric sheets to the students so they can see how they are being graded. Yo! Who the fuck, what the fuck, how the fuck?! This is the most ass-backward, unintelligent bullshit ever! And they expect this to work in classrooms at *Rikers*. Puleeeaze!

My brain is buzzing with a swarm of trapped hornets trying to find a way out. I want to scream. All of the teachers are looking around the room at each other, but the robot is unmoved by our collective body language, which is clearly saying *not pleased*. She pretends to ignore us. Everyone is grunting, sighing loudly, signifying, throwing shade, and shaking our heads. We are *so* bewildered. One of my coworkers asks, "How are we supposed to implement this? It's confusing and very awkward. I don't know how this can work." Silly teacher, not to worry, there will be several subsequent staff development meetings that will be facilitated by two women from Australia, whose company designed this brilliant rubric system. They'll explain it just fine, the assistant principal insists.

My nostrils flare. I glare at her like Nunu from *Sankofa* when she made her slave master choke on his tongue just by staring at him, using her old African magic. I wish I remembered that magic. This meeting and what's coming out of her mouth keeps getting more and more insane. I can't believe the Board of Education contracted a company all the way across the globe, from Australia, to come to New York City and administer a whack-nonsensical-dumb-ass rubric system for kids in jail. What I would like is for these Aussie heifers, along with the bozo superintendent, to spend three days in a regular inner-city classroom in America, in New York City, and then bring their asses to Rikers Island school for three days and *then* tell me if that forty-five-minute lesson plan and rubric system is apropos. What an obvious waste of state money, time, and resources that could and *should* be allocated more productively.

All the teachers look superpissed; we are *not* feeling Evilene, this wicked witch from *The Wiz*.

A lot of side conversations are happening and secret notes are being passed among us. Now *we're* the rug rats. With the staff morale already low, this is nothing less than a bully's fistful of sand in the face. I'll never survive this assault on my creative teacher-flow, a lane that I've *just* found my groove in.

We have all been dealt the most demoralizing blow to the joy of teaching. I'm ready to quit and plan my escape. I feel crushed like a tin can beneath the heel of a rigged system much stronger than me. I cry uncle, they win, I lose…fuck it. But before I throw in the towel and the baby out with the bathwater, I seek advice from one of the seasoned vets. Maybe there is a way around this; maybe I'm overreacting. I reach for insight and discernment from Mr. Shepard, who teaches a few doors down from me. He's an older white man with a lot of gray hair and walks with a funky bop, shoulders slightly hunched over from the weight of wisdom, always clutching a mound of papers. Mr. Shepard is a veteran teacher with major service-duty stripes from this battlefield. He's been teaching on the Rock for twenty-five years and has one of the few advanced academic classes that teaches GED-level curriculum and college prep. Unlike my class, which is pre-GED, Mr. Shepard's class is more focused because the GED test is in immediate sight and graduation is within reach, so the guys don't cut up as much. They can taste success.

Part of his academic curriculum is teaching the guys chess and introducing them to college prep courses. Shepard gets respect and results. I seek him out for counsel on this monstrosity of expectations we were just slapped in the face with. Surely, in his twenty-five years of active duty, he's seen worse and has managed to navigate it successfully. He'll know what this is, what to do, and help me to put it in perspective.

"Ms. Peterson," Mr. Shepard says and pauses to let out a deep sigh, "*never* in my twenty-five years of teaching here have I ever felt so overwhelmed, crushed, and demoralized." Shepard's face turns red, his eyes become bright blue puddles, and he looks like he just might cry. Not Shepard, he's the vet! Oh shit, this is serious. He continues his spitfire lament. "This woman has taken the *t* out of teaching, along with the fun, in one fell swoop! I got my time in, Ms. Peterson, and I could have retired a while ago, but I didn't because I love what I do. I genuinely love teaching these guys. But it looks like I just got my exit date."

This is personal for Shepard—this is all he's known and dedicated his life to for a quarter of a century. I'm just angry and petulant, but Shepard, he's wounded and defeated. He isn't done venting and seems relieved that I'm asking him for his insight. He has no qualm about sharing his strong opinion. "Ms. Peterson, I've seen administrations come and go, but I've never seen anything like this. It's terrible what they're doing," he says, letting out another deep breath as he shakes his head. "I guess I have to figure something out. I sure wish I could have been more optimistic, Ms. Peterson. I have to go sit down for a minute. I just lost my grounding."

Now *I'm* ready to cry. This is completely counterproductive, bureaucratic nonsense. It creates anxiety, erodes morale, and succeeds in providing useless data for disconnected administrators while depriving teachers on the front lines of the experience of actually teaching. It creates obstacles for students to actually learn, think critically, and develop. Perhaps that is the intended plan. The school-to-prison pipeline seems to be playing out, right in front of my face. Urban kids are disengaging from school because so much of the curriculum is not relevant; it's antiquated and the approach is stale. Music programs have been cut. Memorization for testing supersedes critical thinking and inspiration. The kids are tuning out and acting out and being systematically herded from public school straight into the criminal justice system. Just follow the dollars. There is a rush to incarcerate rather than educate. The pipeline is clear: metal detectors and cops in schools. Overcrowded, underresourced classrooms. Outdated textbooks. Overworked, underpaid teachers. Cultural competency not required. Students criminalized for disciplinary issues that would normally warrant a trip to the principal's or dean's office now are whisked away to central bookings and Rikers. I see a diabolical setup. I was shocked, but not surprised, to learn that many states calculate the number of future prison beds they'll need based on failing reading levels of third graders. Funds are allocated based on these projections, so those beds *have* to be filled. It's a prison preorder.

The war on poor, Black, and Latino youth is real in the field. Kids who can't read are more likely to drop out of school and enter the underground (criminal) economy to survive. Kids who can't think critically or creatively usually wind up with mediocre, low-paying line-worker jobs and are more likely to toe the line and not make waves in society, like robots. Work, work, work, and *obey*. Consume a bunch of things you can't afford (and don't need), watch the idiot box, drink and smoke, self-medicate, go to sleep, and repeat the cycle. People who are paralyzed by poverty, racism, and lack of access to adequate educational resources and employment opportunities, and are depressed, are much easier to control and exploit in order to maintain a permanent underclass. Keep the poor poor, and the rich richer.

Money, greed, power, and control are the sole interest of big-business plutocrats who pull the strings in the United Corporations of America. Mass incarceration is big business and works hand in hand with having communities of uneducated, underemployed, uninspired people; both feed the appetite of a caste system designed to keep the superwealthy in power and in control. If you're poor and want freedom, education, and justice, you've got to snatch it off the shelf, because it's not meant for you in the first place. The game is rigged. Poor Black and Latino kids are fighting against a well-oiled machine. The prison system is a racket and the current public education system is its partner in crime. Kids have to be anomalies and teachers have to be renegade third-eye warriors to counter *this* Matrix. My older sister, Leslie, and I talk about this and other conspiracy theories all the time. We speak the same *tongue*. She said, when you look at the history of racism in this country and the relentless violent and economic assaults on African Americans, starting with hundreds of years of slavery, then the Civil War, followed by Reconstruction, thousands of acres of land and property being stolen from us, thousands of lynchings, decades of segregation/Jim Crow terrorism, murderous attacks on the Black Panthers, COINTELPRO, all the way through to today with merciless police brutality and state-sponsored murders of unarmed citizens and unyielding mass incarceration and hyper-unemployment, how can *any* serious thinking Black person *not* connect the obvious dots and see a strategic campaign of terror and conspiracy against us? She also said public schools aren't designed to really teach the poor; they're designed to program them and keep them obedient and complacent citizens who aim low. I can't wait to call her when I get home. After today's meeting, I need some reinforcement and a lifeline from my swami big sis.

My rage against this unfair machine and my conspiracy theories are riled up, making my blood pressure rise. Stress is a trigger for my migraines and I feel one coming on after all that ranting I did in this overactive head of mine. I drift off into a freestyle soliloquy.

I'm convinced that this new rubric system they expect us to implement is designed to fail. How else do you explain piling bureaucratic red tape on top of teachers who are already underpaid and overworked, with obscenely overcrowded classrooms and out-dated materials? And how do you *not* support teachers who have to navigate layers of complex behavioral issues with students stumbling into class from urban war zones? How do you document measured outcomes for a super-shy or super-angry student who never participates but suddenly, through consistent encouragement, gradually begins to take risks and participates...even smiles? How do you determine measured outcomes for the immeasurable?

I work myself into a tizzy.

I know *I'm not* the problem and I know I'm working in a Goliath of an oppressive system, but yet I still manage to leave the meeting questioning if I am a good teacher. Doubt is mounting at warp speed. The meeting unleashed my inner gremlins. Those ANTs, automatic negative thoughts, begin running amok again, marching loudly. I am spiraling fast into a self-deprecating morass of self-sabotage that sounds like: *You suck, you're weak, thought you had this shit, didn't you? You big dummy. Loser. Your artist failed and now your teacher has too, Miss Georgetown University...ha! And you still ain't got health care or two pennies in savings...your plan ain't working, hussy! You ain't ringing no bells, honey. And you lonely. So just what the hell are you doing with your life anyway?*

God, I am so mean to me. I hate when I bully myself into depression.

This afternoon, after the crippling meeting, I decide to let the kids watch a movie when they come up from lunch. I reach for *Ray,* the film about Ray Charles's life, brilliantly played by Jamie Foxx. I want to listen to the blues and sit in the dark. This'll take me to the end of the day and then I can go home, crawl into bed, call my sister, and cry myself to sleep.

I walk in slow motion back to my classroom to get ready for the rug rats, who will soon be returning from lunch. Killa's squeaky art cart can be heard rolling down the hallway and I poke my head out to wave him over. The kids are late coming back up from lunch, so we have some time to chat it up in my doorway for a bit. Still exhausted and reeling from that obnoxious, deflating staff development meeting, I shake my head nonstop in stunned disbelief. "Killa, what was that straight-out-of-bizarro-land meeting all about, really? It felt like an assault. Is she serious? I'm kinda fucked up right now and…I don't know how much longer I can last in this place. What a load of jumbo bullshit! My God! Christmas break can't come fast enough. I'm crossing off days on the calendar like I'm serving time."

Killa leans on his cart, which overflows with construction paper, colored pencils, markers, art books, and his infamous radio with a collection of hip-hop mixtape CDs on the lower tier. "Sis, did you see the expression on everybody's face? Nobody was feeling it, not even the assistant principal's usual ass-kissers. All it takes is one administrator to suck the life out of a place. She's the reason why I stopped doing my annual Christmas play for the guys. I'm not doing it this year because I didn't feel like being bothered with all her restrictions and no support. The woman doesn't have a creative bone in her body, nor a humorous one either. She's too uptight and, quite frankly, mean and weird."

I'm still stuck on Killa mentioning a Christmas play. "Wait, you used to put on Christmas plays for the guys?" I ask, totally and utterly intrigued.

"Aww, man, sis, a few years back, this place used to be really fun. Me and a couple of teachers got together to put on a Christmas program for the guys. You know the holidays are rough, so we wanted to do something to cheer them up. Now, in the past, they used to have people come in to sing corny Christmas carols and have these dry presentations. So I decided one year to do a Christmas skit and got the teachers and even a couple of COs down to play different characters."

I know this Christmas play he's fixing to tell me about is gonna be a riot.

"Killa, you did a play with characters and the actors had actual lines?" I ask, hyping up the suspense and drama—not that he needs it, but it makes story time more fun, being his hype man and all.

"Sis, I had more people wanting to be in it than I had room for. First, I started off with a rap about Santa getting robbed in Brooklyn, which was the introduction. I had the whole auditorium of two hundred guys cheering me on. It was great. Then the play just took it over the top..."

"Oh, my goodness, I know it was crazy—what was the play about?"

"Sis, it was a dope play if I do say myself. I played Santa and I had a crew of Black and Puerto Rican elves working for me, but for low wages. The elves got tired of the low pay and devised a plan to get paid to supplement their income. I was a stingy and mean, Scrooge-type of Santa, the kind of boss you hate. Like assistant principal lady. So, behind my back the elves started moving cocaine through the toys and were getting their hustle on right under my nose. The cops got tipped off and when they searched the toys, Santa gets busted and goes to jail. So I'm in my Santa outfit going to central booking, getting fingerprinted, and I wind up on the Rock, at Rikers Island. The guys extort Santa for his boots and hat and wouldn't let him touch the phone."

I am rolling with laughter. "Oh snap, Santa was *food*!"

"Exactly, sis, it was hilarious 'cause I used all the jail slang the guys were used to, so they were going crazy in the auditorium, laughing, having a good time. Even the COs were laughing. It gave them a chance to escape. Everyone was human and for just a moment it wasn't jail; we were at a Broadway show."

I start clapping my hands like a giddy kid. "Killa, this is fabulous. Finish, *finish* before the kids come up!"

"So, Santa had to fight for the crib and got sent to the bing because someone planted a banger* on him. Mrs. Claus finally bailed him out and, for Christmas, Santa hit everybody off with commissary. It was one of the best assemblies we had here. Everybody, staff and kids, was talking about it for weeks because some of them never experienced anything like that in their lives, let alone in jail. It was a positive experience in a place full of violence and rage. I did it out of love, sis. I saw a need for laughter, because it helps the guys get through the day. That's why I tell jokes and clown around with the guys in class; it makes it easier for them to learn."

I see a couple of boys in beige khakis walk by. Their government-issued uniform indicates they've been sentenced and have a release date—they're either going home or upstate. Sometimes, for some reason, the sentenced guys are the first ones back from lunch. I know the rest of the gremlins are about to flood the halls at any second.

"Wow, Killa—that was great! Damn, I wish I could have been here to see that. That sounds classic!"

Killa beams. "It was truly classic, sis. Things have changed a lot; the morale is not the same. Even though this was jail, we still knew how to have fun in between the madness. But this lady here, forget it. She's not a happy person."

I sigh in agreement. "She's miserable. I don't know what I'm gonna do, Killa. You know I love the kids but this shit here—who can work under her grip with no flexibility, no freedom, no fun... no room for creativity!"

Killa tilts his head and pauses in thought as he looks at me with sage eyes. "Sis, I always told you, don't let this place rob you of your essence. Remember, you're an artist first. I have a wife and four kids so I can't be as impulsive as I used to be. Do what you gotta do, sis; this is just a pit stop for you."

Just then, one of the rug rats pretends to turn on Killa's radio,

---

*Banger: in jail, a shank or a sharp weapon; on the streets, a gun.

making Killa go into a martial arts stance, playfully challenging the kid. "Yo, son, don't touch my radio, or I'mma have to make it hot."

The kid laughs and asks, "Yo, Killa, we got you next?"

"Yeah, man, I'm coming to your class now," Killa responds as he shoos him away and pushes his squeaky cart out of my class.

"Oh *aight*, 'cause my son told me you was nice with the freestyle rapping. You gonna let me hear something, Killa?"

"Go to class, man. We'll see."

The kid pushes. "But I wanna hear how nice you are."

"I don't just rhyme on demand like a circus monkey... it depends on the vibe. I'm an artist." Killa cuts his eye at me, punctuating "I'm an artist," and then winks.

Killa has a reputation for entertaining the kids and they all enjoy his playful antics. He knows how to talk to them using slang while introducing new vocabulary at the same time. Like a big brother or favorite uncle, he's skilled at engaging them in thoughtful discussions, offering new perspectives on life, all while the kids are working in class drawing or sketching something, being creative. Killa has Zen magic. He's like the black-and-white yin and yang ring he wears on his finger.

"I'll catch you later, sis," he says, bouncing down the hall and swerving his cart through a sea of dusty boys, constantly swatting them off his cart: "Ay yo, will you get off my cart and go to class, man? You starting to irritate me." Killa is shooing away another rug rat obsessed with the markers and bright colors poking out of his art cart, but the kid is really fishing for some older male, big brother, fatherly attention, which Killa always gives. Killa is therapeutic, good medicine for the kids... and for me too. And he's right about laughter; his funny story helps me make it through the rest of the day. It's lifted the weight of that meeting off me and the air doesn't seem so thick now.

I have the TV and DVD player up and ready to go in the front of class. As students trickle in, Shahteik enters and sidles up next to me while I'm sitting at my desk.

"Yes, Shahteik, how can I help you?" I ask with irritation. I really don't want any drama with this boy and he's the last person I want up in my face right now.

"I just felt like coming up here to keep you company. That's all, Ms. P."

Lord knows I'm not in the mood for combat with Lil' Rumbles. I look at Shahteik sideways, giving him a curled lip as my response. He continues, "Ms. P, do you know how to surf?"

I don't have space in my spirit for his shenanigans. I reply, flat and monotone, "No, I don't know how to surf."

Shahteik strokes the top of his head and says, "Oh, 'cause if you did, I was gonna let you ride my waves."

"Boy, you are not wavy!" I respond through the cracked smile he manages to pry from me.

He gets playfully indignant. "What? You trynna say I'm not wavy? Wait till I get my haircut this week, you gonna see."

I chuckle. "Boy, go sit down."

Noticing that he's penetrated my stoic force field, he says, "Aaah, see, I made you smile. You like that," and he bounces to his seat. My nemesis tried to cheer me up. Well, I'll be damned.

There are only a few objections to the film I selected for our afternoon movie time. Some of the kids ask for the typical testosterone-driven boy flicks full of gun-busting, car-exploding action adventure, and adrenaline-pumping fantasy. But once the movie starts, those same naysayers are glued to the screen, nodding their head to Ray Charles's intoxicating rhythms. The movie is a hit; they are shushing each other to hear the dialogue. As the credits roll at the end, Raheim gives me the thumbs-up. "Ms. P, you know who else I like? I like Sammy Davis Jr. too."

"Really, Raheim? He was a great entertainer. I'm surprised you know about him." I am genuinely surprised he knows who Sammy Davis Jr. is, let alone has an appreciation for him.

"Ms. P, I got an old soul. My Grams said I been here before," Raheim exclaims with pride.

Mekhai the Muppet chimes in: "Yo, son, I heard after Sammy Davis Jr. died, Michael Jackson called Sammy's wife and asked her do she want a job as a home attendant for his pet chimpanzee, Bubbles."

Shahteik snaps, "Nigga, what kind of crack you got up in your Pop-Tart, son? You sound 730,* nigga! Bubbles? Nigga, you wilding out!"

The class is cracking up and Peanut is out of his seat doing the moonwalk.

I laugh out loud along with the class. "Mekhai, that was so random! Boy, you crazy as you wanna be. Peanut, sit your butt down, boy." The gremlins are in a good mood and manage to lift mine. Just then a CO barks, "Walking out!" The kids scramble out of class, leaving the desks in a hodgepodge mess as they line up and count off in the hallway before being escorted off the school floor for the day. I straighten out my rows and clear off a few desks that have half-finished worksheets left on them. I laugh to myself, thinking my dusty angels are a trip.

---

*730: legal term for classification of mental instability; a lawyer for a criminal defendant must file a 730 motion to receive a psychiatric evaluation to determine if a defendant is mentally fit to stand trial.

CHAPTER TEN

Artist vs. Civilian

The trees are naked, squirrels are fat, winter winds are howling, and I can see steam streaming from my nostrils with each breath I take. It's *brick* outside—but not too brick to venture out to grab a late afternoon cup of double espresso with warm soy milk from the new trendy café around the corner from my apartment on Franklin Avenue. The upside of gentrification, I guess.

Along the way to and from, I enjoy the festive holiday displays. Folks in the hood have blinged out the front of their homes with decadent decorations. Windows and railings are lined with Christmas lights, blinking angels, and gold trumpets. Tiny front lawns are jammed with huge inflatable Santas, illuminated Black Nativity scenes, snowmen that dance, and reindeers that sing. Kitschy Brooklyn charm.

During this entire Christmas break I've been in a conundrum and here I am, the day before school on January 2, being forced to make a clear choice. Continue to teach? Or pursue my dream? Both come with a cost. Today is my last day of lounging and lamping. Tomorrow I'm back on the grind, punching a clock too early in the damn morning. The twelve days I've had off weren't nearly enough time to decompress and rest my weary mind. I still need more time to reflect on the year that just ended and contemplate what's next.

The new year is staring me in the face, asking, *So, what you gonna do, miss honey? Can't keep doing the same 'ole same 'ole. What's the new game plan?*

I don't know just yet. I haven't figured it out; I'm on autopilot like a programmed laborer. Thinking about the vast unknown future seems so daunting—like staring at a blank page waiting to be filled with words and ideas, colorful language and stories. I'm blocked. Not good. Fuck it, following routine is simple. No risk, no thought, *easy breezy*. I pull out my teaching materials to begin to prepare for the first week back to school. Suddenly my body gets hot. A surge of heat starts to consume me and the moistness has left my mouth; my saliva feels like paste. My heart begins pounding hard, fast, chest heavy. I take deep breaths to steady myself and reach for the wall for support. OMG—could this be what a panic attack feels like? Am I actually having one? The hell is going on? Stress has pounced on me in a *Crouching Tiger, Hidden Dragon* surprise ninja move. I'm under siege from *me,* kicking my own ass. I wobble over to my bed to lie down. I need a long nap. Perhaps some rest will bring calm and reset my equilibrium. Maybe clarity will be revealed in a dream. It's time I face the inevitable conversation.

I love working with the rug rats; they actually bring me immense joy in spite of their wild shenanigans, annoying ADD antics, and foul mouths. But the schedule is killing my spirit. My "passionate artist" and my "practical civilian" are in conflict. My two selves are face-to-face, squaring off like two lovers fighting for my affection, demanding I choose one over the other for the new year.

The civilian in me demands that I focus on financial security and only wants to discuss income, health benefits, dental needs, bills, rent, food, and survival. The artist in me demands that I make self-expression, inspiration, and creating art the priority. She misses being able to write a new play, write a new poem, getting back onstage to perform, and acting in film. My artist needs to conceive something, *always*. It's not what I do, it's *who I am*.

My soul sings when I give my inner child permission to play in the divine realm of the imagination, bringing forth an artistic idea to fruition, actualizing a piece of work. By bitter contrast, my civilian is the practical adult and could give a rat's ass about an esoteric dream because *she* needs the rent and taxes to be paid, she needs groceries bought, new rain boots, jeans without holes, lights on, and the phone working, by any means necessary. Teaching at Rikers full-time just barely gets the rent paid, but it satisfies my grown-up civilian with steady, reliable income. And although I absolutely love working with the kids, my artist is paralyzed in pain and on life support, close to death.

I lie across the bed and close my eyes, but the espresso is surging, slip-sliding through my bloodstream like a wild water park, making my much-needed emotional nap impossible. I take seven deep breaths and reach for the phone to call my swami—she who always has answers for everything and gives the best advice, she who knows my heart and holds it gently in the palm of her hand, she who loves me unconditionally as if I was her own child, she who wipes my tears and makes me feel strong—my big sister, Leslie. I dial. It rings and rings and... "Hi, you've reached two-one-five..."

I hang up before she can tell me to leave a message.

I call the second in command: my bestie, Sun.

"Hey, chica!"

"Gurl, I think I'm having a fucking panic attack. I don't know what's going on. You ever had one?"

"No, I haven't. But I heard you have to take deep breaths and drink water. What's going on, gurl?"

"I can't do this Rikers shit anymore. As soon as I pulled out my materials to do my lesson plans, that's when I got lightheaded and hot. This schedule is breaking me; I haven't written in months and haven't been on an audition or performed even longer than that. I'm *suffocating*. It feels like my dream is dead and I don't know what to do. I failed...I fucking failed." I begin weeping and sit up to blow my nose. Crocodile tears continue to fall as Sun talks me off the ledge of hopeless despair.

"Whoa, whoa, whoa. First off, you are not a failure. You have a beautiful apartment that you are maintaining on your own, which is no small feat. Might I remind you that several months ago you had no idea how you would pay rent and thought you might have to leave New York and move back to Philly? Success number one. And Miss Thing, you *are* and will always and forevermore be an artist no matter how much time off you take from your craft. So shut them gremlins up! Your artist is crying out because she needs attention. When you've reached your threshold of discomfort, it means you're being pushed to take action and do *whatever* it takes to relieve the discomfort...so I think it's time for you to get back onstage and do a show. Yup, that's what spirit is telling me. Time for a 'comeback' show. Mugs ain't seen you in a minute."

"I know. I get asked all the time when am I performing again. But I don't have anything new. I haven't written anything new." I'm whining.

"Gurl, all that material you've got, you could do a fucking retrospective. Bitch, *please,* you got hella material that's classic. You *are* Liza Jessie Peterson. Your name rings more bells than you realize. And I'm not just saying that 'cause I'm your gurl. You're an important and prolific artist—your work is timeless. Matter of fact, you should do a show called *I'm Back...A Retrospective of LJP* and do a medley of your greatest hits. Poems and monologues, combination-style."

Sun's words are resonating with me. I need this pep talk. She puts a battery in my back and begins helping me to visualize the show. "*The Bitch Is Back!*" I exclaim with excitement. "That's what I'mma call it."

"Yes! That's brilliant. *The Bitch Is Back...A Retrospective!* And gather up your band, Ghetto Orchestra. Incorporate music, poetry, excerpts from your solo shows, and do some straight-up storytelling about your journey in prison. Folks wanna know where you've been. And miss honey, you've got *quite* a story to tell."

My pillow is still wet, but my tears have dried. I'm feeling renewed. Energized. Perspective is everything. Sometimes you just need someone to remind you of who you are. Sometimes you need help fighting off the gremlins. Sometimes you need someone to encourage your dreams. Sun is great.

I am charged up, dreaming and visualizing again. And then, within minutes, jealous of my artist's confidence, my civilian starts throwing shade in typical jilted-lover fashion. She poses as my rational mind, but the bitch is a doubting Debbie Downer with a strong voice. *What will you do for income? How will you survive? Do you really think you'll be able to support yourself as an artist? You're being irrational, Liza; your art is just some pipe dream you've sold yourself. Bet you wish you had a sugar daddy. Maybe you could strip, heifer. Your art? The gig is up, honey, don't be so irresponsible, suck it up and be an adult and go back to work. By the way ... rent is due in three weeks!*

She's putting up a fierce fight, but I've made up my mind to choose my boo. My artist is stronger than my civilian and her bullying gremlins (this time). There is no match for the power of inspiration. I'm taking a leap of faith and leaving Rikers. It's no longer a debate. The thought of leaving is no longer resting in the far recesses of my mind; it is now front and center. I have no idea when I will make my move, so I pray for a sign.

I lie awake in bed thinking of my show, wired with excitement. I think I finally fall asleep smiling despite having just a few hours before my alarm rings. Nothing like waking up energized with purpose. I haven't felt this motivated in a long time. Yeah, I like this feeling.

My brain is so preoccupied with creating the performance set list and flow of the show, for which I have no date or venue yet, that I forget to present my ID to the officer at the control booth. He stops me dead in my tracks. "ID?"

"Oh my goodness, my mind is still on holiday break. I'm so sorry."

The corridors leading to the school floor look drab and grimy and smell hella musty, like a boys' locker room. The constant sound of airplanes taking off and landing at LaGuardia Airport is grating.

A nasty water bug scurries into the corner behind a turtle's riot gear vest that's lying on the floor. I pick up my pace and step over someone's hog spit on the stairs leading to the school floor. I head straight for the bathroom to wash my hands. I have the heebie-jeebies and feel icky. I know I'm up out of here, that much is clear, but I don't know when or how. I pause to pray before I leave the ladies' room. *"Mother Father God, I need your direction. Give me a clear sign it's time to go. You know I have to go, I know I have to go—please orchestrate the 'how' and the 'when.' I am praying for discernment. I need your direction. Please hear my prayer. Thank you in advance for your grace and mercy. Thank you, thank you, thank you, God. Amen."*

I walk in the main office to make photocopies of handouts for my social studies lesson on Marcus Garvey and get my daily class list. I notice there are many new names today. Phil pokes his head out of his private office. "Ms. Peterson, would you come into my office for a minute? There's someone I want you to meet."

Standing in the middle of Phil's office is a heavyset white woman with short dark hair, lightly streaked with silver, who looks around sixty years old. She's giving me "Anna Wintour funky *Vogue*" style with her black thick-rimmed eyeglasses trimmed in burgundy. Definitely not a stiff corporate type. She greets me with a warm grin as if we know each other. I don't know her from jack, but I politely smile back and exchange pleasantries.

Phil jumps in, "Liza, this is Kathy—she is the new executive director at Friends of Island Academy, a place you know quite well. They're going to be doing outreach again, here on the island, and I told her one of our teachers used to work at Friends." Phil turns to Kathy. "Liza worked at Friends for many years, when Myrna was the director, before we got lucky and scooped her up here at Rikers Island. I consider it one of my greatest coups. How many years did you work at Friends before you came to us, Liza?"

My mind is percolating at the idea of returning to Friends of Island Academy. I pause momentarily before I give a mini-rundown of my resume. "Oh, I worked there for quite a while, six, maybe seven years, and wore a bunch of hats. I did outreach with the adolescent girls here at Rikers; I ran the women's group, facilitated Urban Folktale, which is a playwriting workshop I developed; I did poetry with the students, conflict resolution, court advocacy, and—"

Kathy's eyes glisten as if she's falling in love. She can't contain her excitement and cuts me off, saying, "I've heard wonderful things about you, Liza, and as you know, Friends has gone through a tough fiscal crisis. Their doors almost closed and I was asked to come and help revive the place and keep their doors open. We're not out of the woods yet, but there is hope. That's why I came back on board, because I believe in Friends; I know what it used to be and what it can become. What I wouldn't give to have someone like you with your expertise who knows the culture of Friends, right now. Boy, we could use you!" It sounds like she's pleading. She looks like she's about to cry.

Phil jumps right in to draw the line in the sand and nip that shit in the bud. "Well, you're a little too late for that, Kathy. She's on our team now. Team *Rikers*." They both give a phony laugh laced with acid. I feel awkward. Wait, are they fighting over *me*? Could it be my escape route has come to the rescue? Okay, God, you are fierce!

I politely smile and excuse myself, explaining how I have some prep work to do before next period. "It was nice meeting you, Kathy. I wish you all the best. Friends deserves to thrive. It's a great program," I say as I twirl out the office, feeling an incredible goose-bump tingling sensation surge through my body. I do believe my angels are conspiring to save me. Working back at Friends of Island Academy would be great. I'd still be working full-time, but at least my travel time to midtown Manhattan would be under an hour. I wouldn't have to leave my house until 8 a.m., as opposed to 5:30 a.m. And I could take breaks for fresh air, walk outside and be free. I wouldn't be in jail; no bars, no barbed wire, no gates, no COs, no alarms, no water bugs, and no pigeon-shit windows. I wouldn't be so drained and my artist will have energy and can finally find time to create and play. Gurrrl, *this* is the sign!

Hold up…wait, pump the brakes. I'm speeding and getting ahead of myself. The woman didn't offer me a job; she didn't even give me her card. But she did give me hope. My brain feels like a pinball machine—bells ringing, lights flashing, a ball zipping around the tracks. I float back to class.

Quickly I scan the room and notice unfamiliar faces sitting in seats the Bosses used to occupy. Several of the Bosses—Tyquan, Tyrone, Mekhai, and Miguel—must have left during the winter break. A bunch of my lil' rug rat homies are gone. A few of them were released home, one turned nineteen and got sent to the greens,* aka the adult building at Rikers, and a couple finally got sentenced and shipped upstate to serve their prison bid. There were no goodbyes or advance notice that they were leaving; they were packed up at a moment's notice and *Poof.* Damn. I wanted to give Tyquan a journal, impart some final words of encouragement, tell him how smart he is, that he was my favorite rug rat, and send him off with a loving smile, a prayer, and a fist bump. I wanted to salute Tyrone and remind him how strong a leader he is and to use it for good. I wanted to tell Mekhai how much he's grown and how much potential he has to become someone of importance. And I wanted to tell Miguel "'sophagus" to make him laugh, and to also remind him to keep working on his English; it'll get better with practice. The energy in the room is different. I miss those knucklehead Bosses already. I still have a few of the original rug rats from the beginning of the school year, but it's not the same crew.

The constant flow of new kids in this setting is par for the course, but knowing it doesn't make it any easier, especially since I had developed a relationship and rhythm with the rug rat Bosses. We were a team. The frequent turnover of students greatly changes the dynamics in the class, especially if the core group of original kids significantly dwindles. It feels like starting from scratch to rebuild

---

*Greens: the adult inmate population at Rikers, who wear dark green uniforms to distinguish them from the adolescents, who wear light beige.

a rapport and reestablish rules. I know it's jail and they're inmates; and according to this criminal injustice system, technically they're criminals, all guilty until proven innocent. I'm not supposed to get attached or overidentify with my students, but I did. I cared. They seeped into my skin and became my lil' roughneck brothers, my badass cousins, my hardheaded nephews, and my beautiful way-ward sons.

Luckily, I still have enough students who were with me from day one to help maintain the standards and rules of my class and can let the new jacks know "Ms. P is a little throwed off and will make it hot." I can count on the veteran rug rats to school the newbies about thug mama and the legend of Poof. I pull out the CD player and plop it on my desk.

Marquis yells out, "Word, Ms. P, you letting us rock the radio today? You must be in a good mood."

"Word," Raheim says, "'cause Ms. P be stingy with the radio. Them other teachers let they class listen to it all the time for *incentive*, but not Ms. P." Raheim emphasizes the word *incentive*, then sucks his teeth, trynna signify. I just roll my eyes at him.

"Marquis, I *am* in a good mood, so don't ruin it. I wanna play something for y'all." The entire class groans in unison with the collective assumption that I am surely gonna play some old-school tunes, something they don't wanna hear.

"Come on, Ms. P, don't do that to us. I thought you was in a good mood," Shahteik pleads.

"I am in a good mood," I reply just as bubbly as a kid at Chuck E. Cheese. I fish through my CD mini-collection and pull out Isaac Hayes.

"Then don't you want *us* to be in a good mood too? Why you just thinking about yourself? I know you gonna play some shit don't nobody in here wanna hear. You be liking corny, played-out, whack music, Ms. P. No disrespect, but you being selfish, yo," Shahteik whines with the rest of the class. They can be such babies over the littlest things. I promise to play just one of my songs, then I'll play

Ghostface, Jay-Z, and Nas, but no Lil Wayne 'cause I don't want to hear no damn Weezy today. I'm feeling encouraged and Ghost, Jay-Z, and Nas get me pumped. I really want to play some Mos Def and Dead Prez, but most of the guys don't like either one too much because their senses are so dull and dumbed down, they're ill-equipped to appreciate intellectual revolutionary lyricists. I don't want to struggle, so Ghostface, Jay, and Nas it will be. But first, some Isaac Hayes.

"I want y'all to hear what I think is one of the baddest intros to a song of all times. It's only sixty seconds, literally." I challenge them. "The song I am about to play was used in a famous gangster movie and whoever can name the movie it's from gets to request *one,* and I mean *one,* Weezy song." Everything is always about making a deal with these brats.

"All right, play the song, Ms. P, 'cause I know my old-school shit and movie trivia is my *forte,*" quips Raheim, with emphasis on *forte* to impress me.

"Nice word, Raheim."

"Yo, Harlem, if you get it right I wanna hear that Weezy joint"— Shahteik snaps his fingers several times, trying to remember the name of the Lil Wayne song he wants to hear—" 'Hustler Musik.' That shit is fiyah!"

"Ms. P! Play 'Fireman'!" demands Rashid.

"Nigga, they play that shit all day on the radio. Why you wanna hear some shit we can hear anytime? That don't make no fucking sense, Harlem…" Shahteik says before turning his attention back to Raheim, who has the ball in his court. "You already know that 'Hustler Musik' is what it is."

The pressure is on Raheim, who is now in a quandary. "Yeah, but I like that slow joint, number fifteen. I can't remember the name of it but it's that love song."

Shahteik flags him in disgust. "Harlem, you a soft-ass nigga!"

"Watch that word."

I am not prepared for the intensity that choosing *one* Weezy song ignites. I have to remind them, "You know what? I won't play diddly-piddly if you all don't relax. It's just a song, the CD isn't going anywhere, and Raheim might not even get the answer right."

"Ms. P, you straight-type weird. *Diddly-piddly?* Really? Who talks like that, son?" Shahteik says, giving me the screw face.

Rashid jumps in. "Word, Ms. P, you throwed off."

I put the Isaac Hayes CD in and cue "Walk on By," and then ask, "You ready, Raheim? Tell me either the artist or the movie it's from."

I absolutely love this song. I remember listening to this over and over again in my headphones for inspiration on my way to an audition a few years back. The film was *American Gangster,* starring Denzel Washington. It was a seventies period piece and my character was a gangster chick who ran the drug spot for Frank Lucas, the notorious kingpin. I got a callback for the role but didn't book the job. It was close, but not a score. Every time I listen to this song, I feel like a G. The intro is so dramatic, with an incredible string section that builds up to a massive crescendo before the beat drops. I wave my hand like a conductor in an orchestra and when the bass finally plummets and says "hello," I let out a "Whoo! What y'all know about that! Now *that's* music!"

I hit rewind and replay the intro. "I gotta hear that one more time—just the intro, not the whole song, before y'all start crying."

Peanut closes his eyes and starts swaying to the music. "That *is* kinda funky, Ms. P."

Raheim is nodding his head while shaking his finger, trying to remember the movie. "Wait, wait, umm, shit...*Dead Presidents!* Right, Ms. P?"

I give Raheim a thumbs-up and a big smile. "Yup, now who is the artist?"

"Yo, Ms. P? You said I could name the artist *or* the movie, not both. That's messed up. You straight pulling a swindle," Raheim cries.

"Word! That's not what you said, Ms. P! You playing games! I knew you couldn't be trusted!" Shahteik shouts. He *really* wants to hear his Weezy.

"Boy, will you relax. I'mma play your Lil' Weezy peezy," I snap back at Shahteik, and then turn to Raheim. "I just figured you might also know the artist since you obviously have a good ear for music. Just take a guess; I'mma play your one Weezy song either way."

"Umm, Al Green?" Raheim replies, shrugging his shoulders. He knows he's wrong.

I suck my teeth, which prompts him to try again. "No wait, Teddy Pendergrass?"

I grab my heart in dismay and look up toward the sky. "Lord, please, please, I *can't*."

Peanut blurts out, "The O'Jays!"

"Just stop! Y'all are hurting my *Soul Train* feelings! I see I'mma have to do a whole lesson on old-school soul music because *this* is a tragedy. Y'all don't know Isaac Hayes? The *great* Isaac Hayes! Lord Jesus, help these babies and grant me grace!"

My response tickles Marquis. "Ms. P, you crazy. You sound like an old church lady."

It's important my boys hear the old-school great legends of soul and connect the dots with rap music. We have an extraordinary, rich legacy of music and they need to be aware of the evolution of Black rhythms and the artists who have shaped our iconic, soulful sound, generation after generation. The boys need constant cultural enrichment and I try my damn best to make sure they get it. Not all lessons require a formal lesson plan. Or a stupid-ass rubric.

I play two Lil Wayne tracks for the crybaby rug rats, then satiate myself with Ghostface's *Fishscale*, Nas's *Illmatic*, and Jay-Z's *The Black Album*, which they don't mind one bit. Ghost, Nas, and Hova have us all head nodding. It's a win-win.

I work in C-74, the building where most of the kids are still going back and forth to court and haven't been sentenced, which makes them a particularly transient group. Some boys stay for a long time, languishing in Rikers because they're waiting to go to trial, which can take months, even years. A lot of kids don't have money for bail and keep going back and forth to court, getting their court dates adjourned for months with their fate in limbo, just waiting to receive an actual sentence. And some are just waiting for their court-appointed attorney to work out a deal with the DA, like getting time served, or probation, or an alternative-to-incarceration program, or some combination of the three. Some kids age out at nineteen and get transferred to the greens. Some eventually go home, and some go upstate to prison. I was fortunate to have a pretty consistent core group of students for as long as I did.

Charles, one of my quiet, studious rug rats, has been with me since the beginning. He knows he's headed upstate and has been sitting in Rikers in my class for months waiting to be sentenced. When you are poor and have a court-appointed attorney, nothing is speedy. If you can't post bail, you sit in jail and wait for a date on the calendar for your case to be called and then you pray your attorney shows up and pray he or she is prepared and pray some more that it doesn't get adjourned for another month...or two

Charles is poor and waiting. His attorney sucks and his case has been getting adjourned for months on end. He finally gets sentenced and could pack up any day now. He took the plea and is looking at a minimum of five years in an adult prison. Yet, in spite of his fate, he manages to stay focused and academically productive. He hasn't given up on himself or his future. I enjoy having him in my class. When all the other Barnum and Bailey circus clowns are cutting up, Charles gives me his undivided attention and does my work. So when he asks me if he can take a GED workbook back to his housing area to work independently at night and on the weekends, I don't hesitate to break the rule and loan out the book. Usually I don't let books out of my classroom; we're not supposed to, especially instructional workbooks, because we only get a limited number and supplies are already scarce. But this kid is *hungry*, always working, always asking questions, is eager to learn, and is a sponge for Black history. I make it a point to feed him extra work and push him because I see something special. I see a yearning.

There is a bright light of potential in him. So, yeah, I give him the workbook, trusting that he will bring it back, and if he doesn't, I know he's going to put it to good use. This kid is determined to educate himself out of poverty and I want to help. He deserves a chance. He needs a break. I give Charles three essay prompts and tell him to choose one to practice writing a five-paragraph essay, which is one of the requirements for the GED.

"I got you, Ms. P, thanks. I'mma work on it tonight and bring it in tomorrow for you to correct," Charles says, with a half-sad, half-smiling face. Charles always looks sad. He used to be gang-affiliated, homeless and sleeping on trains and in parks. His mother lives in a shelter and he felt safer out on the streets than in the seedy temporary housing. Heartbroken and disappointed in his choice to run the streets with gangs, his mother tried in vain to hold him close, knowing that her love wasn't enough. He needed what she couldn't offer—safety, manhood, and money. Charles, like many fatherless boys, searched for his manhood on street corners and in alleyways. The gang provided a stream of income and an identity, a family, a sense of belonging and masculinity, albeit unsafe, warped, and false. And although he loves his mother, she couldn't guide him through his rite of passage to manhood, so the streets filled the paternal gap.

Charles's teenage sweetheart became a lifesaving distraction from the gang. He fell in love and became so disenchanted by his gang affiliation that he dropped his flag* and told me he was prepared to suffer whatever consequences may come from leaving the gang. He didn't care about the repercussions because he was tired of

---

*Drop your flag: to quit the gang. The flag, represented by a specific-colored bandana, is what gang members proudly wear. To drop the flag means to give up your gang status. It can sometimes have dangerous or deadly consequences.

being, as he put it, "deaf, dumb, and blind, following the ways of the devil." He shared a lot with me. "God sent me to jail to save my life, Ms. P, but I couldn't see it at the time. When I first came to Rikers, I was ready to hang it up and give up on life. Then something told me to go to school and I was assigned your class. Soon as I saw all the pictures on the wall and you was teaching us about who we are as a people, I knew you was like an angel. God keeps saving me."

I am rooting for this kid big-time. Several days have gone by and I haven't seen Charles in class, which in this setting isn't abnormal, but I'm still disappointed. There's nothing like teaching a kid who wants to learn and is hungry for information.

A rotund, baby-faced boy walks in, bounces over to my desk, and chirps, "You Ms. P?"

"Yes, how can I help you?" I reply, bracing myself for a scam.

"My boy Charles told me to give you this. He got transferred to the adults this morning. He's nineteen now."

Charles told me that he might be going to the greens, but he said it probably wouldn't be for another week or two. I didn't expect it to be so abrupt, which is silly of me because everything in this place is tenuous, sudden, and unpredictable.

I unfold the loose-leaf paper. The child has done his homework. Charles selected one of the three essay prompts and wrote an essay like he promised. My heart swells. I beam at his friend. "Your boy Charles is gonna make it," I say. "He's very focused and smart. They say birds of a feather flock together. Are you getting your GED, brother?"

The rotund baby-faced kid stands up taller. "I'm in the GED class now. I passed the predictor and I can take the test next time they give it, in like a month."

"Excellent, brother, excellent! I love hearing that. Stay focused. Your education is your ticket up and out." I tell baby-face to come by before the end of the day and pick up the corrected essay to mail it to Charles in the adult building. Though I can barely get a minute to myself and am swamped with grading work, I will make time to give Charles's essay priority today. Briefly I glance at the essay to see what topic he chose.

Question: Schools miseducate Black and Latino youth. Do you agree or disagree? Explain.

In the government school system there's a format that is set to educate youth. In the essay before you I will give my opinion with reasons why I feel that schools mis-educate Black and Latino youth.

In the school system there are formats for the teachers to teach. All students have to take tests, such as the regents, in order to make it to the next grade. To finish school you have to pass all of the regents. There are classes that are for students with behavior problems or have low academic skills. This is called special education, which the majority are Blacks and Latinos.

The school system is set up to teach youth European History, which means to me, His-story in Europe. Why do we have to take tests that make us think that people like George Washington and Christopher Columbus are important men and men of honor? We study these men by the facts that the government show, but there are two sides to every story and we never get the other side.

The Blacks and Latino's history is only a small part of the test and are taught in short lessons in class by some teachers. There are more things that Blacks and Latinos should know about when it comes to our struggle. Our ancestors paved the way for us to have freedom today. This battle has been going on for centuries. We must learn, study and not forget our history. It builds our self-confidence, self-discipline and allows our self-esteem to grow, feeling better about ourselves and our culture.

This current education system really mis-educates us. Once we are open with a better and clear vision, we can take back the empire that's truly ours.

This isn't quite a standard five-paragraph essay required for the GED test (which I duly noted and explained at length to him), and he clearly needs to work on sentence structure and fleshing out his argument more coherently. However, I find his critical thinking and revolutionary spirit to be promising. I saddled him with a page of notes and a thick Black history packet of handouts for him to read and work on independently, including a Ms. P–recommended book list.

The beauty of adolescents is that, in spite of their annoying narcissism and reckless decision making, they are still growing and maturing. The prefrontal cortex in their brain is still developing and is a work in progress. There's hope. Normal teenage years are about testing the boundaries of authority and doing dumb shit. Many of these kids are brilliant dummies; smart, gifted kids who did something really dumb. But once on the Rock, many of them finally see their experience of being incarcerated as a wake-up call, a moment to slow down, pump their brakes, reflect on their decisions, and reevaluate their choices and so-called friends. Great awakenings happen in the quiet of the night in their cells. It gets real.

But not all of them get it. There are those who are so entrenched in a cycle of abuse, who know nothing but a negative self-image, who have been abandoned, in and out of foster care, whose spirits are so broken that being institutionalized is an accepted, normal existence. I pray for them all because I know anything can happen at any moment of their development. The lightbulb can finally go on for the ones you least expect it to.

I believe that most of the kids won't come back. While they are with me, I try to plant seeds of hope, encouragement, and knowledge of self into their fertile minds. I'm an optimist, a dreamer. I'm able to see more for them than they see for themselves. I remind them of their potential and keep the standard high. I keep it real and I get results. I get them and eventually they get me. They see I genuinely care. Like the kids say, "Real recognize real."

Facts.

CHAPTER ELEVEN

Paradigm Shift

I never imagined, in a kazillion-billion-million fantasies, that in *my* lifetime, I would *ever* witness a Black man elected to *actually, really, truly* be president of the United States of *America*. I never dreamed it possible for a Black commander in chief, leader of the world's most powerful nation, to be living with his *very* Black family in the *White* House. And never did I think I would be so excited about a president being inaugurated that I would take three personal days off from work and leave the boys to travel to Washington, D.C., just to watch it in person. Puuuleease! Hell, I've never even watched the presidential inauguration on TV. It's always been *white man, white man, white man,* year after year after year. Same 'ole, same 'ole. *Sooo* not interested. But *this* was different. *Very* different. I made sure I left detailed, specific lesson plans for the person assigned to substitute my class while I was off witnessing history. No freestyling while I was gone; I didn't want my boys to skip a beat.

"That was fucking surreal. I'm still numb, it's so overwhelming," Gary says as we exit the capital city and veer onto I-95 North, headed back to New York. "And I gotta tell you, I had a fear that he might be assassinated during the inauguration—I kept expecting something to happen."

"Word," says Ajamu. "I had that same anxiety. Like, okay, when is America going to show her fangs we know she has? I think every Black person felt that collective fear for Obama's life. Shit, Black folks *know* more than anybody how America gets down." Ajamu is a visual artist and shaves funky, artful designs on his head; a beautiful Black nappy canvas. He used to be a barber and traded the clippers for a paintbrush but still cuts fly.

"Well, I know one thing, the country will never be the same, *ever*. I feel hopeful. I know that sounds corny, but I actually expect better and more for our people…and for the country, like, in a real way," Gary admits. "Kinda the same feeling I had coming out of the Million Man March. Something huge has occurred. I really think this is just the beginning."

"It's a lot to digest. I'm kind of speechless. And you know a bitch like me always has something to say. It's a lot to think about…the implications of Black excellence on the national stage. The shit is fucking awesome," says Ajamu's wife, Nucomme, jumping in. She's a singer and social event producer who runs a grown and sexy after-hours speakeasy joint in Brooklyn. No signs, just a peephole and secret password. You gotta know somebody to be somebody, to get in. Authentic, clandestine, old-school underground New York–style. Nucomme's a modern-day maven, a "big-titty saloon broad with a razor tucked into her cleavage" kinda chick. Raspy voice worn down by whiskey and full lips painted red, framing a soft, southern smile. Reminds me of my girls from Philly…honey-on-the-blade pretty tooth-chippers.

I lean my head against the window. "I thought a Black man would be elected president 'when hell freezes over,' and yesterday damn sure felt like the coldest day in history. I guess America froze over, huh?"

"*Word*," says Gary. "It was so cold, it was bizarre. Kinda ironic. I gotta admit, seeing so many white people cheering him on, people of all races, children, old people, families…everybody smiling and so happy for this Black man and for our country, was very validating. Very encouraging, like that 'hope' shit is real. A great moment and movement in history is happening. It's going to take me a while to really process it and properly articulate what this means," says Gary.

"Word. I just wants to sleep right about now; shit wore me out emotionally," Nucomme comments as she leans on her husband's shoulder to take a nap.

"Gurl, who you telling?" I turn up the music slightly, bumping on Gary's dope playlist. A Tribe Called Quest has us head nodding at the moment.

It seems as if every car we pass on the interstate has an Obama bumper sticker. All of them are positive except for one sticker that says *NObama* written across an image of the Confederate flag. I roll my eyes at the driver. Gary honks his horn.

"There's white people, and then there's crackers we, unfortunately, still have to contend with."

"Fuck 'em," I reply. "We won this round. Can't allow them to steal our joy."

"Word."

We aren't nearly as talkative driving back as we were driving down the night before the inauguration. There isn't the guitar-playing, singing, and shit-talking excitement from last night. All of our brains are unraveling the layers of profundity we've experienced, and exhaustion is definitely setting in. I'm glad I took a few days off, including tomorrow, but I can't wait to share my experience with the boys. My sinuses are congested and I keep sneezing. I'm sure I caught a cold. *Dammit.* But it was worth it. I couldn't miss *this.* I *had* to see it. I had to see him. I had to be there to witness this mind-blowing, paradigm-shifting mojo moment in history. The energy feels atomic. The planet is buzzing, I'm sure of it.

My mind is dancing wildly with colliding thoughts jumping all around like an Afropunk mosh pit. Something in me has significantly shifted. I am *so* inspired to take a risk, to change. Seeing Barack and Michelle Obama strutting down Pennsylvania Avenue as Mr. and Mrs. President, literally right in front of my face, reflected the immense possibility of my own dreams. It challenged me to push beyond my fears, my self-imposed limitations, and my consciousness of lack that was holding me back from greatness. Shit, my president is Black. The impossible *is* possible.

The Obamas are a huge breakthrough. Change is here. Barack is fearless. Michelle is bold and beautiful. Yes we can and yes we *did*. Everything is resonating. Witnessing such a grand parade of excellence and seeing a far-fetched fantasy-dream manifest right before my very eyes has awakened something fierce in me. I feel brave again. Clarity is coming into focus and now I get why I came. This inauguration is about *me*. I came to be reminded and encouraged. It's about *my* breakthrough, *my* change, *my* fearlessness, *my* bold, *my* beautiful, and *my* dream coming true. The universe is speaking to me through the Obamas. Yes *I* can and yes *I* will. Nothing is a coincidence. *This is another sign.*

As the New York City skyline comes into view, I sit up and yawn, happy that we're almost home. Gary is now playing Biggie Smalls and turns the volume way up, 'cause it's Biggie, which triggers an instant-reflex, heavy head-nodding, shoulder-shake swagger dance in my seat. *Notorious.* I'm convinced New York has a powerful force field that gives you an energetic charge upon the mere sight of the shiny skyscrapers and bright lights that decorate the shimmering Big Bling Apple. New York, New York, so nice they named it twice.

Yellow taxis and gypsy cabs beep and bully us as we veer onto the Brooklyn Bridge. My mind drifts back to Rikers and I think about some of the changes that are taking place at the school.

A week before I left for the inauguration, word on the grapevine was that the principal, my buddy Phil, was resigning. There was some skullduggery going down in the superintendent's office and Phil was being pushed out. I didn't know the details, nor care to inquire. As far I was concerned, Phil was good people. He gave me a shot at becoming a full-time teacher, which rescued me from the brink of having to "Tootsie Roll on the pole" to pay rent. It's sad to see him go because he's one of the rare and few administrators who really supports the methodology of arts and education to enhance literacy, and I believe he genuinely cares about our kids. Phil's leaving was such an abrupt changing of the guard that I think this too is yet *another* sign from the universe. It's time to quicken my departure date from Rikers.

There's a new "interim" principal on board. This makes resigning even easier. I don't know her, she doesn't know me, it'll be easy. I'll call Kathy at Friends of Island Academy and let her know I'll be a free agent in two weeks, see if she offers me a job. I'm sure she will. I already feel a weight lifted.

CHAPTER TWELVE

The Hardest Part

I walk into class and Shahteik blurts out, "Took a lil' vacation, huh, Ms. P? Well it *sure* was pleasant not hearing you nagging us all damn day!"

Aww, my Lil' Rumbles missed me, I think to myself. Then I playfully roll my eyes at him.

"Psyche, Ms. P, lemme stop playing 'fore you get all crazy and start yelling for real. You went to see the president though?" Shahteik inquires.

My throat hurts and I'm hoarse. I struggle to talk at an audible decibel. "The inauguration was absolutely fabulous. It was incredible. Historic. I got to see the president and first lady up close when they got out their limousine and walked down Pennsylvania Avenue. I had a really good spot at the front of the barricade. Millions of people came out. It was something to behold." I sound like an old barfly with a cigarette dangling from the corner of her bourbon-stained lips.

"Yo, Ms. P, you lost your voice?" asks Raheim.

"Yeah, she was probably screaming *Barack Obama Barack Obama,* wasn't you, Ms. P?" Malik jokes, imitating my voice.

"I was screaming, I was crying. I witnessed history. A Black man is president of the United States of America. A Black family is moving into the White House. Everybody out there was crying when he took his oath and gave his speech. I don't think you truly understand the magnitude of what just took place. You will in time, though. Oooh, but it was cold as a brass monkey. I got sick." The term "brass monkey" draws some chuckles.

Malik, aka Far Rock, is donning a fresh haircut. He's such a handsome kid. Looks just like my nephew, Tyler.

"Ay yo, Far Rock," Rashid calls out to Malik, "when we see that nigga Shams, we gonna give him the brass monkey; knock that nigga out cold." Rashid demonstrates a knockout punch.

"Watch that word," I say instinctively.

In an instant they have taken something old, "brass monkey," and remixed it to create a new metaphor. They are something else. I love these badass lil' boys.

Rashid, aka Leaky, is no longer wearing his dark gray sweat-shirt and pants but has on state-issued khakis. He must have had court and been sentenced while I was out. The pants are too long for him, and even though he's rolled them up several times into a thick cuff, they still manage to drag off his heels. The thug hobbit flashes me a smile, proud of his creative new slang.

Shahteik is now out of his seat and one of the fairly new kids, Diaz, is casually eating a Pop-Tart like he's home. Just brazen.

"Shahteik, sit down. And my brother, you . . . yes, *you*, please put that Pop-Tart away. You know better than that. No eating in class. The sheriff is back; don't play with me."

Shahteik puts his fingers to his lips: "Ms. P, *shhh,* watch your voice; don't talk so much."

I squint my eyes and glare at him. "Boy, don't shush me."

"What? I'm looking out for your voice, my Nubian Black queen. Can't a brother have your back? Shhhh, be easy. That's all I'm saying."

The class snickers and Raheim adds a dose of his own sarcasm. "Word, Ms. P, relax. Take care of your voice—we wouldn't want you to lose your voice altogether now, would we?"

They're on a roll. "If Ms. P lose her voice for real, that would be music to my ears," Malik comments, leaning back in his seat with his feet up on the desk, hands clasped behind his head like he's lounging on a La-Z-Boy recliner.

"Boy, if you don't get your feet off that desk!" I am straining my voice at this point.

"*Shhhh,* Ms. P!" he replies dismissively.

My hand flies on my hip and before I can open my mouth, Malik says, "Psyche, psyche, *psyche,*" quickly, in an effort to avoid my wrath. He switches the subject back to the inauguration. "You saw the president for real though, Ms. P?"

God, they know me so well. "I sure did. He and Mrs. Obama walked right in front of me. They were about the distance from me to you. They are a beautiful power couple. Michelle Obama is divine…and the president is *fine.* I'm just saying." The class grumbles and sucks their teeth. I laugh, enjoying their jealousy. They tickle me.

"Ms. P, next time you decide you gonna take a lil' vacation and whatnot, you run it by *me.* Don't be leaving us like that, ya heard. Had a nigga thinking you wasn't coming back. Three days is a little much," Malik yells out, half-playing, half-serious.

The boys depend on me so much. Telling them I'm leaving is going to be incredibly hard. I've been avoiding it all morning but I know I'm going to have to eventually break the news of my departure. Here it is I finally got the battery in my back to make the huge decision to leave, opting to roll the dice and focus my attention on my artist, but I can't muster up the courage to tell the boys. Being back in the class with them, a doubting thought of *am I doing the right thing* flashed into my head. But it was immediately overrun by a quick inventory of signs that affirmed my brave decision in the first place: the panic attack, the exhausting, draining schedule, running into Kathy from Friends of Island Academy, the new rubric malarkey, Phil leaving, and hearing President Obama talk about change, leaps of faith, and making the impossible possible. There's no doubt in my mind, *I'm out,* but when it gets down to the nitty-gritty and I have to tell the boys, my knees start knocking and I am momentarily stuck-on-stupid. I only have two weeks left before my last day and it'll be here before I know it. I don't feel like telling them today. I've already been gone three days and they've missed me. It can wait.

Lord knows I don't want to abandon them. They're going to be so angry and disappointed at me for leaving them. These boys have endured broken promises and chronic abandonment with people coming in and out of their lives *all* their life. And now here I come, loving them up and then jumping ship. I know they've grown to trust me and rely on me. And they care about me too. What's going to happen to them when I go? Who will stand in the maternal gap for them? Who is going to love them the way *I* love them? Who will inspire them? Will the next person give a fuck about them and *really* want to see them learn? Will they keep the standards high and *demand* it? Who will nurture them and challenge them and know how to balance the "iron fist in a velvet glove" approach? Because *I know* my boys need both.

I have become attached and territorial. I am not looking forward to breaking the news to my funky, dusty lil' rug rats at all. But I have to leave. I am an artist and, as much as I love these kids, I can't stay confined in prison. Damn, this is so hard.

Clarity is a blessing and, as difficult a decision as it is for me, I am crystal clear. I sashay into the new principal's office with confidence. It's my first time meeting her, which makes handing in my resignation easy breezy. Our conversation lasts all of three minutes. She gives me a firm handshake, thanks me for my service, and wishes me "all the best." Wow. I did it! I'm outta here. *Deuces.*

An entire week has gone by and I still haven't gotten the courage to tell the boys. But today is the day. *I must.* It's Monday, and Friday is my last day. That will give us five days to slowly bring closure. I sound crazy saying that. These are my babies though.

"Guys, so, I have an announcement to make. Um, this is really difficult to say to you guys…" I pause and fidget with my nails.

"Yo, Ms. P, just spit it out. What's good?" Rashid says and gives me a look like, "Come on already!"

"This Friday is my last day and the hardest part about my decision was thinking about y'all. Because, believe it or not, you guys, each and every one of you, really mean a lot to me and I really, really care about you…" I clear my throat and swallow the lump rising in it. They give me blank stares.

Shahteik jumps up and cuts me off. "Yo, Ms. P, I'mma remember your Poof. When I go upstate, I'mma be laughing about that shit."

His comment prompts a bunch of "Word…word, son."

He broke the ice and lightened the mood. I love that rascal. Amazing how he's grown on me and seeped into my skin.

Raheim blurts out, "Hell yeah. Ms. P went crazy!" Then he imitates me doing my Poof, stands up and yells, "Poof, Poof, Poof!"

The entire class joins in and begins Poofing me. This is my official rug rat salute.

Malik is not Poofing me. He remains seated just shaking his head. He's not smiling, He's clearly not feeling the news. I want to explain to him why I have to do this and how much they have helped me to grow and that I really do love them. I want to tell him that I will continue to pray for them and root for them. Malik deserves more than an announcement. They all do. By now, Peanut is standing up and doing the Harlem shake, prompting the class to cheer him on.

"Go Peanut, go Peanut!"

"Boy, sit down," I say, laughing

"Ms. P, can we listen to the radio today?" Peanut asks, still shaking.

I smile and get the radio out of my locker.

"Yes! Thank you, my Black Nubian queen." Peanut gives me a military salute and a bow.

I let them listen to Weezy all afternoon because I think they could use some comfort music. Seeing them happy and cooled out makes me feel good. I tell them to do independent reading without any talking, which I know is a joke. So I make it clear that any *loud* talking will guarantee the radio gets deaded. I wasn't serious, but I had to say it.

Malik is still brooding. He hasn't said anything to me or anyone since my announcement. He has his nose buried in his favorite book, *The Collected Poems of Langston Hughes.* I want to do something special for Malik. I'm going to write him a letter. While the guys are pretending to work, I sit at my desk to compose Malik's letter and decide I should probably write something for all the guys. They deserve it. After I finish writing Malik's letter, I start writing each rug rat a personalized student evaluation/inspiration letter. I need to leave them with something tangible and they need to know how much I believe in them.

As I am writing their evaluations, Shahteik plops into the conference chair next to my desk holding a checkerboard on his lap. "Ms. P, nobody can beat me at checkers, *nobody.* Not even you." This is an invitation and a dare.

I put my pen down and glare at Shahteik. "Boy, I will wax your butt so bad, you'll have to wear Pampers." I accept the bait.

He whips my butt at all three rounds of checkers, talking shit the whole time. Then, as if the thought of me leaving has finally dawned on him, he says, "Yo, Ms. P, even though you really, and I mean *really* got on my nerves, I ain't gonna front, you were the best teacher I had. Now, don't get too excited 'cause I'm giving you some love."

"Shahteik, I know that must have been extremely painful for you to admit." We share a laugh.

"I'm about to go upstate so I won't miss seeing you here at Rikers, Ms. P."

"Yeah right, Shahteik, you're gonna be thinking about all those vocabulary words I gave you but you refused to write down."

"Ms. P, you *wilding.* I know my vocabulary; I ain't have to write them down 'cause I'm nice like that. I'mma damn sure miss your Poof though. Ms. P, you crazy, yo." He shakes his head and laughs.

"I'mma be laughing 'bout that shit for a minute. I'mma be Poofing niggas upstate, watch."

"Watch that word," I say as I beam.

"My bad, Ms. P. Yo, where you come up with that Poof thing, though? That's really type crazy—it's original, but *damn* that shit is crazy."

"Y'all rug rats inspired it. There was no Poof before I started working with y'all."

"Oh, word?" Shahteik is proud of that.

Wow, my archenemy, the black-gnat nemesis, bane of my existence, Lil' Rumbles rug rat supreme, is actually warming my heart. Well, I'll be damned. We finally bonded.

I hand out their evaluations, which are full of positive encouragement and constructive criticism. When I get to Malik, he asks, "What's this?"

"An evaluation and personal letter from me to you, because you're one of my favorites."

Malik stares at me momentarily before he cracks a warm smile and begins reading his letter.

"Everybody got one?" he quietly asks.

"Everybody got a personal student evaluation. But you got a letter *and* an evaluation. Don't make it hot. Keep that between me and you," I whisper, making Malik feel extra special.

"I got you, Ms. P. Thanks…I'm kinda tight you leaving though. But I'mma be all right. I'm up outta here soon anyway, so it's all good."

"You better be up out of here. You've got a bright future. And I still got my peoples up here, so I better not *ever* hear about you being back up in this place, ya heard?"

"Naw, never that, Ms. P. I'mma be a poet."

My heart swells.

"You already are."

Malik lights up and leans back in his desk, showing all of his teeth, flashing me a warm solar smile with luminous rays. Malik is gorgeous.

Then it dawns on me. I need something tangible from them too, so I ask, would they mind writing an evaluation on me? I want honest feedback about what they thought of me as a teacher. I let them know it isn't mandatory at all, but it will help me to improve as an educator. They all begin writing on pieces of paper. I am so curious to know what they got from me and what they have to say about Ms. P.

Raheim aka Harlem:
The way I think of Ms. Peterson as a teacher is she shows and teaches her students how to learn. When Ms. Peterson teaches her class we are interested in learning because we want to know about our community and our history. One of Ms. Peterson's weakest points in teaching is that sometimes she has no patience. When Ms. Peterson stops teaching, her class will not be the same because most teachers don't care to teach you if you don't care to learn.

Shahteik aka Lil' Rumbles:
Tu Ms. Peterson better known as my Black queen you noe that you gets me so mad I just wish I could erase you but you teach some gud work. I be mad at the world and you jus ache my nerves but I still love you and I apologize for disrespecting you cause if someone disrespect my moms I'll come rite back to jail. I'm sorry my Black queen. Out of everything you taught the only thing stood out was the essay. You are a very special teacher and you tried to teach me a lot.
Lil Rumblez

Diaz:
Throughout my time here I've enjoyed learning and spending time in Ms. Peterson's class. Ms. Peterson is a very intellectual teacher. She focuses mainly on making sure that the lesson's learned, the goal is reached and assuring the task

gets completed. She is a great teacher overall. She reaches out to the kids when needed.

Rashid aka Leaky:

High Points
1. Black History: You teach me a lot about Black History that I didn't know cuz I was blinded by the white mans way of teaching Black History
2. Getting work finished and done: I never did so much work in jail in my life. Shaking my head
3. Keeping your Kool: If I was you I would be right here with everybody else
4. Last but not least Don't Touch My Radio: Goddamn!

Low Points
1. Making it Hot: it's the next kind of hot
2. Yelling at another person cuz somebody else got you mad

Malik aka Far Rock:
   Ms. Peterson I'm really going to miss u. What I'm going to miss the most is the Poof and just bugging u til u get belligerent, but besides that you are a great teacher. U taught me a lot about Black History and the class is going 2 try 2 keep the same thing going. U even taught me a lot about poetry and I hope to get some more poems even one valentine's.
                                                              The End

My rug rats brought out the best in me, forced me to confront my fears and walk boldly and humbly through my insecurities, *all day*, every day. I *had* to show up, daily and consistently, for something greater than myself. My dusty boys taught me Yoda-like patience and compassion under pressure. They brought out dynamism in me, proving to myself that I *can* indeed teach and reach the seemingly unreachable. The universe clearly put me here for a reason and these loud potty-mouth rascals had a profound impact on me, helping me to grow as an educator, an artist, and a human being. Most importantly, they forced me to discover a deeper purpose that isn't about me at all. We undoubtedly had a symbiotic relationship. I'm going to miss this motley crew of criminal-minded, dangerous minds, menace II society, bad-news bears who I carry in my heart. These beautiful wounded warriors. These kids with potential. My rug rats.

On my way out I found this in my teacher's mailbox. Someone left it there anonymously:

I Do Make a Difference (by Dr. Chaim Ginot)

I've come to the frightening decision that I am the decisive element in the classroom. It is my personal approach that creates the climate. It's my daily mood that makes the weather. As a teacher, I possess tremendous power to make a child's life miserable or joyous. I can be a tool of torture or an instrument of inspiration. I can humiliate or humor, hurt or heal. In all situations, it is my response that decides whether a crisis will be escalated or de-escalated, and a child humanized or dehumanized . . . I Do Make a Difference.

CHAPTER THIRTEEN

MoMo and Friends

As I exit the A train on Thirty-Fourth Street, starting my new job at Friends of Island Academy, I feel *free*. People are zipping by, zigzagging around; some of us are slowpokes, like myself, easy-walking to our office. I wonder if the speed racers even like where they're rushing to.

Working in midtown Manhattan, beginning my workday at 9 a.m., is a far cry from waking up at 4:30 a.m. to travel two hours to clock in at 7:30 a.m. Now I'm *waking up* at 7 a.m., out the door by eight, and I don't punch a clock. This feels normal. This I can manage. I stop into Starbucks and order a Doppio Soy Espresso Macchiato. Fancy shit. Then I quickly duck into the gourmet deli on the corner and get a sesame bagel toasted with chives cream cheese, tomatoes, smoked salmon, and capers. *Foo-foo, chichi*. I'm rolling. I didn't even need to bring lunch today because there is a plethora of cute lunchtime dining options in the vicinity I can stroll to. Sipping on my overpriced designer coffee feels great. I smile and do a happy-bop to work.

Kathy, the program director, is thrilled to have me back on board at Friends of Island Academy to help resuscitate the program, and she gives me a hero's welcome. Because I worked there during what we former employees called the "glory days," I know the culture of the place and what it takes to keep the kids engaged. I've worked with many teenagers in the past who, as a result of their involvement with Friends, have turned their lives around and evolved into dynamic, responsible young adults. I've seen kids coming straight out of Rikers or off the streets walk through the doors of the program and, within months, begin to develop and exhibit their true potential. My coworkers and I worked hard to chip away at the gangster-thug survival façade they desperately clung to. We were the dream team. We helped untangle each kid from the grips of the criminal justice system and from the negative lure of the streets by employing various methods of tough love and doing court advocacy to achieve our collective goal: helping youth stay alive and free. I've also seen my share of knuckle-busting fistfights, rearrests, and relapses back into the gang/drug/fast-money culture—enough to dishearten staunch optimists like myself. But I've also witnessed enough triumphs from tragedy that give me just enough hope to keep believing in unexpected, unpredicted, sudden change. The X factor.

Now that I have official Board of Education teaching experience under my belt, I've been asked to coteach GED classes in addition to other responsibilities. My business card reads *Senior Youth Advocate Specialist,* but it should say "Cirque du Soleil–juggling contortionist." I do a lot and my range is wide.

I teach the coed GED class in the mornings from 9:30 a.m. to 12 p.m., and one day out of the week I travel back out to Rikers Island to do outreach with the adolescent girls detained at Rose M. Singer Center. I meet with potential participants, one-on-one, to make an assessment of her needs and tell her about the various support services that Friends has to offer upon her release. Meeting a girl behind the wall and developing a rapport while she's still incarcerated helps strengthen the chances of her walking through our doors when she gets out. Seeing a flyer posted on a bulletin board in the jail doesn't compare to meeting me in person. Human contact is much more effective and offers me an opportunity to personally connect with the girls before they come home.

I enjoy spending that one-on-one time with the teen girls at Rikers because I become like a big sister–favorite aunt to many of them, offering life-skills advice, a boost of needed encouragement, honest "real-talk" feedback, and sometimes, many times, a shoulder to cry on. I've been doing it so long, I'm "Oprah Master Class Yoda" with it. I get the girls to open up and talk, which doesn't take much because they all need someone to confide in who will listen without judgment.

Another male coworker does outreach with the adolescent boys in the sentenced building, a different building altogether from where my lil' rug rat rascals are housed.

I wonder how they're doing, who's home, who's upstate, who's still at Rikers—and are they learning? Tyquan jumps in my mind and I say a silent prayer for his safety up top. I hope he takes his GED while he's there and remembers what I told him: "Don't serve time, but let the time serve you." I catch myself reminiscing about their shenanigans, laughing to myself thinking about Shahteik, my Poofs, and Peanut's spontaneous Harlem shaking. I miss my boys. I pray they're somewhere winning.

On the days I'm out at Rikers doing outreach with the girls, David holds it down in the class, drilling them with mathematics. He's a wiz at math and excellent at explaining the alchemy of numbers, dissolving algebraic mysteries for the shorty-rocs to easily digest. The kids feel accomplished and smart after they tackle challenging equations. He hits 'em with numbers; I hit 'em with words. We make a dynamite teaching duo.

My new classroom is open and airy, on the second floor, and overlooks the ground-floor main entrance, which is street level. The office space used to be a trendy, split-level clothing warehouse with huge frosted windows that don't have pigeon shit on them.

Now that I have my official teacher badge and earned my stripes on the Island, I step into the classroom at Friends with confidence. I mastered working with a roomful of rowdy rug rat boys, so I got this. However, this *new* dynamic, adding loudmouth, hard-as-nails firecracker Betty Boop girls into the mix *with* the boys, I wasn't quite ready for. Like MoMo, a tough cookie from Brooklyn who makes her presence known as soon as she enters the building. Her entrance is performance art. Walking in with loud music blasting from her earphones dangling around her neck, MoMo feels compelled to talk extra loud on her cell phone while popping gum all at the same time. And her strut is classic hood couture. Babygirl has hips that switch to the beat of her own soundtrack and she walks harder than Naomi Campbell in an Alexander McQueen runway show. MoMo's walk serves high drama. And if by some miracle she's not yakety-yak-yakking on the cell phone when she walks in, not to worry, she's singing loud and abrasively off-key some random lyric to her favorite song playing on her ghetto playlist. And, if by another miracle from the iPod gods, she's left her pocket-sized boom box at home, not to worry again; MoMo is singing her very own entrance theme song with lyrics she done made up in her own mind: "Owww, you already know MoMo's in the house, yes, yes y'all, to the beat y'all...*owww.*"

Sporting a bright pink tongue piercing, which is in full view every time she throws her head back and belts out a deep-rooted, gutbucket-belly laugh, MoMo has an endearing charm just beneath her 'groid grit. There is something about the heavy register of her laughter that sounds like home. It feels familiar. Authentic. I never did trust a woman who talked or laughed like Minnie Mouse, all squeaky-like from their nasal cavity. MoMo has an earthy, grounded tenor with a straight-no-chaser resonance that reminds me of my Hennessy-sipping homegirls. MoMo is a teenage saloon broad, a loud and honest mirror reflection of my seventeen-year-old self. A fashionista rumbler. Unafraid of bright neon colors, which are highlighted by her dark mahogany skin, MoMo is certified "Brooklyn fly." Always sporting a ladylike pocketbook, acrylic nails, dressy shoes (the kind usually reserved for the club), and big, bold costume jewelry, she wears Cookie Monster–blue or Ronald McDonald–red streaks of synthetic weave in her hair. This week she's giving us Smurfette. Electric blue.

"Ay, yo, who the fuck got my phone?" MoMo has a mouth like an auto mechanic, always barking at the boys. There are usually ten to fifteen students on any given day, with two to three girls mixed in. Female numbers are low. Today she is the *only* girl, which means nothing to MoMo because she hangs with the boys with pool hall ease.

I snap, "Watch your mouth, MoMo!"

"Excuse me, Sista Liza," she says so politely. Then she rephrases her pit bull attack: "Which one of y'all niggaz got my phone?"

I first met MoMo at Rikers. She hadn't been there long and was about to be released on bail. Her family had some resources, so she could fight her case while home. She was one of the lucky ones. Though she was looking at a possible three-to-five-year sentence, her paid attorney said there was a good chance she would get off with just probation since it was her first offense. What a difference a paid lawyer makes. The case looks like it might swing in her favor but she isn't quite out of the woods—anything can happen. MoMo needs to stay productive, out of trouble, and focused in school. Our program is perfect for her.

During our initial conversation at Rose M. Singer, aka Rosie's (the female facility at Rikers where the women and adolescent girls are housed), MoMo presented me with the not-so-spicy mild-chili-pepper version of who she is. I meet Emily Post: *Yes ma'am this, yes ma'am that*—she was so polite and sweet as pumpkin pie. Her smile could melt butter. Seeing her walk through the doors of the program asking for me a few weeks later was a victory. Many girls I meet and connect with behind the walls never come. I was really glad MoMo showed up. Half the challenge has been met. The tough part now is getting her to come to class consistently, on time, and not high, while monitoring her involvement with classroom soap operas—the "he-said-she-said-who-you-talking-to?" drama—that she always seems to get tangled up in.

After the morning classes are over, the kids break for lunch and are expected to come back for the scheduled afternoon groups. Group is mandatory. The primo bargaining chip and main incentive to get the kids to show back up after lunch and not just tear ass and go home is giving them a round-trip MetroCard at the end of the day. If they attend a full day until 3 p.m., they get a full fare.

Today's afternoon group is with the International Center of Photography. ICP conducts photography workshops teaching kids the art form, using it as a tool to help young people see themselves and their community differently while fostering self-reflection and development. It's one of our favorite partnerships. Today ICP is bringing in a world-renowned guest star photographer, Jamel Shabazz, to show his work and help the kids with their photography projects. Of all the days to *not* show out, today is the day, but *of course* the rug rats seem to love showing out in front of company.

Jamel Shabazz's photography work is iconic. He's most famous for his body of work that chronicles the 1980s era of urban life. None before him have documented it so brilliantly and authentically, *ever.* His books *A Time before Crack, Back in the Days,* and *Seconds of My Life* archive images from the early eighties, during the dawn of hip-hop. Having grown up in the eighties as a young teenager myself, I find the fashion, people, poses, and scenery in his photos to be absolutely riveting and nostalgic. To have Jamel Shabazz come to our little bad-news bears program is an honor, so I am beyond mortified that he is witnessing what is fast escalating into a full-blown dramatic escapade with firecracker supreme MoMo leading the charge. I have to defuse the situation as quickly as possible and douse her flames before they rage. I tell MoMo to wait in another room as I address the group of boys already seated around the table ready for group. I figured if I frame it as a bad prank and not a theft, maybe the person who has taken MoMo's cell phone will return it under the guise of *just joking.*

Before I can address the boys, MoMo is back in the room yelling, "Y'all niggaz play too fucking much—niggaz better get up off my phone! Who got my phone, yo?"

"MoMo! Your yelling is not helping the situation. Go wait outside of the room *now*! Let me handle this. Go!" I command.

Of all the girls *not* to fuck with, it's MoMo. But the boys get a kick out of pushing her buttons and getting her riled up just to watch the MoMo-go-crazy show. She is their postlunchtime entertainment. Lord have mercy on me. We've got guests. I'm cringing, but there's no time to be embarrassed. I have to go into Sherlock-Kojak mode before MoMo goes beast and we're all facing Godzilla.

Her phone was sitting on top of her pocketbook one minute and no sooner than she turned her head to talk to someone, it was gone. Whoever lifted it so blatantly did it in front of others who are clearly in on the joke. But the prank has gone too far and needs to end. We have *company,* goddammit.

"All right," I lay into the boys, "who has her phone? Where is it? I know this is a practical joke, so let's end it. Joke's over. Give up the phone, guys."

Kadeem sucks his teeth. "Sista Liza, who would want to steal her phone? She got a bum-ass phone, a Sidekick…don't nobody want her old played-out phone."

Marcus agrees. "It ain't even a phone worth stealing."

"Like I said, gentlemen, I don't think it was *stolen,* but somebody *is* playing a prank and it's time to stop it. It's not funny anymore and it's causing a major problem and disruption."

Jamel Shabazz is on his laptop quietly sifting through images he's prepared to show the group while patiently waiting for the whodunit drama to be resolved. While my coworker David has the boys undergoing a voluntary search, emptying their pockets and backpacks one by one in a private office, I'm in another room with MoMo, having her empty her purse, checking every nook and cranny. She empties the contents: comb, brush, lip gloss, iPod, headphones, lotion, cigarettes, wallet, nail polish, keys.

"Argh, I want my phone! Who got my phone?" she roars in frustration.

I come up with a eureka idea! "Hey, let's call your phone."

"Sista Liza, my phone is on vibrate!" She's on the launchpad of going ballistic. MoMo tries to sneak past me to leave the room and confront the boys. In a split-second ninja swerve, I block the door, foiling her escape and potentially saving a life.

"Sweetheart, they are looking for your phone. We are going to find your phone, baby." I make a promise I can't guarantee.

"I need my phone! Niggaz got my fucking phone and shit is not funny! Lemme out! *Aaagh,* let me go get my phone from them bum-ass niggaz!" Still screaming at the top of her lungs, tears are now sprinting down her face in a mix of fury and frustration. She punches the wall and immediately grabs her fist in pain, making the tears flow like a fountain. A coworker hands her a soft, round, squishy stress-reliever ball to squeeze.

I answer her ridiculous request in my well-trained Miss Crabtree clinical voice, smothered in honey: "Now MoMo, you know we can't let you out of here just yet, not in the state of mind you're in and not until we find your phone, baby. Let us handle it, sweetheart."

MoMo takes a deep breath and serves me an exaggerated super-calm voice. "Sister Liza, I just want to go in there and let them know how I feel, that's all." We're playing ping-pong with the phony pleasantries. She is trying anyway she can to get out of the room. I can't contain my laughter at the absurdity of her request and the inner actress that she has mustered up.

"Girl, you're a damn good actress; that was a good one. Now you know if I let you back in the room with the boys, you're gonna *turn it up* and turn it out. Come on, ma, even you know that." I chuckle and she cracks a smile. "Give me a minute, MoMo, lemme go back upstairs. I'll be right back. Be easy, okay?" I won't leave until she promises me that she'll sit tight with my coworker and let me handle it with the boys.

The search with the boys is unsuccessful; nobody has turned

over the phone. I attempt to use a stern but reasoning tone with them, trying to spank 'em with a little guilt. "Guys, look, this has truly gone too far. Y'all are friends with MoMo and how would you feel if the shoe was—"

Kadeem cuts me off, laughs flippantly, and says, "This is ridiculous, why would anybody want—"

I snatch the mic and cut his ass back off. I think it was his dismissive laughter and that smug look on his face that tripped the switch on the lamp. It's this group's first time getting a lil' taste of thug mama.

"Do not interrupt me! I am talking. This is not funny. It's a bad joke and whoever took her phone trying to be cute, you know who you are, and you're being straight-up foul and disrespectful. I am so ashamed and embarrassed . . . today of all days—when we have a guest! Whoever took it and hid the phone is dead wrong."

My nostrils flare with steam rolling out of them. I take a deep breath to calm down. I really want to lay into their asses, but we have company. One of the ICP teaching assistants suggests that we call the phone. I tell her the phone is on vibrate and she comes up with a plan B. She suggests we get everyone in the room to be supersilent and call the phone with the slight chance we might hear it vibrate. I think her idea is like trying to stab an elephant with a toothpick, useless. But I'm willing to give it a whirl. It takes a minute to get the boys silent and I call her phone.

"*Shhh,* I hear something," Jason blurts out. "Over here, I hear something vibrating."

Jason, who is sitting next to a tall metal file cabinet, presses his ear to the cabinet. "It's in here. I hear it vibrating in here!"

Jason is a stoner and looks like the ancient pharaoh Akhenaten, a tall, handsome, gangly artist type who loves poetry. He reminds me of Malik, aka Far Rock, and sort of looks like him too. Jason could have easily been in my class at Rikers, but he got lucky and was sentenced to an alternative-to-incarceration program and reports to probation twice a month. Besides his occasional purple-haze-hydro, glazed-eye mornings where we have to send him home for coming in high, he is otherwise a supernice, jolly hood nerd. I keep telling him he's playing with fire, getting high. If his PO decides to random-drug-test him, he could get violated and the judge could send him to jail instead of our "second-chance" program.

I fling open the file cabinet and there's MoMo's phone. "Here it is!" I yell and roll my eyes at the boys as I make a mad dash down to the first floor into the room where MoMo is contained doing deep-breathing exercises. I burst through the door holding the phone up in the air like an Olympic torch, prompting MoMo to leap to her feet and give me a bear hug. I hook my arm in her arm and pull her close. "See, I knew nobody stole your phone. The boys like to pull your chain and they play too much. I told you I was gonna get your phone; I got your back, girl."

MoMo puts her hand on her hip that's poking out and smiles. "Yeah, Swagga Sisters get it done, you already know. Thank you, Sista Liza." We walk arm in arm out of the building like besties. I want her to take a fresh-air-and-sunshine bath to reset her energy before going back into the room with the boys. I make her promise me that she won't say one word to them and absolutely no side-out-the-mouth, signifying-monkey comments either. She's the queen of saying some snide, slick shit under her breath, throwing backhanded batteries. MoMo pulls a cancer stick out of her purse, lights it, and drags on it, slow-inhaling toxins and years of accumulated stress. "Nah, I got you, Sista Liza. I ain't gonna say nothing; I got my phone. I'm good now."

Letting her back in the room with the boys is a dice roll but I gamble and take the risk, praying she'll keep her word and not antagonize the boys by hurling a Molotov cocktail with fighting words. When MoMo and I enter the classroom, Jamel Shabazz is already addressing the group of testosterone rascals. Quietly we slide into two empty seats. I make sure to sit next to MoMo so I'm in arm's reach; I'm still nervous she might pop off, turn it up, make it hot, and be the first one to shake.

Jamel Shabazz has an ominous, impressive presence that commands attention, standing at six foot six, broad and diesel. The brother is well dressed—as my daddy would say, he's "clean as the board of health," sporting a tailored, raw silk, short-sleeved silver shirt with finely pressed matching slacks that lightly graze the top of his shoes just enough to slightly break the crease. He's immaculate from head to toe in a military/Nation of Islam kind of way; hairline razor sharp, posture erect, crisp suit, and wingtip shoes spit-shined to damn near see your reflection in them. He's addressing the boys.

"I am in a lot of pain right now. It pains me to see my young brothers and sisters, *our children,* fighting with each other with no regard for the other person's feelings. Especially when I know you all have so much potential and greatness inside of you. I don't even want to show my photographs, which is why I came here today to share my work and look at yours, but I just want to talk to y'all."

Let the read begin. Two nincompoops put their heads down on the desk, pretending to sleep in an act of quiet resistance and rebellion. I have the urge to pluck them in the back of the neck, but I don't. Jamel continues. "I used to work on Rikers Island. I was a CO for twenty years. I'm fifty years old."

One of the boys, Kevin, cuts him off: "You're half a century?"

I can't tell if Kevin is being a smart-ass or just dim-witted like normal. Jamel doesn't break stride, ignoring the irrelevant question, and keeps going with his story. "And I worked at C-74 in 4 Upper, which was the baddest, absolute *worst* housing area you could be in. Sending you to 4 Upper was a punishment. But I worked with the young brothers and gave them guidance and knowledge of self. I had them doing workout regimens. I can do a hundred push-ups easy, and I had those brothers in shape. My partner was a Puerto Rican CO who spoke Spanish. And, ideologically speaking, we were on the same page because, just like me, he saw the value in investing in our youth and he gave the Spanish perspective, so we had our bases covered with the 'knowledge of self' study groups we ran."

I'm getting goose bumps. He's a kindred spirit speaking my

language. That was exactly what I tried to achieve with my rug rats at Rikers, teaching them knowledge of self. God I wish I knew Jamel when I was teaching at the Rock; I would have had him come talk to my rug rats and do a life skills class in a heartbeat.

Jamel wipes the sweat from his brow, pushing his glasses back up on his nose; they had slipped down to the tip. Preacher man is warming up. "I turned those young brothers around because I talk to people. I want to hear what you're going through, what you're thinking, especially the youth…especially! That's my mission, to save as many young lives as I can."

He is talking straight from the heart, unscripted, in a complete stream of consciousness. The energy in the room is supercharged with the intensity of Jamel's passionate conviction. And the sermon has just started; it hasn't reached fever pitch yet, which I know it's headed toward. I'm leaning on the edge of my seat, his power pulling me forward like a magnet.

"It's *real* out here, y'all, I've seen some things…I've *seen* some things. I've seen a guy come into intake at Rikers, go through the strip search and he's got on a pair of fresh kicks because he's just come from central bookings, still wearing his fly clothes from the street. And there's two other inmates fighting, cutting each other's throat over who's going to get the new dude's sneakers. So if they'll fight *each other* over the sneakers that you *still* have on your feet, what the hell you think they'll do to *you* for the actual sneakers… that are *still* on your feet? Oh, I've seen some gangster things go down!"

It's super quiet. All the kids are wide-eyed and fixated on Jamel as he bobs and weaves through Rikers Island war stories like a professional heavyweight storyteller rope-a-doping thug rats, holding court with words. The two ornery juveniles still have their heads down on the table and I really want to mollywhop them on the back of their heads and tell these two little disrespectful gremlins to sit the fuck up, but I am so riveted by Jamel's spontaneous sermon that I dare not create an interruption that would cause a hiccup in the service—which is in full, high-spirit swing. I let them silently protest and pretend to sleep.

"And it hurts my heart to see Black men treat other Black men with such unjustifiable rage and violence. When I was a CO, I was promoted to captain and could have become warden but I disobeyed orders. I didn't play by the prison rules. I treated the brothers with respect because I'm not better than anybody, so I referred to the inmates as gentlemen and I'd say 'Good morning, gentlemen.' The higher-ups didn't approve and told me to stop calling them 'gentlemen.' They said they're scumbags, dirt, and no-good mutts. You have to understand, I was a righteous Black man in a plantation atmosphere, and because of it I lost my rank. I refused to disrespect and humiliate the inmates. I was considered dangerous to the status quo, so I was demoted. I never made warden because I was bringing a righteous consciousness in a place that rejected the inmates' humanity. But how am I any different? We're just wearing different uniforms. They're in green, I'm in blue, but we are both Black men trying to survive in a hostile society and toxic environment. I couldn't buy into the 'overseer' mentality. I learned a hell of a lot about human nature in that place."

Jamel pauses to retrieve a handkerchief from his left lapel and dabs the perspiration from his forehead, the anointed warrior water seeping through his skin. I do believe the minister is about to take us to the river for a baptism. "I didn't plan on talking this much, much less about my life, but I *gotta* talk! I gotta just talk to y'all. My camera has taken me all over the world, across the country. I've had so many conversations. I've been able to photograph the leader of the Bloods, the Crips, Ñetas, Latin Kings, all the major gang leaders—"

Kadeem's eyes get big with starstruck wonder and he cuts Jamel off in childlike excitement. "You went to Los Angeles and met T. Rodgers!"

Kadeem's Blood, so he's superanxious to know if Jamel met one of the original LA-based founders of this notorious gang that he has pledged his adolescent life to—willing to die for a general he's never met. T. Rodgers is a big deal if you're Blood; he's a real, living OG. It's sort of akin to meeting Huey P. Newton if you were a Black Panther, or Kool Herc if you're a hip-hop DJ, or Steve Jobs if you're a computer geek. T. Rodgers created a crime organization of epic proportions that has captured the imagination and lives of thousands of wayward warriors across the nation. The mere mention of him has Kadeem's attention, sitting up like a soldier.

Jamel seizes the moment with masterful precision. "Not only did I *meet* him, I shot the cover of his book and kicked it with him at his house. And what's so deep about it is, the brother has diabetes and has a rare symptom where his disease, his diabetes, makes his eyes constantly run so it looks like he's crying nonstop. How ironic is that? The leader and founder of the Bloods, a gang that has shed a lot of blood and pain in the streets, has an illness that causes him to cry nonstop."

Kadeem takes out his phone and shows Jamel a picture of a picture that he has of T. Rodgers: "See, that's T. Rodgers right there." Kadeem is so proud to have an image of his gang-guru and is naively looking for Jamel's approval. Jamel lifts the glasses off his nose to examine Kadeem's picture on his cell phone and gives an unimpressed, "Ok, ok."

Kadeem keeps fishing. He's still in weird starstruck awe and asks, "So what was T. Rodgers like? Was he a cool person? Like, you actually sat and *talked* to this man. That's deep!"

The rest of the class commences sucking their teeth at Kadeem's obsession with the Bloods leader, especially since most of the people in the group aren't in gangs and the two who are gang-affiliated are Crips. They've never fought. I learned it's possible for a Blood and a Crip to occupy the same space without knocking knuckles so long as their respective neighborhoods don't have beef.

"Everybody has a story they want to tell and photography has given me entrance into a lot of people's lives," Jamel responds graciously. "The brother was a cool dude to talk to and he's a very smart man, but to be honest, I wasn't impressed. Here's a man who is so powerful and smart but wasted all his potential in creating a gang which is hurting and killing so many of our young Black and Latino men—"

"Anybody ever tell you that you look like Minister Farrakhan?" Since Jamel didn't give T. Rodgers the props Kadeem was looking for and eloquently criticized his sacred king, Kadeem felt compelled to interrupt our guest, totally off topic. "I mean not exactly, but your facial features, some of them." Jamel looks nothing like Minister Farrakhan; however, there *is* something about Jamel's Nation of Islam *Message to the Black Man* consciousness-raising energy, powerful presence, and minister-like delivery that seems to conjure a Farrakhanesque aura, which Kadeem picks up on. I feel it too. Jamel is bringing a critical testimonial to the boys in all of his alpha male command, grabbing their attention like a gladiator. If I had a tambourine, I'd be shaking it. If I had a fan, I'd be fanning it. If I had a bell, I'd be ringing it.

Jamel gives Kadeem a slight smile at the compliment. "Thank you, brother. I try to be a righteous man with integrity who loves our people. Our people are in so much pain, ignorance, and confusion. We have to save our youth by telling y'all the real deal, what's really going on in the world." Jamel briefly pauses to reflect on the thought, on the state of Black people. "I tell you, there is nothing like the drug crack cocaine. Crack did a number on our communities and was allowed to be sold and distributed in our communities with the assistance of the U.S. government. It was like dropping the atomic bomb on our people."

Okay, now my body temperature is beginning to heat up and I am on the verge of doing a praise dance in the isle. This is *exactly* what I shared with my rug rats at Rikers. I even gave them a handout that I compiled with information about Gary Webb's scathing investigative report exposing the unholy alliance between the CIA, the Contras, and crack. It has always been my belief that crack was like Hiroshima to Black people, ripping our communities and families apart, and we are still struggling to recover from the chemical hit. I must sound like a deaconess, all the *mmhmm, yes yes*, and finger waving I'm giving from my lil' amen corner, consisting of just me.

Jamel is getting more and more animated, using his hands to help tell the story and conduct the electric energy shooting out of his body. "I remember hearing about unmarked vans that would drive into the hood in LA and you'd open the back of the van and it was full of guns, Uzis, AK-47s!"

By now, the two little couldn't-be-bothered, defiant knucklehead rug rats lift their heads from the table. Jamel is striking a chord and now they're more interested in listening and learning than faking their resistance with phony apathy.

"Crack makes you lose your soul," Jamel says with a loud, impassioned whisper. "I've never seen a drug as deadly as crack. The level of dehumanizing and desensitizing is sick. Crack ushered in the culture of pornography to a mainstream level. I remember when brothers were rapping about love, politics, and verbally sparring with intelligence; the more facts and information you had in your rap, the doper you were. But after crack, now all you hear about is money, hoes, *nigga this,* drugs, and killing. We lost the concept of family and community. Money and pornography is now the dominant theme, and brothers wearing their pants sagging down—"

At this point, I can't contain my excitement and I shout, "Teach! Break it down!" This prompts the boys to collectively suck their teeth and grunt.

Jamel continues. "That came right out of prison culture. Anyone *without* a belt was considered weak because the prison would take your belt away if they thought you might try to hang yourself, so brothers without a belt were seen as suicidal and weak. The brothers who were smart would take a sheet and tear it up to make a homemade belt to hold their pants up and not look weak. That's where *that* came from. I remember I had to cut a young brother down in his cell, he was trying to hang himself, and when I cut him down I asked him, 'Why do you want to kill yourself, brother?' And he said because his mother's boyfriend raped him and gave him HIV and when he told his mother, she put him out. I've seen some things and I carry a lot on my heart, brothers."

The room is silent. Jamel stops in painful recollection. "I'm sorry, y'all. I didn't mean to go where I went. This surely wasn't planned— in fact, I was about to leave when the young lady's phone went missing and no one owned up to it; I was about to walk out because it took me back to an ugly place. A place where I experienced a lot of pain at C-74 Rikers Island. But something in me said, 'No, just speak to the brothers and tell them what's on your heart, let them know the pain I'm feeling, and impart some wisdom. I didn't even know what I was going to say, but I knew I had to say something."

Kevin is nodding his head affirmatively and starts to clap. He's a self-taught visual artist born and raised in the Bronx who was in and out of foster care most of his life and has a strained relationship with his abusive mother, whom he loves in spite of her dark rearing. A seasoned pessimist, Kevin grasps for guidance, showing signs of hope. I'm so glad he's here for this today. His homeboy, Jason, joins in to clap and says, "Word, I'm glad you did speak. You have a lot of wisdom. I was feeling everything you was saying."

Jamel reaches over and shakes his hand. "Thank you, brother, I appreciate you saying that." Then he addresses the group: "How many of y'all have younger brothers and sisters or cousins that look up to you?"

Every hand in the room shoots up.

"Wow! See, y'all have a responsibility for the shorties, for the younger ones coming behind you to leave them something positive. You have to make changes now to show them the way so they don't have to suffer ignorance."

Jamel begins to share some of his photographs. All of the kids are laughing at the old-school images and are feeling good. It's almost 3 p.m. and time for the workshop to end. We all gather in the main entrance to take a group photo. MoMo has stepped out for a cigarette, prompting Jamel to ask, "Wait, where's my girl? Blue hair?"

And, as if she heard the call through the brick walls of the building, right on cue, MoMo walks through the doors, sees us positioned about to take a picture, runs toward us, and does a baseball belly-flop slide on the floor into position, lying sprawled across our feet with her hand on her hip, as usual. In the span of two hours, the group overcame a huge obstacle, which was, ironically, the theme for the photography workshop: Overcoming Obstacles. And it's not just a metaphor but also a reality for their lives. Overcoming. Obstacles. An Olympic category for urban kids.

My boys at Rikers, like my current roster of rug rats at Friends, have to face a myriad of obstacles to overcome. Alongside the mega-triumvirate of poverty, racism, and violence, most of what they'll have to overcome is self-produced and internal. Anger masking the pain: obstacle. Immediate gratification: obstacle. Hunger for fast money to catapult themselves out of poverty: obstacle. Addiction to the streets: obstacle. Finding a sense of identity and belonging outside of gangs: obstacle. Materialism: obstacle. Peer pressure: obstacle. Self-regulating emotions: obstacle. Optimism: obstacle. Visualizing and believing in a better life than they've experienced: obstacle. Self-love: obstacle. And for me, dealing with a coed group of hormonal trickster boys, showing off for pepper-head, potty-mouth girls: *major* obstacle.

The kids at Friends and the kids at Rikers are the same peas in different pods. They both are tangled up in the criminal justice system and they're all wounded children battling an internal struggle to be emotionally healthy and mentally free. Poverty, police brutality, gang violence, addiction, the lure of fast money, peer pressure, lack of guidance, miseducation, and greasy processed fast foods drag them down like quicksand. It's a gravitational pull into a dark vortex of pain, fear, and survival of the fittest. The ones who make it out are genius Olympians anointed by a powerful guardian angel.

Most urban kids have witnessed or experienced some type of trauma early in life, ranging from violence to abject neglect, poverty, abuse, and abandonment. The psychological effects of unacknowledged and untreated traumas don't disappear but show up in behavior that is directly connected to their teenage act-outs and the inability to regulate their emotions—not always, but more often than not. I became acutely aware of this during my years at Rikers, first as a teaching artist and later as a schoolteacher, when my students would share snapshots of their childhood, like Tyquan, and others before and after him. They're all wounded children employing different methods to mask and cover the pain.

The girls, however, bring an added layer of intensity, an extra serving of explosive emotion along with their firecracker attitudes, which they wield like a protective shield. The tears and screaming come easy for them. The vast majority of the girls carry on their hearts the scars of sexual abuse. They hide behind their loud-mouth, eye-rolling, teeth-sucking, and neck-swerving armor of self-defense. The boys are not exempt from sexual assault by far, but rarely do they talk about it as openly as the girls do. All it takes is for one girl to disclose her experience and it is usually followed by a litany of testimonials. The girls require much more energy to deal with. My spidey-sense estimation, drawn from empirical evidence in the trenches on the front line for more than a decade, is that working with one girl is equivalent to working with four boys, energetically speaking. The girls demand more attention, time, and patience. They are what hip-hop artist Wale calls *lotus flower bombs*.

Today is a scorcher. The weatherman predicted sweltering heat and, by 9 a.m., the humidity is hostile, squeezing the life-force out of the morning air. Surprisingly, the class is focused and on task and, despite the trickling in of latecomers, the morning is going smooth without a hitch of drama. Nobody has been sent home, nobody came in high, and nobody needed a time-out. David and I high-five each other as the kids walk out for their lunch break, and we congratulate ourselves on what was a smooth day of instruction, so far. It's noon and heat is rising from the concrete like hell's furnace is beneath the surface. The kids are going to the basketball courts around the corner for lunch break. MoMo bounces out of the building with the boys, swinging her cobalt blue hair, wearing bright orange patent leather sandals to match her neon orange tank top, along with a multicolored pocketbook dangling from her arm. Her plaid poom-poom Daisy Duke shorts are *way* too short, making the boys gawk and drool at her kadonk-a-donk booty. I had to remind her of the dress code school rules—nothing too suggestive—and gave her a warning; next time, she gets sent home.

As soon as the last kid walks out the door, the building immediately becomes serene and quiet, like an office should be. Not more than twenty minutes have gone by before MoMo bursts through the door, making her usual loud, dramatic entrance talking on the phone. All I hear her say is, "Let me call you back, shorty!" Shoving her phone into her purse, she plops the latter on the front reception desk and hightails it back out the front door. *Strange.* Her behavior gives me pause for a split second but I quickly shrug it off, leaning back in my chair to return a call to Kevin's probation officer.

No sooner than I hang up the call, I hear a commotion like someone bumping into the frosted windows that we can't see out of. "*Thump thump thump.*" I look up toward the direction of the thumps and all I can see is a silhouette of arms flailing. Then I hear the kids yell, "Whoa…*Whoa!*"

Oh shit, MoMo is fighting! I can make out her hourglass figure through the frosted windowpane. My coworker Jay leaps over his desk in a gymnast/capoeira move and beats me out the front door. He grabs MoMo and yells, "Not out here! Not out here!" Our building is located four blocks from Times Square, which is swarming with police and undercover detectives ready to arrest any natives scaring tourists and blemishing Disney, not to mention the landlord is not too thrilled about having an "urban" (read: Black and Latino) youth organization housed in his prime real estate, midtown Manhattan office building. The lease was issued to Friends on the condition there would be no security issues that would negatively affect the other business offices and tenants in the building. That meant no graffiti, no stealing, no loud loitering in front of the building, and no fighting. The program constantly stays skating on thin ice.

Jay has MoMo pinned up against the wall while the crew of sweaty, musty boys walks inside the building, shaking their heads and uttering, "Yo, son, that's crazy." "MoMo be wilding; I ain't saying nothing, son." "I'm on probation. I just want my MetroCard and I'm out of here, son."

MoMo is struggling to get out of Jay's grip. *"Get the fuck off me! Let me at that motherfucker…Get the fuck off me!!!"* Homegirl manages to Houdini her way out of Jay's grip, making her way into the vestibule of the building. I block the door to the office and try to contain her in the small space. I have no idea who she is fighting or why. My first order of business is to calm her down, keep her out of the office away from the boys, and find out what the hell just happened.

"Sista Liza, *get the fuck off me*! Tell that punk-ass nigga to come outside! Come outside, motherfucker! Come on, motherfucker!" Her voice has transformed into a bloodcurdling growl and there is pure homicidal venom in her eyes. I desperately try to restrain her, but her adrenaline has created a beastly superstrength that requires the help of another adult. She has turned into the Incredible Hulk. I try stroking her hair with my one free arm, while my coworker has her in a body grip. I do my best to get eye contact with her. "Baby, what happened? I need to know what happened. Who are you talking about?"

"Kadeem! That nigga put his hands on me…Kadeem punched me in my face! *Let me go!*"

I'm taken aback by this. "What? Kadeem literally punched you in the face?"

I ask the question because if I can get her to tell me the details of what happened, hopefully that will take some of the stream out of her supernatural fury. I try to get her to talk and slow her down, engaging in the specifics.

She struggles to breathe, panting. "Yes! That nigga punched me in my fucking face and I'm 'bout to bust him in his fucking punk-ass face! *Get off me! Let me at that nigga! Come outside, you fucking pussy!*"

The Hulk has not yet waned and she is now a heat-seeking missile looking right through me, searing a hole in the door toward her target. It's blazing hot outside; she's sweaty and her skin is slippery like a watermelon seed, making it possible for MoMo to slither out of the grips of both me and my coworker. And, like a bionic roach, she slips through the door into the office. Oh shit! She's in! My coworker cuts her off and thank God I am able to grab her around the waist from behind and pull her into my body as I lean against the front office desk for reinforcement. I have her in a full bear-hug grip, using every bicep and tricep I have, which are flexed beyond capacity.

"*Get the fuck off me!*" MoMo is blinded with rage.

I whisper in her ear a calm, repetitive mantra, "I got you, baby, I got you, baby... I got you..."

"*Come outside, you punk-ass nigga! Let me go!*"

She doesn't even hear me, but I am just as relentless. "No, baby, I got you, I got you."

She realizes her force has met its match because my clutch is secure. There won't be any wiggling out from me this time. Running out of steam, she begins speaking in a staccato pant, "That nigga. Punched me. In my. Face. I wanna. Fight that nigga. He put. His fucking. Hands on me!"

I begin rocking her like a baby, side to side. "I know, and we're gonna deal with it. Didn't we get your phone back yesterday? I had your back *then* and I got your back *now*, but I can't let you handle it your way, so you gotta calm down so I can get the whole story and know the facts, baby."

I get MoMo to agree to step outside to tell me the whole story and she gives me her word that if I let go of her and release her from my bear grip, she won't run upstairs after Kadeem. She keeps her word. Outside, she begins telling me the dramatic details of how the fight unfolded.

While the kids were on lunch break at the park, in typical MoMo fashion she said some disrespectful and dangerous words to Kadeem. There were some other boys in the park who were not from the program, and Kadeem went over to them to "peace the homies," meaning he gave them the secret gang handshake. It's akin to fraternity brothers acknowledging each other, throwing up the hand sign for their frat.

"Nigga, you ain't Blood," bigmouth MoMo blurted out to Kadeem.

I cock my head to the side and give her my *why-did-you-do-that?* screw-face look of disapproval. She knows she was wrong and laments, "I know, I know, Sista Liza. My mother always said my mouth always gets me in trouble. But I was just playing, we was all joking. So all right, after I said what I said, he gets upset and starts popping shit, talking 'bout, 'Don't ever disrespect me like that in front of the homies. I'll spit in your face, *blah blah blah.*' So I start popping shit back like, 'Fuck you, you soft, you ain't shit, you a fake-ass Blood slob* nigga.'"

Sticks and stones can break your bones but *those* words can get you murdered. I try to assess when the actual first blow was swung. "So that's when he hit you?" I ask.

"No, he ain't hit me, we was just popping shit back and forth, or whatever, while we walking back from the park to school. And I'm on the phone talking to my shorty and *then* that's when the nigga cocks his fist back and punches me in the face out of nowhere."

I'm still confused with the sequence of events and need more specifics of the timing because it isn't adding up. I ask, "So wait— while you were on the phone, he punches you in the face?"

"Yes! He punches me and all the boys is like, 'Whoa, shit!' 'cause they *know* how I gives it up, but I keep walking. I eat that 'cause,

---

***Slob**: slur; what Crips call Bloods as a disrespect.

what! That's all you got, nigga? You think that did something? Plus I knew if I swung on him right then and there, all my shit, my phone and everything in my purse, would be all out in the street and I can't be losing my shit over some bum-ass nigga. So I start walking fast like, 'Let me get back to school and put my purse down, then I'mma bust his fucking ass and—'"

I cut her off, amazed at her stealthlike ninja strategy. "So, let me get this straight. He punches you in the face while you're on the phone, you take the blow, keep walking and talking, come into the building, and put your purse down *before* you went back out to fight him?"

MoMo gives me a devilish grin and says, "Yeah, you know I keeps it sexy, Sista Liza."

My coworker cracks up, and I howl with laughter while MoMo reenacts the showdown, full of her animated flair. "So I put my cute lil' brand-new pocketbook down, run back outside, squared that nigga up, and punched the mutherfucker dead in his face, like this."

MoMo is a sure-enough buckshot, shorty-roc, firecracker pepperhead. She begins demonstrating for us the boxing move she put on Kadeem, taking us through the fight blow by blow. "I got a brother who used to whoop my ass, so I handles mine. I got that nigga real good too, got him square in his jaw. I hooked him like a grown-ass fucking man and the nigga was shook!"

Normally I would have shut down her flagrant use of the word *nigga* and interjected with my infamous "watch that word," but I let her talk freely since it has been having a calming effect on her, and rationalizing with her might be possible now. Just like out at Rikers, knowing how and when to choose your battles is important. I try to reason with her: "Well, since Kadeem hit you and you got him back with a good one, then it should be even Steven. Let it drop."

But MoMo wants blood. "Nah, fuck that. That ain't enough for me. I want that nigga leaking. Plus, my mother told me if a man put his hands on you to find the closest brick, bottle, stick, or whatever, and don't stop swinging till you see the white of his bone!"

"Damn, MoMo, you don't play. I swear you are a stone trip. One minute you're miss prissy diva with your cute outfits and pocket-book, next minute you turn into a beast on some Incredible Hulk–type presto-chango, punching dudes in the face. Girl, what I'mma do with you? You ain't no joke, ma."

Acknowledging her gangsterness makes MoMo grin. Smiling is a great sign for rational entry. I seize the moment. "MoMo, I know you want revenge, but hear me out. You still have an open court case and so far it looks like it's close to getting dismissed. Remember, mama, you were looking at a possible five years upstate, so if you pop off *now* and get rearrested, it's a *wrap*. I can't let you go out like that, sweetie. And besides, you know you can't wear your cute poom-poom shorts up at Bedford Hills, Albion, or Taconic."

MoMo starts shaking her head affirmatively. I think she's taking it all in, looking at the big picture. Thank God. "Besides, nobody is worth you risking your freedom, to be sitting in a cell while they're home free, enjoying the summer. And trust and believe, you gave Kadeem something to think about. You clocked him nice and got the last punch. Let *us* deal with him at this point. As for you, I need to know it's dead."

She makes a promise to dead it, and since she has proven to be a young woman of her word, I believe her. But then it dawns upon me—she's slick. "And I need you to tell me that you're not gonna get your shorty or anybody *else* to come up here and make it hot, either. Any more drama in and around the building could get the entire program evicted from the premises because you already know they don't want us here. And this is a safe space, neutral territory for all the youth who come here, regardless of whatever set* you represent back in the hood. We need it to stay that way. Don't bring the hood beef to our front door. Promise me that, ma. Look me in the eye and give me your word, 'cause word is bond, right?"

---

*Set: the group of homies you roll with and pay allegiance to; your posse, usually from a gang.

MoMo shakes her head in disagreement. "Well, I can't control what my shorty do, 'cause once he gets his mind to do something, there ain't nothing I can say or do that's gonna stop him. That's just how he is."

Oh, Lord, it's gonna be a wild-wild west Brooklyn brawl at our front door any day now. "Now, MoMo," I say with my hand on my hip, head tilted, poised to court her ego, "you know *you* run your shorty; you got his nose wide open and on lock. If you dead the beef and say it's done, then it's done. I already know you pull *his* strings, not the other way around."

She basks in the accolades, giving me her signature sheepish grin and coy giggle. "You already know how I brings it. Damn, Sista Liza, ain't no winning with you. All right, I got you, word is bond, I'mma tell my shorty to fall back."

Whew. The remainder of the afternoon, Jay and I hold a peer mediation with MoMo and Kadeem. MoMo takes responsibility for throwing the Molotov cocktail with her words. I'm proud that she has taken the high road. But Kadeem refuses to admit to hitting her and, though I'm disappointed, I am not surprised that he chooses to remain infantile, taking the cowardly road of denial. MoMo is willing to grow and self-reflect, albeit kicking and scream- ing. Kadeem stays closed and unwilling to change, refusing to do self-inventory.

MoMo eventually got her case dismissed; Kadeem got rearrested months later for robbery.

It is a constantly changing flow of motley-crew characters and band of bad-news bears that come through our doors on a reg- ular basis. Some have stayed around for years, some for months, but almost all come back periodically to touch base and say hello because this is a safe place that doesn't judge them. It's a place that helps them navigate the rough terrain of urban adolescent life and untangle from bad decisions. It's a place that advocates for them in court and lambastes them in private, all the while recognizing their potential and applauding their successes, no matter how big or small. It's a place where second and third and sometimes fourth chances are championed.

My days frequently flow between calm and chaos, and no matter how colorful and draining, the kids keep me coming back and showing up. If it weren't for the obnoxious schedule of traveling to Rikers so ridiculously early in the morning, I would probably still be out on the island, because I grew to love my boys. Now with this new job and normal schedule, I am at least able to carve out time to write in the evenings and on weekends.

I took Sun's advice and created a performance piece that combines some of my classic poetry hits with music along with excerpts from my one-woman show, *The Peculiar Patriot*. It's a musical narrative of how a starry-eyed actress-turned-poet wound up teaching incarcerated kids for fifteen years and performed *The Peculiar Patriot* in thirty-five prisons for three years.

People often asked if I was still performing and where had I been all this time, so I answered their question onstage. Writing and performing *The Bitch Is Back* (which later became *Down the Rabbit Hole*) was a perfect comeback show. My artist is alive again. I have my mojo back and I hit the stage, performing the work in Manhattan and Brooklyn. My old boss and former principal, Phil, even came out to support. My passion is resurrected. I'm thinking creatively again and my dream is back in focus. Even though I am still working a full-time job to pay bills and support my art, I know that the day will come when my art will financially support my life. I still believe in *that* dream. And working with teenagers, wayward rascals, and urban rug rats keeps me fully present, authentic, and grounded. The kids give me profound inspiration and purpose. The wounded teenager in me connects with the wounded teenager in them, which creates a spontaneous bond I seem to be unable to shake. My sister, who always believed in my dreams, frequently reminds me: "Lee-Lee, you're an artist; it's what you're born to do—act, perform, write, create art, and tell stories. And working with kids is a part of your purpose that you can't separate from. It too, like your art, is a calling. If you had one without the other, you wouldn't be happy or fulfilled. Pray for balance, baby." This journey has indeed taught me balance.

The dream of writing and acting for a living is the pulse that's driving me. It's alive and percolating, and it's no longer in conflict with my purpose for teaching. It's not an either-or, but rather, it's that both the Dream and the Purpose can harmoniously coexist. How they will merge and what it will look like in the end, well…(insert shoulder shrugging), I don't quite know. God is in the details for that. But what I do know is watching kids grow and seeing their potential blossom ever so slightly right in front of my eyes is enough to convince me that I must continue to sow seeds of love in what some would consider barren ground. I've seen moss grow on rock.

Afterword

It's been eighteen years. I never thought working in jail with incarcerated youth would become an integral part of my life's purpose and now, my identity. As my art continues to blossom, grow, and demand more and more of my time, walking away from the barbed wire, the slamming of electronic gates, the jingling of CO keys, the ringing of alarms, and the shouting, fighting, crying, and laughing of young captive souls trapped in cells isn't easy. Who am I if I'm not in jail being challenged by and going head-to-head and heart-to-heart with my hard-rock, shorty-roc foul-mouth lambs...okay, lil' lions? I am first and foremost an artist, a creative being wired to give testimony on the stage and on the page, using my instrument to tell stories by weaving poetry, theater, and prose, fact and fiction, and a combination of it all to reflect a slice of our human experience. I aim to edutain—educate and entertain. But this journey in the trenches of mass incarceration for almost two decades has solidified the warrior-abolitionist-freedom-fighter-revolutionary spirit in me. It's who I am and what I do. I want to liberate these young people.

There is something profoundly divine with each opportunity I am given to bear witness to a young person at their lowest point, at rock bottom, scared, confused, temporarily broken, and to be able to stand in the valley with them and speak life into their future, shining light on an otherwise false, dark vision. Where they see despair and a dead end as inevitable, I see a flickering flame, a glimpse of the sun they can't quite see. I know their future is still unfolding. I am convinced God is still working on them and that their journey in jail, oddly enough, has the ability to connect them to their spiritual and emotional growth. The misadventure in the bowels of the beast many times serves as a much-needed wake-up call that redirects their focus and is a speed bump to slow down their race toward destruction in the streets. It's a gift inside a curse. The younglings are no different than our sacred Black ancestors, who were genius alchemists able to bloom like a lotus out of the wicked, treacherous swamps of violent oppression. If prison is the new plantation, then my boys (and girls) at Rikers are the crops, Black and Brown cotton bursting with laughter and life. As the late, great Tupac Shakur once said, "I might not change the world but I want to be the spark in the brain of the one who does." This is my prayer.

During my eighteen-year sojourn working with incarcerated youth in various capacities (freelance teacher-artist, Board of Education teacher, re-entry specialist, program counselor, court advocate, big sister, thug mama, and friend), I learned that our children who wind up in the bowels of the mass incarceration beast have bountiful resilience, breathtaking creativity, and tremendous promise. They deserve our fierce attention, unyielding nurturing, and iron fist with a velvet glove kind of love. They don't need sympathy but rather compassion. They don't need coddling but discipline and direction. They don't need to be lectured to but listened to and skillfully challenged. They don't need to be condemned but encouraged. They don't need to be written off but reimagined. First and foremost, they need to be seen. My hope is that in this book they *will* be seen and heard and their humanity recognized.

Much of the behavior we abhor in incarcerated youth is a mere reflection of a racist, violent, materialistic, celebrity driven, low-bar mediocrity celebrated, instant gratification society. They are showing us what they learned. Our collective social pathologies, bequeathed to them, have legs and teeth and hungry bellies staring us in the face. They've been watching us. So it is up to us to show them something different. It is up to us to give them the language needed to understand and navigate multiple systems pimping their poverty, hustling their pain, and profiting from their loss of freedom.

We must find the courage to tell incarcerated youth the ugly historical truth about white supremacy and the racially biased, profit-driven prison system that was designed to entrap them before they were even born. Fear of making members of the dominant culture feel uncomfortable holds back the truth. It is time to stop protecting the privileged from discomfort, tiptoeing and playing nice-nice to sanitize Black and Brown suffering and mitigate white guilt. Our children are in crisis. Author and scholar Dr. Neely Fuller said, "If you do not understand white supremacy, what it is and how it works, everything else that you understand will only confuse you."

One antidote for racism and white supremacy is Black love. When we love ourselves, our culture, our heritage (which didn't start with slavery), our hair, our features, our complexion, our style, our uniqueness, our flaws, and our potty-mouthed, sassy, beautiful children, we are better inoculated from the disease of both external and internalized racism. The Black community has a lot of healing to do. We survived a lot of trauma. We have to practice being gentler with ourselves and each other. We've been grossly wounded and beat up pretty bad. Laughter and love is the medicinal balm.

Let's begin to tell children in jail the whole story of history. When Black and Latino kids think their ancestors contributed nothing to the world, how can they consider themselves a positive and necessary part of society? How are they supposed to act when their sense of self is warped or nonexistent? How can a child aspire to be anything great when they have not been educated to their culture's great gifts to civilization? Knowledge of history sparks the imagination and inspires self-knowledge, self-love, and a sense of purpose. It helps kids recognize they have a place in society and are not thugs, monsters, savages, natural-born criminals, and other degenerate identities that society has labeled our children. Teaching them true history, exposing them to the depth of their stunning ancestors, will connect them to something great and vastly impact how they see themselves in the larger world and influence how they act and feel.

Children in jail (and other high-risk kids) reflect spiritual and psychological problems caused by the environment in which they live, the low-frequency music they listen to seemingly hypnotized by lyrics of death, the videos they watch, the toxic foods they consume, the complex traumas they've experienced, the poverty they navigate, and a cobweb of failing systems they are embroiled in (economic, educational, judicial, and mental health). But we have the power to change the narrative.

Over the years I had the privilege of working with many uniformed staff at Rikers—COs, captains, deps, and wardens who were committed to helping the youth. Those extremely rare, select officers possessed the gift of knowing how to relate to and engage the adolescents and young adults in custody. I witnessed them wield their magic, dropping jewels of knowledge, building a rapport, connecting, listening, and lifting a kid's spirit. These spiritual soldiers, this small group of agents of change who wore shields, were *in* the system, but like me, they were not *of* the system. Their ability to connect with incarcerated youth may have been because the officers came from the same communities as the detainees and reflected the population.

Preventing our kids from going to jail is paramount, but getting them out and helping them stay out requires reaching them while they are in custody, feeding them empowering information and then providing a network of support upon their release.

Along with receiving education and strong cultural curriculums, youth behind the wall could greatly benefit from learning trades such as barbering and cosmetology, automotive, carpentry, printing, culinary arts, and more to arm them with employable skills to earn a decent coin instead of committing crimes against poverty, hurting others, and risking their freedom. Changing their daily diet (and commissary selections) from heavy starch, high sodium, and sugar will have a huge impact on their behavior. Having real in-depth conversations with formerly incarcerated men and women—the OGs and former gang members who have successfully turned their lives around—can help demystify the allure of gang culture and de-normalize prison. Tell the children the truth. Have real-talk discussions on manhood, womanhood, and how to handle adversity. Deconstruct, dissect, and psychoanalyze racism, current events, hood politics, national and global politics, and relationship dynamics so they develop critical thinking skills and stronger life skills. And, of course, expose them to the arts, one of the most viscerally liberating and empowering ways to help a young person develop and grow at warp speed.

I don't have all the answers. There is no single solution to a problem entrenched in a centuries-old system of slavery and capitalism that has morphed into mass incarceration, gobbling up Black and Brown people at a dizzying rate, especially our kids. But we can turn this thing around. I believe in our children, our jewels.

This book is my testimony, my offering, my contribution toward the liberation of a marginalized community…my community. It's my imperfect, brassy push toward racial awareness and authentic justice, where Black and Brown lives will matter with equal value as white lives. When the humanity of Black and Brown youth will be seen as just as important as white youth. When courts, judges, and DAs offer the same consideration to children of color as is afforded wealthy white youth. When a poor Black kid and first-time offender will hear the judge say jail will have a negative impact on him like Judge Aaron Persky did for Brock Turner, the rich, white Stanford University student accused of rape who was sentenced to only six months in jail and three years of probation, because the judge thought, "a longer sentence would have a severe impact on him." I want to see a judicial system where collective Black and Brown humanity is equally valuable and fragile enough to protect. I want psychologists to come up with newfound conditions for poor Black and Latino kids that will preclude them from prison time, like they did for rich, white sixteen-year-old Ethan Couch, who killed four people while driving drunk and was sentenced to ten years of probation because he suffered from "affluenza," a made-up condition that psychologists successfully argued in court, saying it was the result of Ethan's parents' having spoiled him to the nauseating point that he didn't know right from wrong or have the capacity to comprehend responsibility. I want that same judge, Jean Boyd, to accept "poorfluenza" as a credible defense for the thousands of poor kids of color so steeped in poverty that their ability to know right from wrong is warped. Our children deserve freedom from inequity.

I want to see equality.

I want to see freedom.

I want the elephant in the room to be courageously addressed.

I want to see compassion.

I want to see the last become first, and the masses at the bottom rock the few at the top and the walls of injustice come tumbling down.

I want to see love manifest in our children as they dance to music affirming their life and their goodness and their necessity.

I want to see them laugh and grow up knowing joy.

I want to see them alive and free.

I want to see them prosper and multiply.

I want to see them win.

May their voices be amplified, because they matter.

Acknowledgments

Thank you Mother Father God Infinite Great Spirit NTR, ancestors, guardian angels of Light for the gift of life and storytelling, this divine assignment and all the doors that open and close in my life.

My Philly fam, "Squad deep!" I love y'all. See me following in big sis' steps. In the genes, I guess.

Krishan aka Freddy Krueger (wink and smile). Thank you for believing in my voice from day one at the Schomburg library with a raggedy journal and Post-its.

Carol and Adrienne, your guidance, wisdom, and patience helping me navigate all this has been tremendous. I've grown so much and learned a lot. Thank you for honoring my voice. Much more to follow...

To every teacher, social worker, youth advocate, and CO with a conscience, I salute you all for your selfless, rarely recognized, underappreciated, astronomical efforts and sacrifice to educate, heal, guide, and save our youth. I see you. Keep pushing; it's making a difference despite appearances to the contrary. We need you!

Shout out from Ms. P aka Sista Liza to all my shorty-roc teenage-rug-rat, loud-mouthed, hard-headed, snarky kids I taught, laughed with, cried with, yelled at, and kicked it with. I can't even begin to articulate just what you have meant and continue to mean to my life. Y'all keep me growing, learning, and showing up with purpose. I believe in you. I want y'all to win. Remember your ancestors and history. Bang against this beast by any means necessary. We need you. You're very necessary.

To my super ninja, homegurl, sista gurl, pot-stirring, shit-talking, loud-laughing saloon broads from Brooklyn to Philly, y'all give me life and sanity...I love y'all so much.

To my close circle of brilliant writer-artist-poet crew of creatives, thank you for keeping my blade sharp and for your loving, constructive advice, pulling my coat when my slip was showing. You inspire me and keep me reaching for excellence.

BBP aka Akh you already know the blessing you are to me. You always had my back. Nothing to say but The Creator linked us up, lovely. What a divine journey. Love and light, QSL aka Lucy.

To my boo...I'm walking loud, baby.

Rikers Rug Rat Slang

Banger: in jail, a shank or a sharp weapon; on the streets, a gun.

Bing: punitive segregation or solitary confinement at Rikers Island; also called the hole or the box.

Booster: a person who steals items and sells the goods on the black market.

Burner: a gun.

Cali or **Caliente:** Spanish for "making it hot," bringing unnecessary attention to a situation, usually from an authority figure.

Catch a body or **Have bodies:** to be incarcerated for murder; to have murdered someone.

City Year: the eight months an inmate serves under a twelve-month sentence. For every thirty days of an inmate's incarceration, ten days are reduced from their sentence. These ten days are considered "good days" or "good time." For example, an inmate sentenced to thirty days in jail will actually serve twenty days; an inmate sentenced to one year will serve eight months.

CO: correctional officer

Commissary: the jailhouse general store where snacks, toiletries, and goods are purchased.

Commo: short for commissary.

Crab: slur; what Bloods call Crips as an insult.

Crib: the housing area for inmates.

Criminal mischief: committing acts of vandalism, graffiti, or destruction of property.

Cypher: a term used in hip hop to denote a circle of freestyle rap artists taking turns "spitting" or rhyming.

Deebo: to take or snatch something from someone without permission and in an aggressive way; a person or bully who has deeboed something, simply taking what he or she wants from a victim. Deebo was the name of the large, menacing character in the film *Friday* who was so intimidating and scary-looking that he was able to take what he wanted from whomever he wanted without a fight.

Doja: synonym for pop-off dummy (POD); a follower on the team or within a group. The doja (like the POD) is the low man on the totem pole who does the bidding or fighting for others with higher rank in the crew or group.

Drop your flag: to quit the gang. The flag, represented by a specific-colored bandana, is what gang members proudly wear. To drop the flag means to give up your gang status. It can sometimes have dangerous or deadly consequences.

Esophagus: "Swallow it" or "Shut up."

Floss: to be fashionable; looking fancy and fly.

Food: a weak kid who is preyed upon for easy extortion and gets "eaten up" like food by the stronger members.

Get light: a specific Harlem shake dance routine where the shoulders move in a syncopated rhythm; it's a frenzied tribal-like praise dance that has a specific accompanying handclap done by the audience/onlookers.

Get money: the literal sense—to acquire cash or enhance one's ability to spend; also to masturbate.

Good days: the ten-day reduction in the duration of an inmate's actual sentence for every thirty days served.

Greens: the adult inmate population at Rikers, who wear dark green uniforms to distinguish them from the adolescents, who wear light beige.

Hang up: to commit suicide.

Herb: a cornball, a nerd, a square; usually a nonfighter who is seen as weak.

House or **Housing area:** synonym for crib; the area where inmates are housed and kept; the dorm area; the cells.

Infraction: a ticket; a recorded incident of an inmate for a violation of a prison rule. An infraction can result in the forfeiting of "good days." If the offense is serious, the infraction can result in a new criminal charge and the inmate being rearrested.

Juvie: juvenile detention.

Knocked or **Bagged:** to be caught by the police and locked up.

Making it hot: bringing unwanted attention to a situation from an authority, usually from a correctional officer (CO) or teacher; creating a scene that could bring trouble; *caliente*.

MO: inmates at Rikers under mental observation; crazy.

Obamas: the most recent state-issued slip-on kung fu–style sneakers that are black canvas with thin white rubber soles.

OG: Original Gangster, an older street player with experience and rank; the leader of the gang.

Patakis: official name and synonym for "pumpkin seeds," the bright neon orange, state-issued canvas slip-on sneakers named after former governor George Pataki.

PC: protective custody; where an inmate is separated from the general population for their own protection.

Plea deal: in criminal proceedings, where the district attorney will offer the defendant a lesser sentence if the defendant agrees to plead guilty to the charge and waives their right to a trial.

Pop-off dummy (POD): the kid who fights battles for a particular set or team. He is willing to take the blame for the "boss" or "OG" in the group. He does this for inclusion and to receive fringe benefits from the group, relating possibly to extra purchase power at the commissary or to obtaining heightened protection by the particular set or team from physical harm by others.

Pumpkin seeds: state-issued kung fu–style slip-on canvas sneakers. They are bright neon orange in color, like a pumpkin, and shaped like a seed; also called Patakis.

Rock, the: a synonym for Rikers Island that was borrowed from the nickname for Alcatraz, which had the appearance of being a giant "rock" on an island. Like Alcatraz, Rikers is on an island, located in New York's East River.

Scrap: homeboy; a term of endearment.

Set: the group of homies you roll with and pay allegiance to; your posse, usually from a gang.

730: legal term for classification of mental instability; a lawyer for a criminal defendant must file a 730 motion to receive a psychiatric evaluation to determine if the defendant is mentally fit to stand trial.

Slob: slur; what Crips call Bloods as an insult.

Spinning: when your hair displays visible waves.

Taking your peanut butter: to be raped by a man; forced sodomy.

Team: synonym for "set"; the group of homies you roll with and pay allegiance to; your posse.

Throwing batteries: to instigate someone to get pumped up to fight; to charge someone up with energy and give them courage; getting someone to do something they wouldn't normally do. A battery can have a positive or negative effect, depending on the situation.

Tight: to be angry or pissed off; wound tight with rage.

Toaster: a gun.

Turn it up: to make it hot; to fight; to become hostile and belligerent.

Turtles: the riot squad at Rikers Island. The correctional officers' riot gear resembles the paraphernalia of the Teenage Mutant Ninja Turtles characters from the iconic children's television show, with all-black helmets and armored vests.

Up top: refers to the plethora of prisons located out of the city limits, in upstate New York.

Washed: to get beat up, tossed around, and pummeled, like being in a washing machine.

Wavy: cool; hip.

YG: young gangster; the younger generation of an OG.